PRESENTED TO

LAEL SCHWAB

BY

BETH ISRAEL RELIGIOUS SCHOOL

UPON CONFIRMATION

MAY 31st, 1970

HEART

OF

WISDOM

A THOUGHT FOR EACH DAY
OF THE JEWISH YEAR

HEART

OF

WISDOM

by

Bernard S. Raskas

THE BURNING BUSH PRESS

NEW YORK

Library of Congress Catalogue Card Number: 62-18076

Designed by Meyer Fecher

Manufactured in the United States of America

This book is dedicated to my

Foreword

There are various ways of bringing home to modern
man the relevance and insight of an ancient tradition. One
is to begin with its classical texts and seek to relate them
to the current existential situation. Another is to start with
a current concern and go back into the tradition to find
guidance and direction.

Since 1940, the National Academy for Adult Jewish
Studies has conducted an ongoing program to tap the
spiritual resources of Judaism for our time. It has published a number of basic books, study guides, and pamph-
lets which have become staples in adult Jewish education.
These have, in large measure, begun with the Text and
intensively expounded Jewish ideas.

The present volume represents a new direction in the
work of the National Academy. It deals with the variety
of concerns of contemporary man and offers him, for their
resolution, the insights of an age-old tradition. This volume
is not intended to serve as a systematic exposition of
Judaism. It undertakes, rather, to offer a framework of
perspective drawing upon forty centuries of human experience in a variety of circumstances. Beginning in each
case with a human concern, it draws upon Jewish sources
via anecdote, folklore and direct quotation from writings
ancient, medieval and modern. In arranging this material,
Rabbi Bernard S. Raskas has brought to bear the wisdom

of a distinguished ministry of service coupled with a profound knowledge of the sources of our tradition and the wellsprings of human experience. The Jewish calendar itself serves as the organizing principle drawing together the rich panorama of ideas, values and experiences.

It is our hope that this collection of thoughts will invite the reader to intensive and systematic study of Jewish sources.

I find it my pleasant task to express our appreciation to Rabbis Samuel Chiel and Simcha Kling who served as readers of the original manuscript and who offered a number of helpful suggestions. Our grateful thanks are also extended to Rabbi Bernard Segal for his sustained interest in this volume and to Mr. Moses Eskolsky for his good counsel in the many technical matters associated with its publication.

May this volume be the first of a series of popular works fulfilling in our time the hope of the prophet that the vision be written plainly so that "a man may read it swiftly."

Marvin S. Wiener

NISAN 5722
APRIL 1962

Preface

"Teach us to number our days, that we may attain a heart of wisdom." PSALMS 90:12

The authentic Jewish tradition knows no division between secular and religious. All of life and experience is bound together by a unity of the divine purpose and the integrity of human character. Upon this very premise — that every moment of the day can be used in service of God — this book was written. It is designed to be used as:

   a. A source book for a *Devar Torah,* for the daily synagogue service.
   b. A book of inspiration to the hospital patient or shut-in.
   c. A reader for Jews in the Armed Services.
   d. An inspirational reader for the Jew who desires to include a devotional thought in his daily routine.
   e. A source of insight into the Jewish mind for the interested non-Jew.

The book, quite logically, follows the Hebrew calendar. All the reader need do is find the Hebrew date corresponding to that in the civil calendar and the sequence is simple thereafter. Although the Jewish calendar adds one extra month during its leap year, this book was aranged for a year of twelve months (354 days).

I wish to express my gratitude to my teachers who instructed me in Torah and other forms of learning, my family, my friends, the members of my congregation, all of whom shared their wisdom with me. I especially want to thank Rabbi Marvin S. Wiener, Director of the National Academy for Adult Jewish Studies, whose manifest ability and devotion to the cause of adult Jewish education has added immeasurably to this book.

I have conceived this work in the classic purpose of devotional literature: *lehagdil Torah u'lehaadirah* — "to extol the Tradition and to amplify it." Some of this purpose will be served if the reader will be inspired to number each day in seeking a "heart of wisdom."

Bernard S. Raskas

PASSOVER EVE 1962-5722
TEMPLE OF AARON
ST. PAUL, MINNESOTA

תשרי
TISHRE

In The Beginning, God

Once, two men became involved in a quarrel over a piece of land. They decided to take their dispute to the rabbi, who would solve the problem. One said, "The land is mine!"

The other retorted, "The land belongs to me!"

The rabbi thought for a moment and then he said, "Why don't you come back and ask me the same question 100 years from now?"

The simple truth is that the earth is the Lord's and we are merely the spiritual renters.

Rosh Hashanah, the Jewish New Year's Day, reaffirms this ancient truth. This day does not commemorate the founding of a religion, nor does it salute the birth of an individual; but rather it celebrates the anniversary of the creation of the universe. To put it simply, Rosh Hashanah is the birthday of the world.

It is especially significant that the second Hebrew word of the Torah is *bara* – "He (God) created." This emphasis on creativity is really the moving force of intelligent and productive living. The very fact that in the Hebrew the act of creation is placed between the word "beginning" and the name of God suggests that we might freely interpret the first verse of the Bible to read: "The beginning of all creative thought and living occurs when we recognize God as the source of moral energy and spiritual power."

In the beginning, God created the heaven and the earth.
GENESIS 1:1

The Ladder Of Education

After hearing a lecture by the late Francis Parker, a great Chicago educator, a woman in the audience asked him, "How early can I begin the education of my child?"

"When will your child be born?" Parker questioned.

"Born?" she gasped. "Why he is already five years old!"

"My goodness, woman," he cried, "don't stand here talking to me — hurry home! You have already lost the best five years."

This episode is an excellent commentary on the inspiring story of Hannah and Samuel which we read on Rosh Hashanah. We are informed in the prophetic selection that Hannah brought her child to the house of God in Shiloh when the boy was "but a child." Hannah intuitively understood what modern educational psychology has confirmed: the earlier a child is exposed to spiritual values the deeper and more lasting these influences will be in his life.

It is important that parents make every effort to surround their children from infancy onward with the beauty of Jewish traditions. A child who has many meaningful Jewish experiences in his earliest years will be given a secure foundation upon which to place the ladder of education which reaches from earth to heaven.

Train up a child in the way he should go,
And even when he is old, he will not depart from it.
                                                        PROVERBS 22:6

3

A Spiritual Examination

Just as the wise physician recommends a "physical" to preserve physical health, so does the responsible rabbi advise a "spiritual" to maintain spiritual well-being. During the period between Rosh Hashanah and Yom Kippur, known as *Aseret Yemai Teshuvah,* the Ten Days of Penitence, each Jew is urged to conduct a *heshbon hanefesh,* a spiritual self-examination. This spiritual examination might very well be conducted in a manner similar to the typical physical examination.

We might survey our reactions. How do we respond to the world? In what way do we react to our families? Do they grate on our nerves or do they please us?

We might test the function of our heart. Do we respond with heartfelt sureness to the needs of others? Do we have the stout-hearted courage of our convictions?

What is the condition of our spiritual eyes? Do we have insight into the character of others? Can we see clearly the worth of people, or are we made color blind by prejudice?

How does our coordination function? Is our entire being coordinated by a definite purpose in living? Do our spiritual goals unite our life so that we do not waste or scatter our emotions? Do we coordinate our reactions, our heart and our eyes so that we truly live a healthy spiritual life?

If a man is concerned for his spiritual welfare, let him examine his conduct.   BERAKHOT 5 a

4

The Big Flash

Following the first atomic explosion in New Mexico, observers were discussing what had gone through their minds when the "big flash" came. Dr. J. Robert Oppenheimer revealed that he had thought of a line of Sanskrit: "I have become Death, Destroyer of worlds." An even more pessimistic observer admitted, "I thought to myself, 'This is the kind of flash the last man will see the last fraction of a second before the world ends.'"

By very interesting contrast, William L. Laurence, the science reporter for the *New York Times*, said quietly that he thought, "This is the kind of a flash when the Lord said, 'Let there be light.'"

Tomorrow at dawn there will flash the first light for the new day. As the day wears on, men throughout the world will gather to welcome the first daylight with prayer and contemplation. With supreme confidence we face this new day, ready to accept what it has to offer and eager to improve our lives as well as our society. We have hope because of the light of love, understanding, mercy, and truth. This is the only true light that can illuminate our world with faith and confidence.

The Holy One, blessed be He, observed, "How long shall the world exist in darkness? Let the light enter!" And God said, "Let there be light."   GENESIS RABBAH, CHAPTER 1

5

Consider The Turtle

Scripture tells us that on the fifth day of creation "God created the great sea animals and every living creature that creepeth." These creatures have mystified, delighted and instructed us. The following is an apt illustration of the manner in which they teach us the art of living.

It is recorded that when James B. Conant was president of Harvard University, he kept among other objects on his desk a little model of a turtle under which was the inscription, "Consider the turtle. He makes progress only when he sticks his neck out." This is a truth. It can be verified by watching any turtle. No turtle ever moves forward when he is enclosed within his shell.

The turtle has a very important lesson for our time. How carefully we guard our necks! We have become afraid of taking risks for a good cause. We fear to stick our necks out for what we believe. But unless we challenge the thinking of our contemporaries and on occasion chance their displeasure, we cannot advance beyond ourselves.

In every generation, in every social circle — indeed any group — there must be individuals who are willing to express their ideas and their ideals, even if they are unpopular. It is through these people that the progress of society is assured and its welfare continually advanced.

The truth is neither shy nor timid.   JOSEPH CASPI

The Goodness Of Life

It is recorded that after each day of creation God surveyed His work and affirmed its goodness; and on the sixth day He reaffirmed the worthwhileness of the entire universe by declaring, "It is very good." This is the basis for the Jewish conviction that life is worth living and that the world is good. Life is a divine gift to be accepted joyfully.

Judaism, alone among the religions of mankind, urges man to enjoy the pleasures of the world. The ancient rabbis boldly proclaimed, "In the hereafter every man will be called to account for the earthly pleasures he rejected."

The rabbis believed that the true way to enjoy God's gifts in the world is to use them with discretion, balance, pleasure and keen enjoyment. The total abstainer is not the finest example of humanity, even as the drunkard is not the model human being. Too much fasting is just as reprehensible as gluttony. Neglect of the body and its needs is just as regrettable as hypochondria.

We serve God best when we enhance the worthwhileness of life by using with appreciation His many gifts. Throughout the ages, Judaism has held firm to the conviction that the world is good, life is worth living, and possibilities for happiness are endless.

And God saw everything that He made, and behold, it was very good.   GENESIS 1:31

7

The Pause That Refreshes

Every beat of your heart is followed by a pause. The first action of the heart is called a systole, and this is followed by a period of relaxation known as a diastole. Because this second function is so vital to life, it is sometimes referred to in medical circles as "the pause that refreshes."

The Jewish tradition has likewise formulated a pattern of six days of work followed by a day of relaxation. That day of spiritual refreshment is known as *Shabbat*, the Sabbath, which literally means "resting." Just as the heart cannot function well without regular rest, so a person cannot live properly without a regular day of relaxation and spiritual refreshment.

Interestingly enough, *Sabbath* is a term that has never been translated from the Hebrew. The reason is that there is no equivalent in any other language for this term with its unique combination of religious feeling, ideals, song, foods and folklore. The Sabbath has thereby become distinguished as a day of rest. It has helped to preserve the Jew as an individual, the Jews as a people and Judaism as a great religious civilization. For the heart of Jewish life, the Sabbath is the pause that refreshes.

Far more than Israel has kept the Sabbath, it is the Sabbath that has kept Israel.   AHAD HA'AM

To Err Is Human

There is an old Yiddish story concerning two community leaders who were involved in a bitter controversy over some imagined slight. Soon their relationship deteriorated to the level that the entire community became a divided camp because of them. The rabbi could no longer tolerate their behavior, and saddened by the state of affairs, he decided to take positive steps to end the feud. After the Rosh Hashanah service he called the men into his study. He pointed out the ancient message and purpose of the High Holydays and asked them to forgive one another. They hung their heads in shame and pledged their renewed friendship. As they were leaving, the rabbi remarked that in keeping with the new year, it was customary to extend good wishes. One man turned to the other, put out his hand and said, "I wish you everything you wish me in the coming year."

The other quickly replied, "Aha, there you go starting it all over again!"

Our broken relationships with others can never be resumed properly unless we have real trust in others. Unless we act in good faith, our actions become meaningless, if not disastrous. We are all human and our acts are fraught with error; we all do wrong and we are wronged in turn; we all hurt and sustain hurt. But the fact that we have a Rosh Hashanah and a Yom Kippur implies that we can right our relationships if we repent in honesty, if we mend our ways in sincerity. The emphasis is on honesty and sincerity. It is human to err, but a mark of the divine to forgive.

He who forgives will himself be forgiven.   YOMA 23 a

Worship Without Words

Judaism is essentially a faith based on deed rather than on creed. This unique concept of worship without words finds appropriate expression in a classic Jewish story whose events occurred on Kol Nidre Eve.

Rabbi Israel Salanter, the founder of the modern Jewish ethics movement, once failed to appear in the synagogue on Kol Nidre Eve. His congregation waited, and when the rabbi did not appear, the members became worried and went out to search for him. After several hours of effort they found him in a neighbor's barn. They wondered what had happened to prevent their rabbi from being in the synagogue on the holiest night of the year. It seems that on the way to the synagogue Rabbi Salanter had found a neighbor's calf which had strayed and become entangled in the brush. With great difficulty he tenderly freed it and brought it back to the barn. When the men of the congregation found him there, he was tending the animal's wounds.

They protested, saying, "How could you do that? Don't you know that your first duty as a rabbi is prayer?"

He answered gently, "God is called *Rahmana,* the Merciful One. An act of mercy is a prayer, too."

It is not external ritual that wins forgiveness, but inward sincerity.   TAANIT 16 a

At-One-Ment

Have you ever wondered why we fast on Yom Kippur? Why did the Bible introduce this strange ritual, this very unusual way to worship God? Why trouble ourselves physically by refraining from food and drink? Why pain ourselves mentally by casting up our sins and our failures?

If these questions have ever bothered you, then you might do well to consider a wonderfully simple epigram uttered by Sakini, the central character of *The Teahouse of the August Moon*: "Pain makes man think. Thought makes man wise. Wisdom makes life endurable."

Here, then is the answer. Only by taking the trouble to set apart a time for meditation and reflection can we right our wrongs. Only by the painful process of soul searching can we literally refashion and reform our lives so that we can be at one with God.

The key word for this day is atonement. We might even consider the word in its divided form: "at-one-ment." To really achieve the full import of Yom Kippur we must strive to be "at one" with God. This means we must make every effort to elevate our lives and ennoble our characters until we have attained a state of "at-one-ment" with the highest values of godly living. When we have learned to be "at one" with God, then surely we will also be "at one" with man.

For transgressions between man and God, repentance on Yom Kippur brings atonement; for transgressions between man and man, Yom Kippur brings no atonement until the injured party is appeased.   YOMA 8:9

11

Sealed Orders

During the Ne'ilah service, the last of the five services on Yom Kippur, there occur several changes that are simple, but at the same time deeply meaningful. One of these basic changes in the liturgy is that the word *Katvaynu* is changed to *Hatmaynu*. Hence, the prayer *"Inscribe* us in the Book of Life," recited in all of the High Holyday services, is now read *"Seal* us in the Book of Life." This phrase expresses the traditional Jewish belief that the destiny of a person's life for the coming year is sealed at the end of that day.

This idea of sealed orders gives rise to an interesting analogy. In time of crisis ships frequently set sail under sealed orders. These orders may be opened only at a specified time and must be followed implicitly. When the captain of such a vessel casts off, he does not know exactly where he is to go, but he has confidence in the orders he carries. His only concern is to carry out the assigned mission, which he knows can best be accomplished by sailing the course planned for him.

This is true of life itself. At birth and every year thereafter we are handed sealed orders. We can best carry out our personal mission by accepting these orders and following them with unshakable confidence in the Commander of creation. We must sail the course assigned to us to help carry forward the movement and purpose of all of existence.

At the Ne'ilah service the gates of heaven begin to close and man's fate is sealed.   JER. BERAKHOT 4:1

A Code Of Honor

Socrates was one of the wisest men who ever lived. He was accused by the city of Athens of corrupting the morals of the young because he was teaching values contrary to those held by the general public. He was tried, found guilty and was sentenced to drink the poisoned cup of hemlock by his own hand. As Socrates was waiting in prison for the appointed day, a friendly jailer left the door unlocked. His disciples urged him to flee. The reply which Socrates made over two thousand years ago should still stir something noble within us.

"When I was a young man," he said, "I studied Anaxagoras' book on physics. He would have me believe that I am sitting in this crouched position on my prison cot because of the tensions in the tendons over the joints in my legs. But what Anaxagoras doesn't seem to know is that I sit here because I will not break the democratic law of Athens. The people have condemned me to drink the hemlock. As a man of honor, I will not creep stealthily away like a coward."

It was not the impersonal law of physics or nature that determined that Socrates should sit in prison; it was the code of honor to which he chose to commit himself.

In a place where there are no men, strive to be a man.
AVOT 2:6

Man's Humanity To Man

We often use the poetic phrase, "man's inhumanity to man," but we just as often forget that there also exists man's humanity to man. The following incident illustrates the truth that in the midst of hate there can also be love.

When the Nazis overran Paris, Mother Maria, a nun, took charge of a secret organization of priests for rescuing Jewish children. A small convent in Paris was established as the liaison point and rescue center. In February of 1943 Mother Maria's home was raided by the Gestapo, and the nun's mother was taken.

During the angry interrogation a Gestapo agent turned to the old woman and said, "You educated your daughter very stupidly. She helps only Jews."

"This is not true," the nun's mother replied. "She helps those in need. She would even help you, if you were in trouble."

Mother Maria was last seen alive on March 31, 1945. It is reported that she committed one last humane act. She exchanged her precious Aryan card for the card of a Jewish woman chosen for the gas chamber.

Mother Maria is a fine example of the heroes of humanity who stand forth in their willingness to help people regardless of color or creed. These people, and they are to be found in all faiths, are the living embodiment of man's humanity to man.

The righteous of all faiths have a share in the world to come.
                                                    MAIMONIDES

Comfort Is No Crime

A rabbinical student once came to a renowned rabbi and asked to be ordained as a rabbi. The rabbi inquired about his daily conduct and the candidate replied, "I always dress in black; I drink only water; I place tacks in my shoes for self-mortification; I roll in the snow; and I order the synagogue caretaker to give me forty stripes daily on my bare back." Just then a black horse entered the courtyard, drank water and began rolling in the snow.

"Observe," said the rabbi. "This creature is black; it drinks only water; it has nails in its shoes; it rolls in the snow; and it receives more than forty stripes a day. Still it is nothing but a horse."

Judaism rejects the concept of needless self torture as a means to attaining a high level of religious feeling. Instead it urges man to take freely of the goodness, the pleasures and the comforts of the world, for these, too, are part of God's gifts to man.

In fact, some comfort is essential to a wholesome life. To read requires that one be seated comfortably. The growing child needs the comforts of family life for his emotional security. A person must have a comfortable income, for when a man is in dire financial stress he needs money and not just sympathy. The comforts afforded by even good food deepen the worthwhileness of life. Every human being has the right to comfort, for comfort is no crime but is essential to living a full life.

Pleasant sounds, sights and smells put one in a good spirit.
BERAKHOT 57 b

Stars In Our Eyes

The festival of Sukkot is centered about building a *sukkah*. According to traditional plans, the *sukkah* must be covered with foliage, but there must be enough space between the greens so that the stars can be seen. The Talmud teaches us an important lesson in this specification, and it can be told through the following literary passage.

In a novel entitled *The Harbor*, by Ernest Poole, a group of boys who lived by the side of the railroad tracks in the slums of a city became bitter and destructive. But one lad, the hero of the novel, developed the habit of wandering out to a small secluded spot on a hill. He found that when he was there, even though the ugly, dirty freight cars banged and clanged about him, by lifting his eyes "he could see the stars above the freight train." This boy became a great man.

Judaism taught the Jew symbolically through the *sukkah* to lift his eyes above the present into the future. It reminds us that all we need do is lift our eyes and we will see the stars. Though our present may be perplexing, our difficulties seemingly insurmountable, yet there is always a source of inspiration and encouragement, if only we can see the stars.

The sukkah is designed to teach a man to put his trust in heaven, for as he sees the universe which God created, he is inspired to trust in Him.

MENORAT HA'MAOR, CHAPTER 3

The Manuscripts Of God

Nature is man's greatest teacher. For this reason Judaism instructs through the symbols of the natural world. The fall festival of Sukkot is celebrated about *arba minim,* four species of growths that are common to the land of Israel.

The *lulav,* the palm branch, is the symbol of the spine. As it stands tall and firm and proud, so man is urged to stand morally straight and intellectually firm.

The *hadas,* the myrtle, is figurative of the eye. Just as it grows in even rows and presents a pattern that is sure and certain, so must a person's temperament strive to be even and his eye behold a pattern of conduct that is sure and certain in responsibility.

The *aravah,* the willow, represents the mouth. As it is gracious, so must the words of man's mouth be gracious and kind.

The *etrog,* the citron, is symbolic of the heart. As a citron is generous in its growth, so must a heart be generous unto all.

This idea is beautifully expressed in a poem entitled, "The Manuscripts of God":

> And Nature, the old nurse, took
> The child upon her knee,
> Saying, "Here is a story book
> My father wrote for thee.
> Come, wander with me," she said,
> "In regions yet untrod
> And read what is still unread
> In the manuscripts of God."

The palm branch is like the spine; the myrtle is like the eye; the willow is like the mouth; and the citron is like the heart. With all thy limbs praise God.

YALKUT SHIMONI 188 b

17

Thanksgiving

The festival of Sukkot is known as *zeman simhataynu,* "the season of our rejoicing," because the holyday is essentially an expression of thanksgiving for the fall harvest. But the urge to express gratitude is not limited to any one religion, and one country, or any one person. The basic idea of thanksgiving is as old as the dawn of time and as young as the face of a newborn child.

The American people have created a Thanksgiving national holiday that has deep religious overtones. The Greek Orthodox tradition has the Feast of Demeter, the Japanese have Kainane Sai, the Moslems observe the Ashura Feast and the Chinese celebrate the Moon Festival. All of them show man's basic need to express gratitude for the bounties of nature and the manner of his good fortune.

But although these expressions of thanksgiving are universal, they may come from different sources. They can be the children of our fears or of our hopes. We can judge whether we are motivated by fear or hope by the way we express our feeling. If it is fear, then we merely mumble a prayer of gratitude and feel a sense of relief, then let it go at that. But if it be hope, then it is expressed in authentic thanksgiving, that is to say, first thanks and then giving. It is not enough to thank; we must also find a way of giving.

In the world to come all prayers will be eliminated except for prayers of thanksgiving, which will never be abolished.
MIDRASH TEHILIM 80:56

The Significance Of The Sukkah

During the week of Sukkot, we obey the Biblical command, "Ye shall dwell in the *sukkah* for seven days." The *sukkah* as we know it is but four simple walls and some leaves or foliage for a roof. We decorate it with beautiful fruits and flowers and it reminds us of the bounty of the fall harvest.

We might well ask why we need to erect a special booth, outside of our homes, under the starry sky to commemorate the beauties of nature. Could we not simply decorate our homes with floral arrangements or offer prayers in the synagogue? Why must we go through the trouble of setting up a new structure?

With a little deeper thought we can discover the reason why we build the *sukkah*. Before the new little hut is erected all that exists is space, just emptiness, devoid of any purpose. Once we have built the *sukkah,* we have enclosed that area and made it into a shrine, a scene of worship and thanksgiving. When we place the four walls and then add a roof, we have captured space and made it serve our purposes.

The meaning of this observance is that man has the power to take elements of nature and make life itself serve his welfare.

We are commanded to adorn the sukkah. And what better ornament can there be than the distribution of charity among those who lack the means wherewith to be glad in the "season of rejoicing"?

HAYIM HALBERSTAM

An Ounce Of Prevention

Dr. Albert Sabin of Cincinnati, Ohio, has developed an oral vaccine which promises to give lifelong immunity to polio. It has been tested and used successfully not only in the United States, but also in Singapore, Russia, Israel, and England. It took twenty-four years and almost 2,000,000 experiments to develop and perfect the vaccine. Recently, when he was asked to comment on the tremendous effort that went into the discovery, Dr. Sabin said, "The art of prevention is difficult indeed, but it is worth it."

His thoughtful answer might impel us to appreciate the men and women in our communities who help prevent illness of the body and the mind — men and women who have dedicated themselves to the healthy physical and spiritual development of ourselves and our children. Not only the professionals — the doctors, nurses, teachers, clergy, social workers — but also the lay people, who sit on boards and give time and thought to running the basic institutions of research, teaching and healing in an efficient manner.

An easy way of evaluating their work is to imagine what a community would be like without a hospital, a synagogue, a school, a library, or an art museum. The presence of these institutions is that ounce of prevention which is worth a pound of cure.

The true guardians of a city are not its armed men;
Its consecrated teachers are its guardians.

JER. HAGIGAH 1:7

The Mature Mind

There is an important distinction between the immature and the mature individual. One may recognize the immature person by his lack of balance. He is overwhelmed by the first assault of misfortune and swept off his feet by the first piece of good luck. Then he believes, through his own slender store of experience, that what happened to him is utterly unique and that nobody has ever suffered his problems or met with his good fortune.

The mature person, on the other hand, knows that to be human means to have spiritual ups and downs and that to love means to experience both joy and sorrow for the sake of those we love. He knows that the Psalms, the Prayer Book, the love of a friend, the steadfast faith of a spouse, the balm of time, and the healing hand of God together make up the great balancing force of life.

A minister has expressed this thought as follows:

Today, upon a bus I saw a girl with golden hair.
She seemed so gay, I envied her and wished
    that I was half so fair.
I watched her as she rose to leave, and
    saw her hobble down the aisle,
She had one leg and wore a crutch,
    but as she passed — a smile.
Oh, God, forgive me when I whine:
    I have two legs and the world is mine.
Two legs to take me where I go,
Two eyes to see the sunset's glow,
Two ears to hear all I should know.
Oh, God, forgive me when I whine:
I'm blessed indeed, the world is mine.

Acceptance of the unanswerable is the beginning of all wisdom.   ZELDA POPKIN

21

The Silent Chamber

In the ancient Temple there was a "Silent Chamber." The room was so constructed that coins could be placed into it by one person and at the same time withdrawn by another without either party ever seeing the other. Thus, the donor and recipient remained unobserved and were completely anonymous. Such a secret treasury existed in every town in ancient Israel. One purpose of this Silent Chamber was to assure that the needy could receive their gifts without any possibility of embarrassment. Another was to teach people that in the highest form of giving, the donor remains anonymous.

It would be a very fine spiritual exercise for every person to create his own equivalent of a Silent Chamber, to give without pride and conceit. The Silent Chamber would accomplish many purposes, for it would enable us to give where it is deeply needed without embarrassing the recipient.

A Silent Chamber would encourage us to . . .

Provide a job for the handicapped,

Increase our pledge to the community,

Help a youngster through school with a scholarship,

Send a CARE package overseas,

Give to the hospital free bed fund . . .

All in silence.

He who gives anonymously is greater than Moses.

BAVA BATRA 9 b

The Source Of Blessing

On the eighth day of the festival of Sukkot a prayer for rain is included in the service. It expresses man's dependence upon Nature and makes us aware of God's daily gifts.

Once there was a clergyman watching a colorful rain dance in New Mexico near an Indian pueblo. He heard his friend comment on the deeply religious prayer for rain. "Religious!" the clergyman scoffed. "Why this is a pagan travesty of real worship."

A wrinkled old Indian squatting in front of them looked up briefly, but said nothing. The visitor continued his harangue. "Do you mean to tell me that these primitive Indians actually believe that this dancing and singing will make their gods send them rain?"

The old Indian chief looked up gravely and said, "We not make; we ask."

We may plant flowers, but we do not make them grow — God does. In humility we must understand the real source of all creation. And when we desire the blessings of Nature, we do not make them ourselves alone; we must also ask. The energy that is contained in the single seed and the creative powers of a tiny plant that can be released through the droplets of rain bear testimony to a great and provident God.

For Thou art the Lord our God, who causes the wind to blow and the rain to descend.

PRAYER INTRODUCED INTO THE DAILY
SERVICE ON SHEMINI ATZERET.

A World Without End

On Simhat Torah, which means literally "the rejoicing of the Torah," the annual reading of the Torah (the Five Books of Moses) is completed and begun anew. This sacred round and its moving celebration testify that study is considered by the Jew a world without end.

While in the morning of time, the human race was wandering about brutish and ape-like, the Hebrew people were already scratching marks on stones that were destined to be called The Ten Commandments. While the world was plunged into the intellectual blackout of The Dark Ages, when even the kings of France and Germany could not sign their names, the typical Jew sat in the synagogue, read his complicated Talmud and debated philosophical problems. Even in modern times, the Jewish love for learning has found ready expression, but in altered forms. In addition to the Talmud, the modern Jew studies law or medicine or nuclear physics. The link is different, but the chain continues.

Dr. Joseph Kaplan, one of the nation's outstanding physicists and chairman of the United States committee for the International Geophysical Year recently made this comment: "I undoubtedly inherited something of my father's love of learning. The atmosphere of my home encouraged study for its own sake. He believed that what we were doing was good, and that somehow it must have its roots in the Torah."

This conscious devotion to study is the uniqueness of Jewish life.

If we look upon Jewish history in its integrity as a simple and uniform power, we find that it was the Torah which stood forth throughout the history of Israel as the guiding star of its civilization.   LOUIS GINZBERG

The Unique Role Of Woman

A woman arrived home in the United States after a long stay in the Orient. She had with her a little six-month old son. When she came to the customs inspection her heart sank as the official looked sternly at her large pile of luggage to determine the amount of duty.

"What articles of value have you acquired abroad in the last twelve months?" the customs inspector demanded.

"Well, there's the baby . . ." began the woman.

The customs official stared at the sleeping infant in the woman's arms. Then waving the woman through with all of her luggage, he smiled and said, "Lady, original works of art are exempt from duty."

A woman can fulfill herself and be creative just by being a woman and building a home and a family. A woman, by carrying a child and rearing him, helps to organize community life in a unique way. Every woman knows that the love of a mother for her child is basic and indispensable to all human relationships. Every woman knows that it is the prime function of women to teach men how to be human.

The woman who understands this will make sure that her outlook and her presence will soften, charm, add graciousness to the life of her family and deepen its faith.

A woman of valor is distinguished . . .
She doeth good all the days of her life.

PROVERBS 31

25

Life Must Not Be Little

The following true story gives us considerable food for thought. Four golfers were once forced to cut their game short because of a sudden rain shower. One of the foursome insisted that since they had only played ten holes, he only owed his caddy a little over half of the eighteen hole fee agreed upon. The rest pointed out that it was hardly the caddy's fault that it rained, but he was adamant. In the end the other three paid the balance of the caddy's fee. The man saved a few pennies, but lost three friends, for as they were in the shower room, one of the men said to the others, "I guess the meanness that he had as a kid will never let him grow up and enjoy life."

One wonders how many of us are still imprisoned by the traits of our childhood that prevent us from tasting the cup of life to its fullest.

What about the person who becomes angry over trifles, or the man who is always running others into the ground, or the one who hasn't accepted the fact that he never went to college, or made the first team, or was turned down on the first date? How awful to be warped by some unpleasant experience of childhood and then to make the rest of a lifetime miserable by taking it out on others!

Life is too short to be little.   BENJAMIN DISRAELI

A Modern Aladdin's Lamp

Prayer does not come easily to the present generation. Our contemporary confusion about prayer was illustrated by the following words that recently came over a radio network. The presiding dignitary solemnly intoned, "And now let us pray for good luck."

Many of us still approach prayer in this immature fashion. We think of prayer as magic, just as we think of God as being a heavenly magician. We say we do not believe in the story of Aladdin and his lamp, and yet many of us would like to be modern Aladdins and use the prayer book as a magic lamp. We naively think that all we have to do is rub the cover of the prayer book and repeat a few magic words for God to appear, obey our requests and give us everything we want.

We pray selfishly: "O Lord, make my business prosper; grant me recovery from illness; give me relief from pain; save my dear one." But we do not pray, "Help me to accept the reality of life and to face the truth to live on with courage and dignity."

Prayer is not a liturgical slot machine in which we insert the coin of words and from which miracles jump forth at the press of a lever. In Greek the word for prayer is *eychomai,* which means "to wish"; in German it is *gebet,* which is rooted in the verb "to beg"; but in Hebrew it is *tefilah,* which means "to be judged." Prayer is a way of standing before God and accepting with equanimity and calm what life has to offer us. Prayer helps us to live with truth, for truth is God.

For I have come to know Thy truth;
I accept Thy judgments upon me
And am content with my life.   THE DEAD SEA SCROLLS

27

A Thing Of Beauty

One family on a particular block had let its home become dirty and dilapidated. The house needed painting, the lawn was filled with weeds and it was an eyesore to the neighborhood. Many friends and neighbors pleaded with them to make an effort to clean and care for their home, but to no avail.

One day in autumn a friend of the man gave him a bulb and asked him to plant it under his front window. It was a gesture of friendship, so he planted it. Early in spring a little green shoot pushed its way to the surface. A while later a yellow flower unfolded. As the family was sitting in their front room, the wife said, "That flower is so beautiful; I think I'll clean the window so we can get a better view of it." After she had completed her task she noted that the curtains looked drab, so she decided to wash them. Her husband, moved by the contrast between the curtains and room, decided to clean the house.

Inspired by this, the next week he hired painters to redo the exterior of the house. Eventually, the entire family worked to make the lawn the most beautiful in the neighborhood. All of this resulted from one friend, one seed and one flower.

When beauty is properly appreciated and understood, it can be an inspiration to beautify our lives.

When you see a beautiful plant, pronounce the benediction: Praised be He who creates beautiful things.

TOSEFTA BERAKHOT 7:4

No Rest

Wisdom is essentially the ability to know what and when to accept and why and how to reject. While there are moments when we must accept what life has to offer us, there are also times when we must not give in to life's circumstances.

It is wrong to pass off life's suffering by saying, "Well, it's a great mystery, and only God knows the answers." While this is true, it is only a partial truth. The ultimate meaning of the universe we can never hope to know, but this does not excuse us from our responsibilities to help whenever we can.

Just a century ago, some clergymen fought a bitter fight against relieving women's birth pains. Anesthetic, they argued, was a blasphemous attempt to thwart the curse laid upon Eve. This attitude is opposed by, and is exactly the opposite of, the Jewish tradition. Thus, Jewish law tells us that even the laws of the holy Sabbath must be broken to help save a life or to alleviate internal pain. This is the Jewish way: not to give way to suffering, but to do something about that suffering.

It is the Jewish conviction that anesthetics, palliatives and beneficial drugs were created for the welfare of man. But it is up to man to probe the secrets of the world through study and research and to apply the resultant knowledge to the welfare of mankind. In constant struggle to heal and relieve suffering there can be no rest.

The Holy One, blessed be He, created the healing before the suffering.   SONG OF SONGS RABBAH 4:5

The Jew In You

Friedrich Wilhelm, the king of Prussia, once asked his chaplain to prove in one word the truth of religion. "Your Majesty," the chaplain replied, "the Jews."

He correctly saw that the Jews, collectively and individually, are the embodiment of a long and continuous history of religious ideas and teachings for which they have struggled to gain world recognition throughout the ages.

Deep within the consciousness of the Jew burns the awareness of this unique spiritual destiny. His personal existence as a Jew is bound up with the deeper meaning of mankind. He is not a lonely individual on an endless road.

A Jew who lives with a sense of history is aware of his identity. He is fully cognizant of himself, of his fellow man, of his past, of his possibilities. He must understand the past, for the past is a foundation on which Jews must continue to build and develop if they would be loyal to the master builders who have laid the spiritual foundations of Judaism.

It is a unique thing to be born a Jew. It is good or bad, depending upon what we do with our Jewishness and what use we make of our heritage. Ultimately, however, the real truth is that to be born a Jew is an accident, but to live as one is an achievement.

I am a Jew because for Israel man is not yet created; men are creating him. EDMOND FLEG

Who Built The Ark?

The story of Noah has eternal charm for the young and deep meaning for the old. Who among us is not fascinated with the story of Noah and the ark? The child sees it as a picture — the march of animals, two by two, into the ark. The adult sees it as the terrifying warning of the possibility of the destruction of the earth through man's evil, which can be averted only by man's greater goodness and the grace of God.

The intriguing part of the biblical account is that God commands Noah to build an ark to save himself during the coming flood. It stands to reason that if God wanted to save Noah, He could have simply created a refuge for him and his family through a miracle. Why then did Noah have to make the ark himself?

One possible answer is that God was telling us symbolically that man must make efforts to save himself if he is to be saved at all. There is a time to rely on God, but there is also a time to rely on ourselves. Noah had to make the ark, for ultimately, only he could save himself by doing things for himself.

This is important to understand. Certain things in life take doing or they will not be done. Specific values must be deliberately sought and taught or they will never be accepted. The future, then, belongs to those who prepare for it.

Only he who takes the pain of preparing on the eve of the Sabbath will enjoy the pleasures of the Sabbath.

AVODAH ZARAH 3 a

חשון

HESHVAN

On Reading The Minutes

Rosh Hodesh, the beginning of each Jewish month, is observed by special prayers. The renewal of each month is an occasion for spiritual stock-taking, for rereading the "minutes" of the previous month.

At a meeting held not long ago, the newly elected secretary of a club was asked to read the minutes of the previous meeting. Equal to the occasion, he arose, cleared his throat impressively and said, "The minutes of the last meeting were one hour and twenty minutes and six seconds." Then he sat down.

Jews are reluctant to merely record the minutes of each month in simple time units. For the more accurate assessment of the month is not the hours spent or the seconds kept, but the measure of human emotions and feelings — the joys and the tears, the hopes and the fears.

Furthermore, there is no reason why a person should not measure himself — and be measured — by the customary ideas of right and wrong; of sin, guilt, repentance, forgiveness, and amendment of life; of joy and sorrow; success and failure. These are the real yardsticks of our monthly activities, and it is exactly these that the Jewish ritual of *birkat hahodesh,* blessing of the new month, tries to emphasize. Ultimately, we will find that if our monthly spiritual statement is correct, then our yearly religious accounting will balance correctly.

Teach us to number our days that we may get us a heart of wisdom.   PSALMS 90:12

The Pursuit Of Excellence

Near the entrance to an art gallery in London there used to be a wastebasket. A visitor once asked the guard at the entrance what the basket was for. The guard answered with a smile, "That is where the students drop their conceit when they go out." He had noticed over the years that as students saw the great paintings in the gallery, their conceit over their own work was diminished.

When we contemplate the great works of art, whether they be in literature, painting, sculpture, or music, we inevitably measure them against our own abilities. While this should not reduce our own efforts into insignificance, yet we should at least maintain a sense of humility in their presence. We should be inspired by the great expressions of the human spirit to reject mediocrity and be satisfied only with excellence.

The magnificent achievements of the human spirit remind us that in every age we are capable of excellence. This degree of attainment comes with the cultivation of our true abilities. To let them rest undeveloped is as sad as permitting them to raise us to a level of conceit that is not honestly within us. We must develop an attitude which will make true artistic greatness the constant vision of our way of life in every expression of the human mind and spirit.

The artist is content with aspiration, whereas the mediocre must have beauty. And yet the artist attains beauty without willing it, for he is striving after truthfulness.

ARNOLD SCHOENBERG

A Person Is Not A Thing

Count Leo Tolstoy, the great Russian writer, was once walking the streets of Moscow on a cold wintry night. Suddenly, he was stopped by a beggar in rags, shivering with the cold. The man's eyes pleaded for some coins with which to purchase food. Tolstoy reached into his pockets, but to his great dismay, he found nothing, for he had left home without his wallet. He placed his hand in the hand of the unfortunate beggar and with a deep sigh said, "I am sorry my friend, I have nothing for you." The beggar's eyes lit up, and overcome by emotion, he whispered, "But you gave me the greatest gift of all — you called me friend."

The real key to resolving social problems is the basic recognition that a person is not a thing. Every individual has wants, needs, and feelings, and only when we understand this, can we begin to practice sound human relations.

Can we appreciate the emotional scars of a child who is rejected from a circle of friends because he is of another religion? Or do we understand what exquisite joy it is for the handicapped to find gainful employment?

When we see someone whose welfare and well-being is in our hands we view him not as a statistic, but rather as a father or a mother, a child or a relative, a soul, a child of God. If we wish to discharge our obligations in life, we must always be able to put ourselves imaginatively in the place of others.

All that we cherish must rest on the dignity and inviolability of the person.   JOSEPH PROSKAUER

The Best Years Of Our Lives

A minister leaving his church one day, noticed three small boys sitting on the steps. One had a toy airplane, one a miniature racing car, and the third a copy of *Esquire*.

"What would you like to be, son?" the minister asked the first boy.

"An airplane pilot," was the quick reply.

"And you?" he said to the second boy.

"A racing driver."

"What would you like to be?" he asked the youngster with the magazine.

The boy grudgingly dragged his eyes away from its pages and replied longingly — "Grown, sir, grown."

Those of us who are grown ought to appreciate and enjoy the fact that we are grown. One of man's greatest needs is to grow, and to grow is to really live. We should worry less about hardening of the arteries and more about hardening of the mind. We should take all that life has to offer and enjoy it fully.

Remember, today and tomorrow are the "good old days" we will miss a decade from now.

Remember to enjoy your son's Bar Mitzvah, savor your daughter's wedding, swell with pride at the graduations, make the most of the birthdays and anniversaries. Remember to share in all the happy events of growth, for these years of growth are the best years of our lives.

For if a man live many years,
Let him rejoice in them all.   ECCLESIASTES 11:8

A Continuity Of Faith

A teacher in a religious school was reading a Bible story to a group of children. Suddenly she looked up and asked, "Why do you believe in God?"

She received a variety of answers, some filled with simple belief and others obviously insincere. The one that stunned her came from a little tot. The little one had answered, "I guess it just runs in our family."

A continuity of faith running through generations is indispensable to establishing the roots of trust. For there is much more meaning to life than any one soul, any one people, or any one generation can ever hope to understand. And understanding is not as important as trust.

Very few of us understand our digestive system, but we eat. Only doctors understand our respiratory system, but all of us breathe. We understand very little about the mysteries of love, but we fall in love, marry, and raise families.

This thread of trust ties the generations together. A family brought up in faith realizes that we did not create all we have, that we are the heirs of the accumulated wisdom of the generations. Moreover, we must remember that whenever we try to understand the universe, we are using our limited minds, to pass judgment on a limitless Spirit. This limitless Spirit is an endless and wonderful sea of mystery. Every time we discover something new, we again experience the wonder of a great God and come to the full realization that the world is more than we know.

Trust in the Lord;
Be strong, and let your heart take courage;
Yea, put your trust in the Lord.   PSALMS 27:14

The Temptation To Do Good

Just after services, a woman came up to a rabbi and said, "I have attended four Sabbath services in a row, twice for Bar Mitzvahs, once for a blessing of a bride and groom, and then again for the naming of a child. I enjoyed all of them very much. In fact, I am almost tempted to be religious."

This woman's conventional conversation might startle us into a most unconventional thought. The word temptation really is bipolar, that is to say, it is both positive and negative. But in our society the word "temptation" is always associated with evil. Say of a man that he is tempted, and the immediate inference is that he is lured to do wrong. Why is this? Why do we habitually think and speak as though life's major enticements are on the side of sin?

The answer is that we have based our society solely upon success and self-seeking. We have come to the erroneous conclusion that life means either driving ahead or blocking someone else's drives. We cannot do either of these without feeling severely guilty, for someone must be hurt in the process. On the other hand, if we are always on our emotional guard, then our corroding suspicions and nagging doubts undermine our lives. What we must do is to begin to restructure our society on the basis of social service and redirect our energies from hindering to helping others. In a sentence, let us tempt ourselves to do good.

Seek the good in everyone and reveal it; bring it forth.
                                            NAHMAN OF BRATSLAV

Down Payments

A lady once walked into a department store and after making a sizable purchase, she said to the clerk, "Charge it." After he finished billing her and gave her the customer's copy, she remarked to her friend, "Thank God, *that's* paid for."

Most of us erroneously believe that the best things in life can be obtained by a simple request to "charge it." The real truth, however, is that anything that is worthwhile must be purchased with down payments of thought, energy, and devotion. Eventually, all the accounts of life must be fully squared, and they can never balance by an indifferent word or two.

A healthy relationship between a son and a father is no mere accident; it comes through the daily down payments of love and mutual respect. A religious person does not achieve the benefits of a life of piety merely by conviction, but rather through the down payments of prayer, sincerity, and good deeds. The many friendships we treasure during a lifetime are not acquired by wishful thinking, but by the down payments of thoughtfulness, understanding and mutual devotion.

When we have real insight, we see that the good and worthwhile things of life are usually paid for in advance and its hardships can be written off against the account of experience.

Your deeds will bring you near or your deeds will drive you far away.   EDUYOT 5:7

The Tongue Of The Prophets

Let us look at some educational statistics. The Protestant child receives an average of thirty hours of church school a year. Our Roman Catholic neighbors see that their children receive yearly about two hundred hours of religious instruction. In marked contrast, our Jewish children annually receive an average of 335 hours of Hebrew instruction! This fundamental commitment to the study of Hebrew is the lifeline of the Jew, for one cannot understand Judaism without a knowledge of Hebrew. It is the language of our faith.

The basic difference between Jewish education and that of other faiths is that Judaism must transmit to its children not only religious understanding, but also a complete culture and a fund of historical knowledge. Judaism is not just a religion; it is a religious civilization. In this civilization, the Hebrew language plays a key role.

Hebrew is the cement that created the cohesiveness of our people. In the long range of experience, the Jewish community that has abandoned Hebrew ceased to endure. We have survived the waves of history — the pogroms, the crusades, the intellectual assaults — but we have never survived the loss of Hebrew as a vital tongue.

To teach Judaism without Hebrew is like trying to carry water in your hands. The living waters of our faith can only be carried in the strong and sealed container of the Hebrew language.

Flowing down the hills of eternity, the Hebrew language has been set apart for truths destined to sway mankind and humanize the world.   SABATO MORAIS

For Whom Do You Work?

According to a popular belief the success of a person is determined by his drive, and it is measured solely by how much he can produce or what he owns. In this new religion, business is worshipped as God; the office or the plant becomes the House of God; the adding machine replaces the liturgy; the closing of the financial books represents Judgment Day. But we have forgotten the sacrifices: they are merely family, friends, and self.

Perhaps the following story could be told about you. A man, let us call him Jim, collapsed in his office. The doctor who had known him well for many years confided to a mutual friend, "Jim sacrificed for his beliefs."

"What beliefs did he cherish?" the friend asked.

"Jim believed," answered the doctor, "that he could live a thirty-year-old life with a fifty-year-old body."

Be honest with yourself. For whom do you drive, run, acquire, amass? Ask yourself these questions:

Is there any widow living on the benefits of a good insurance policy and shrewd investments who would not throw it all away in a moment and take in washing if she could only have her husband back?

Why is it so hard to get a person to leave his work for just a half hour for the welfare of his child? Money he can have every day, but his child he cannot.

Why is it that when lifelong friends become partners, in a matter of days their money relationships can turn them into bitter enemies?

For whom do you work?

For whom do I work during the best part of my years and thereby deprive my soul of goodness and contentment?

JUDAH LEIB GORDON

Self-Forgiveness

Taken At the Flood, by John Gunther, is a brilliant biography of Albert Lasker, the man who created modern advertising. This man's restless energies ranged all the way from politics and sports to Jewish affairs and medical research. In one part of the book in discussing his psychoanalytic treatment, Lasker made this penetrating comment: He said, "You know what it did for me? It taught me to forgive myself."

This is a valuable insight, for self-forgiveness is indispensable to self-understanding, and ultimately to self-development. Because of the inexperience of our childhood, because of the conditions of life itself, because there are so many variable factors in all human relationships, we often burden ourselves with guilt. If it be justified guilt, then we must face it honestly and forthrightly and resolve to mend our ways. If it be groundless guilt, then we must see it for what it really is — namely the product of our imagination, and let it vanish as smoke on the horizon. Very often, we are not even aware that we are motivated by inadequacy or guilt. Therefore, our attempts to understand ourselves, through our own efforts or through the help of a competent counselor, will help us to see the truth and eventually forgive ourselves.

Perhaps we are really too hard on ourselves. Perhaps we ought to discover how to forgive ourselves and thereby live healthier and happier lives.

God loans us the impulse to judge ourselves and to forgive our own actions. If we use this impulse wisely, then we can create an admirable pattern of life. ISRAEL BERGER

The God In You

The simplest events in daily experiences may reveal the profoundest meanings of life. We see this in the story of a small boy bending over the crib of his newborn brother and whispering, "Tell me quick, little brother, before you forget, what does God look like?"

This child might well have been speaking for the whole human race. From our youth through old age, we struggle unceasingly to know and understand God. But He is so vast and so many-sided that each person sees Him, in his own way, and thus each person, no matter how great, obtains but a glimpse of God.

The ordinary person sees Him plainly and straightforwardly. The more thoughtful individual beholds Him in deeper studies and finer meanings. The laborer approaches Him through his strength, the artist through his creative ability, the scientist through his research, and the theologian in the biblical and liturgical word. Each in his own way, but each equally valid and true. There is a spark of the Divine in every one of us. How we preserve this spark and pass it on to others clearly reveals the extent to which God is in us. For a spark dies unless it flares into full flame and makes contact with something other than itself.

The soul of man is the light of God.   PROVERBS 20:27

44

The Heart Of The Matter

There is a child's story that is at once charming and instructive. A certain school introduced the practice of giving the children a physical examination every year. When this first was put into practice, the children in the primary grades were extremely puzzled and skeptical about the whole project. One little girl went in to be examined by the doctor. When she came out, her little friend, waiting next in line, asked what they did.

"Oh," she said, "They cut you open and take out everything."

"Everything?" echoed the friend.

"Absolutely," she solemnly insisted.

"Even your heart?" the boy queried.

"Sure," was the answer.

"Well," said the boy, "if they take out your heart, how can you pledge allegiance?"

The heart of the matter is really that we can not pledge anything if our heart is not in it. All the standards we set up and all the resolutions we make will eventually fail unless we are sincere. Very often we set forth visions of what we wish to do, but they are either too lofty to be attainable or too low to be really worthy of us. Standards must be honest, inspiring and attainable if they are to claim our allegiance.

Never speak mere empty words . . .
Cherish a good heart when thou
findest it in any man.   ELEAZAR (ROKEACH) OF WORMS

The First One Was Abraham

In the Jewish tradition, Abraham is the proponent of the concept of one God. There is an ancient Midrash (Rabbinic story) about Abraham, which is part of the lore taught in nearly every Jewish school. It goes like this:

Abraham's father, Terah, sold idols for a living. His idol shop contained a complete assortment of images, all the way from the god of power to the goddess of soil and fertility. It was a very profitable business. Abraham repeatedly asked his father to give up the business, but Terah refused and would not listen.

One day, Terah went out to lunch and asked Abraham to watch the store. As soon as he left, Abraham took a hammer and proceeded to smash every idol in the shop. He left one idol, the largest, standing, and placed the hammer in his hand. A short while later, his father returned and found his shop in ruins. Abraham gave his father the following explanation: The idols fell to quarreling and started to fight. They destroyed one another, except for the largest, who was the final victor.

His father said, "You fool, idols are made by men; they cannot move or talk. They are really quite stupid." And Abraham asked, "But Father, then why do you worship them?"

The worship of idols is the cause and the beginning and end of every evil.

WISDOM OF SOLOMON 14:27

Married Love

A little girl once turned to her mother and said, "Mommy, I love you ten times." After a few minutes of deep thought she added, "No, twenty times," then, "No, six hundred times." After her mother kissed her she blurted out with, "Mommy, I love you outside the line of numbers." This was true insight, for real love is without measure. We see this real love truly in the family and most profoundly in the relationship between husband and wife.

A couple who have shared a lifetime of devotion can always deepen love by blowing on the coals of the heart. A part of the great gift of God to man is that man and woman in married love may come together freely and unashamedly in the communing of the flesh and spirit in an experience of re-creation. Having shared the rearing of children, having seen and faced the death of dear ones together, having carried together many problems, having tasted the joys of happy events, the confidence of friends, the warm pleasures of intimate thoughts, married love becomes ideal love.

A man who really loves his wife will understand and accept her moods and appreciate her abilities. A woman who truly loves her husband will share his concerns and compliment his real achievements. A happy marriage is one in which each partner gives the best years of his life to the one who has made them the best.

O make these loved companions greatly to rejoice . . .
Blessed art Thou, O Lord, who makest bridegroom and
bride to rejoice.   JEWISH MARRIAGE SERVICE

Compassion Is The Badge

Ben-Zvi, the President of Israel, is essentially a scholar. After Chaim Weizmann died, he was called to the presidency from his small cottage in Jerusalem where he had been living with his wife Rachel. On the day he was made President, he returned home at night and found a sentry marching up and down in front of his dwelling. He asked the man what he was doing there. The young sergeant replied that he had been sent by the Chief of Staff as an honor guard before the home of the President.

Rubbing his head in amazement, Ben-Zvi entered the house. It was winter in Jerusalem and the night was cold. After a few minutes, he came out and said, "Look here, it is cold tonight. Won't you come in and at least have some hot tea?" The soldier replied, "I cannot leave my post. Orders are orders." Foiled, Ben-Zvi re-entered his house. After a while, he turned to his wife and asked her to make some tea; then he went out again and greeted the soldier. "Look here, I have an idea. You go in and have tea, and I will stand outside with your gun and take your post."

This compassionate regard is typical of the Jews throughout the ages. Through years of oppression the Jew has acquired a sensitivity to suffering. It may well be said that compassion is the badge of the Jew.

When a person has compassion for humanity it is a sure sign that he is a descendant of Abraham, our father.

BETZAH 32 b

Training Our Tensions

Once a small boy was shouting out the headlines to sell newspapers on a street corner. A kindly passerby asked the lad if he was making much money. "Oh, I don't make any profit," said the boy, "I get my papers from my friend for five cents each and sell them for a nickel." The stranger then asked, "Then why do you sell papers?" "Oh," said the boy, "just to get a chance to holler!"

All of us need to holler now and then, but we must be wise enough to train our tensions so that no one gets hurt in the process. We must be able to express our pent-up emotions in a very healthy manner. We can release our burning energy in sports, gardening, volunteer work, simply walking, or in any of a hundred other outlets. Even housecleaning and dancing are often wonderful ways to relieve the pressure built up by a personal problem.

Anger is in all of us and we must learn to recognize its danger signals long before it overpowers us. Those who are alert will learn to handle angry feelings safely and even profitably. The next time you see storm clouds gathering upon the horizon of your emotions, why not make it a point to recognize them and immediately begin an activity which offers you relief and release?

Who is strong? He who is master of his impulses.

AVOT 4:1

49

The Untouchables

During the beginning of the Russian revolution, a Communist approached his friend and told him that religion was unnecessary — and was therefore to be eliminated. The friend asked how this was to be done. The Communist replied, "We will tear down all religious buildings, burn all prayer books, and destroy all symbols of God." The friend replied, "Yes, but you can never touch the stars."

Ultimately, the stars symbolize the everlasting presence of religion and God among us. If every religious mark and symbol were to disappear, the stars would still remain as reminders of the everlasting nature of the universe, the timelessness of religious values, and the source of all life.

We must always remember this lesson in dealing with the daily issues of life. We must always abide and cherish the deep feeling that certain values are unshakable and certain religious convictions are untouchable. There are certain teachings that are lofty and claim our ultimate loyalty. These truths remain with us and give us the strength to meet the difficulties of life and to resolve them. For as the stars are untouchable and everlasting, so is the essence of God.

Lift up your eyes on high and see who created these. Then to whom will you compare Me, says the Holy One.

ISAIAH 40:25-26

Conscience As Carpenter

Once there was a contractor who had employed the same carpenter for many years. One day, he approached the carpenter and said, "Every time you have built a house for me, I have given you a plan in advance. This time, I would like you to build a house on this empty lot any way you wish." The artisan, wishing to finish as quickly as possible, was careless and shoddy; the foundation was weak, the walls were slightly crooked, nails were left out, and in a few years, the house would undoubtedly begin to sag.

On the day the carpenter had finished, the contractor walked up to him with the key to the front door in his hand and said, "I have always wanted to give you a home as a gift; since you built this home the way *you* wanted, it now belongs to you." He handed him the key and left.

We are all given the opportunity to build the house of our character. The blocks are time, the cement is our ideals, the foundation is our faith. The contractor is God and our conscience is the carpenter. When its structure is fully erected, we live in it — for the rest of our lives and for all eternity. We can build straight or crooked, firm or weak; it is really up to us.

How do you build? How skilled and true is your carpenter?

Be master of your will and slave to your conscience.

JUDAH LEIB LAZEROV

Source Material

Some people say that we should seek the essence of Judaism and ignore ritual observances. These people forget an interesting analogy. If we put on the essence of cologne, it will evaporate overnight, unless, of course, we have a source to continually draw upon.

Similarly, the essence of Judaism's beliefs is stored in its rituals, and only those who have a storehouse from which to draw upon the fundamentals of Judaism will live creatively as Jews.

We fix a mezuzah to the door and thereby fix our principles upon family living.

Every morsel of kosher food we prepare testifies to our reverence for life. For we do not kill wantonly; we do not take a life without divine permission.

Every Sabbath day we keep means we reject commerce as the control on our lives. We are not money-making machines; we are men, and we say this with our beings every Shabbat, from sunset to sunset.

When we insist upon Hebrew as the language of our prayer, we testify that the words of Moses still ring in our ears in their authentic form. We maintain our link unbroken in the golden chain of Judaism.

Judaism functions only so long as it is co-extensive with the whole of the Jew's life.   MORDECAI M. KAPLAN

The Cradle Of Civilization

While in Israel, Billy Rose, the internationally-famed showman, drove to Jerusalem to visit the site of the sculpture garden which he is giving to the people of Israel. As he was leaving Haifa, his driver pointed proudly to the beautiful slopes of the Carmel Hills. Rose was unimpressed and he said, "If this were Westchester, I wouldn't even look."

The driver then suddenly changed his course, switched off the main route and headed into the hills. He kept right on despite Rose's protests that they were going in the wrong direction. A short while later, the driver halted the car in front of a cave and said that in that particular cave was found the first recorded information about man, 600,000 years ago. "You don't have that," he said, "in Westchester!"

Israel is the source of the most precious memories of man. It is the scene of the genesis of the conscience; it is the stage on which were enacted the supreme moments of the spirit; it is the Holy Land of the major faiths of the Western World. Its every rock and rill are filled with sacred memories. It is the spiritual cradle of civilization.

The very name Israel stirs within us the most elevated sentiments. All find consolation in that land, some by its memories, others by its hopes.   SOLOMON MUNK

Let 'er Fly

There is the wonderfully warm story of the minister who was appealing to his congregation for funds. He became enthusiastic, and as he reached the climax of his talk, he said with deep feeling, "This church must walk."

The immediate response from the congregation was "Let 'er walk."

Encouraged, he continued, "It must run."

And back came the reply, "Let 'er run!"

Extremely excited, the minister proclaimed, "It must fly!"

And once more the congregation echoed, "Let 'er fly!"

Then he went on, "And that will cost money."

Back came the response, "Let 'er walk."

Many of us are genuinely enthusiastic about many causes. We do not hesitate to expound high-flying ideals, but the moment we are asked for money, to translate our values into reality, we lose our enthusiasm. This is actually a kind of hypocrisy. To be really mature, we must understand that ideals cannot be created and fostered cheaply. Values cannot be built on words alone. They require the support of energy and money. We must never be ensnared by the pseudo-sophisticated notion that to mingle money and ideals is beneath our dignity. Actually, it is a test of our conviction to be able to ask for money and to give money for what we deeply believe.

Giving is equal to all the other precepts put together.
BAVA BATRA 9 a

Everyman

According to a Yiddish story, a man one day meets his rabbi on the street, and after the exchange of the usual pleasantries, the congregant tells his spiritual counselor of his despair because of the sad state of the world. He winds up with, "I tell you, Rabbi, it's enough to make a man lose his religion."

The rabbi reflects for a moment and then tells him quietly, "Seems to me, it's enough to make a man *use* his religion."

This anecdote shows that everyone thinks of changing humanity, but no one thinks of changing himself. We never really like to face ourselves with the basic questions of living: Who am I? Why was I born? What shall I do with my life?

We evade these questions in a hundred ways. Our hyperactivity is an index of our deep restlessness. In the middle ages, this restless spirit would have been compared to the knight who jumps on a horse and rides off in all directions at once. Today, one might aptly say that our motor is racing, but it isn't in gear.

The way to a meaningful life is not through random activity, nor is it through its opposite — passive withdrawal. We give meaning to our lives by trying to understand who we are, what we believe, and what we can do by realizing that each of us is a child of God with unlimited potentiality for good. What each of us thinks and does, matters — to ourselves, our society, and our God.

Salvation is attained not by subscription to metaphysical dogmas, but solely by love of God that fulfills itself in action. This is the cardinal truth of Judaism.

HASDAI CRESCAS

Gam Zu Letovah

There are many heroes in the tradition of Judaism, but the one man of rabbinic times whose personality has most impressed Jewish students is the great Akiba ben Joseph. Akiba actually distilled his faith into formula; it has now become classic: *Gam zu letovah* "Whatever God does is for the best."

The following true story illustrates this principle. Once while Akiba was on a mission from Jerusalem to Rome, he and his group came to a certain city at nightfall. There they found all the inns filled. They were forced to sleep in a field, and Akiba, without the slightest disturbance, said, "This is for the best."

They had with them a donkey, a rooster, and a lantern. During the night, the wind extinguished the light, a fox carried off the rooster and the donkey was killed by a lion. Akiba awoke, noticing the havoc, and he simply remarked, "It is for the best." Then he turned over and went to sleep again.

The next day, when they entered the city, they found it in ruins. During the night, an invading army had sacked it. Akiba turned to his companions and said, "Did I not tell you that whatever God does is for the best? Had we found accommodations in the city, had light been burning in the field, had the donkey brayed or the rooster crowed, we would not be alive. My friends, it is always *gam zu letovah,* for the best."

All my life I have been waiting for the moment when I might truly fulfill the commandments. I have always loved the Lord with all my might and with all my heart; now I know that I love Him with all my life. AKIBA BEN JOSEPH

You Are More Than You Are

We often wonder what effect our conduct and our religious faith have upon others. An interesting example can be found in a true story gleaned from the Talmud.

Simeon, the son of Shatah, lived during a period of dire poverty. One day, he sent his pupils to buy a camel from an Arab. When they brought him the animal, they gleefully announced that they had found a precious jewel in its collar. "Did the seller know of this?" he asked. When they said he did not, Simeon retorted, "Do you think I am a barbarian that I should take advantage of the letter of the law by which the gem is mine together with the camel? Return the gem to the Arab immediately."

When the heathen received it back, he exclaimed, "Blessed be the God of Simeon ben Shatah. Blessed be the God of Israel!" We are told that this exclamation was dearer to Simeon than all the riches of the world.

In everything we say and do, we must remember that to others we represent the living image of our faith. Others base their judgments on the way we act. If we act as we are taught by our faith, then we have not only fulfilled ourselves, but we also reflect glory upon our religious heritage. We must therefore be fully aware of what we say and do, so that others may look upon the way we live and say, "Blessed be the God of this man."

A man is always responsible for his actions, whether awake or asleep.   BAVA KAMMA 3 b

The Tie That Binds

When Sholom Aleichem, the popular Yiddish writer, came to America, he was introduced to Mark Twain in New York City. Sholom Aleichem said to his fellow craftsman, "They call me the Yiddish Mark Twain." Whereupon the other responded, "And they refer to me as the American Sholom Aleichem."

In point of fact, the real name of Sholom Aleichem was Sholom Rabinowitz, and Mark Twain is the pen name of Samuel Clemens. Both men adopted popular and ordinary terms for their writing names because they had a deep feeling for people and because they wanted to identify with people. Indeed, it was this genuine compassion for humanity that made their works so similar, even though one wrote in Yiddish and the other expressed himself in English.

If anything, this confirms the truth that people are alike the world over, and that nations everywhere share common hopes and fears. The particular expression varies only to the extent of the cultural and the linguistic difference. But it must never be forgotten that all mankind is bound together with the ties of humanity.

It is not the seas that divide the peoples, but the peoples that divide the seas.   SHOLOM ALEICHEM

When God Says No

There is an interesting and inspiring story about a little girl whose doll was broken. Her brother laughed as she prayed to God to put the pieces together again. "Do you expect God to answer your prayers?" he scoffed and mocked at her. But she insisted confidently, "You will see that God will answer." A few hours later, when the brother returned and the doll still lay broken on the floor, he demanded, "Well, has God answered?" "Oh yes," she replied, "He said no."

To be sane about living means accepting the fact that there are times that God says no to our prayers in His wisdom and for our welfare. We must not expect the impossible to suit our own narrow desires and selfish interests.

We cannot pray that God strike all the Russians dead, for we must not seek that which is immoral.

We cannot desire that we suddenly grow younger, for we must not expect that which is unnatural.

We must ask for what can be and accept what we receive.

Prayer is the bridge that carries man to God, but he must not, while praying, think of a reward. Do not ask God to change the laws of nature for you. It is enough to find God through prayer.   HASIDIC ANTHOLOGY

The Price Of Success

One spring, a small Indiana town received its first tornado warning. At 3 A.M., warned by telephone, sleepy neighbors gathered in the basement of a large house. For the most part they were clad in a motley assortment of slacks, nightclothes and bathrobes. One woman who came last caught everyone's attention. She wore rings on every finger. Her throat was hidden by her pearls and necklaces, and she had thrown a blue mink stole over her fur coat. To her husband's hoot of laughter, she replied, "It took me twenty-seven years to get these, and if I go, they go."

This woman contains a little of all of us. We hunger so to fill our lives with the symbols of success, but we do not realize that it often costs us our serenity and at times even our sanity. We are bound so firmly to the economic wheel that our values become warped. There is nothing wrong with a beautiful gift as a symbol of love, but there is a great deal wrong when the symbol becomes a substitute for love and an end in itself.

True morality requires of us not to despise wealth, but to appraise it rightly. But never must the desire for riches become a fetish to which we sacrifice our moral health and tranquility of soul. MORRIS JOSEPH

As A Mighty Stream

An ancient Talmudic teaching, whose lesson is especially meaningful in our time, reads as follows:

"The Torah is compared to two paths, one of fire and one of ice. If a man turns to one, he will be burned, if he turns to the other, he will be frozen. What shall he do? Let him walk in the middle."

This is one of the finest insights our tradition can offer us into our own position with regard to the past and the future. The true function of religion is to combine a vast awareness of the past with a deep sense of the future.

Those Jews who want to return to the "old-time religion" will find a temporary escape, but no permanent refuge. Their children will pass them by. Those who ignore the past completely in their desire for modernity, will find themselves restless, and like the tumbleweed will roll off the plain of Judaism at the first blast of prejudice or challenge.

We must maintain a steadfast loyalty toward our faith, but at the same time be willing to experiment, and thereby permit the living waters of Judaism to flow surely and serenely. In order for Judaism to live, it must follow between the frozen ways of static faith and the fires that indiscriminately destroy the values of the past.

The old must be renewed, and the new must be made holy.   ABRAHAM ISAAC KUK

The Road To Paradise

An ancient Hasidic story tells of a soul that went to Heaven. When the soul arrived, he immediately asked to see the rabbis who were in Paradise. He was led to a room where he saw a group of rabbis sitting about and studying. The soul was surprised and said, "There must be some mistake. These rabbis do not appear any different, they are not in Paradise." Whereupon the guide turned and said, "There is no mistake. You see the rabbis are not in Paradise; Paradise is in the rabbis."

Very often we seek peace and contentment through all kinds of external devices and amusements. We scurry about tasting the latest philosophy or sampling the newest fad. But, when we arrive at maturity, we learn that the world is simply a reflection of our own state of mind and soul. If we are at peace within ourselves, we will see unity and integrity in all of our activities. If we are troubled and confused, then we see chaos and unhappiness in everything we do. To substitute one activity for another will not give us the peace we seek. Peace can be found only if we look inward with courage and honesty.

The grass may look greener elsewhere, but it is only an illusion, for wherever you look, you will find that happiness lies right in your own backyard.

You cannot find peace anywhere save in yourself.

MARTIN BUBER

כסלו

KISLEV

Be Yourself

It is told that when Rabbi Zusya was on his death bed, surrounded by his family and disciples, he suddenly began to weep. They turned to him and asked, "Reb Zusya, why do you weep? You have nothing to fear. You have been the noblest example of our time." And he answered, "I weep because in the coming world they will not ask me, why were you not Moses, nor even why were you not Abraham or the Baal Shem Tov, but they will ask, why were you not Zusya? And what will I answer?"

Every moment of living, we are being asked, "Why are you not yourself?" Our responsibility is to develop ourselves to our fullest capacities. We have hidden resources, abilities and talents that atrophy because we are content to accept the deadening routine of life.

A housewife prepares over a thousand meals a year, and how easily she could bow to routine, and how great a lift is given her and her family when she comes up with a new recipe! A businessman must concentrate on his business to earn his livelihood, yet when he finds time for a hobby, it changes his pattern from existing to living. Nothing is more boring than a teen-ager who talks only of clothes, dates, or the latest record; but nothing is more enchanting than a young person who can carry on an intelligent and informed conversation about world affairs. The world is filled with opportunities for self-expression and growth.

The full development of each individual is not only a right, but a duty to society.   LOUIS D. BRANDEIS

Reason And Ritual

In India, holy men often practice mortification. That is, they systematically try to harm or inflict pain upon their bodies. In this way they think they are worshipping God. Once such a man bound himself in chains. Each year he added another section of chains to his body until he was hardly able to move. One day he wanted to travel to another province, but he was so weighed down with chains that he could not fit into the passenger compartments. So they lifted him into the freight train and the conductor labelled him "baggage."

Many of us often lose sight of the real value of religion. We become so laden down with ritual that we forget that the fundamental purpose of a ritual is to express a relationship with God. Ritual serves as one of the bridges between man and God and must always be seen as such. Ritual is never an end in itself, but always the means to a greater end. Therefore, every ritual must be performed with understanding. When ritual is mechanical it defeats its purpose, but when it is sincerely practiced and its proper function understood it becomes the finest link between man and God.

God considers not only the form of the worship, but also its sincerity.   ME'IL TZEDAKAH 346

The Trifles Of The Hour

A friend once called on Michelangelo, the great artist, who was in the process of finishing a statue. Some time afterward, he called again and the sculptor was still at this work. His friend, looking at the fine figure exclaimed, "Nothing much has changed. You must have been idle since I last came."

"By no means," replied the sculptor, "I have retouched this part and polished that; I have softened this feature and brought out this muscle; I have given more expression to this lip and more energy to that limb."

"Well," said his friend, "but these are all trifles."

"It may be so," replied Michelangelo, "but I believe that trifles make greatness and greatness is no trifle."

Greatness is found in a concern for some of the trifles of life.

A little card of congratulations.

A few words of encouragement.

A short expression of condolence.

A small donation.

A short hospital visit.

A brief prayer.

All these trifles add up to greatness.

Be careful in the observance of a small commandment as of a large one, for you do not know the merit of each commandment.   AVOT 2:1

How Much Are You Worth?

We sometimes wonder about a person — how much is he worth? We usually mean by this — what are his financial assets? — but this is actually a very limited view of someone's true worth.

Consider J. Paul Getty, the richest man in America. Not long ago, his eleven-year-old son died. On that day, how much was he worth? Shortly thereafter, by chance, an article appeared about the women who wear America's most fabulous jewels. A third of them had been divorced twice, and a half had been divorced once. On the day they received their divorce, how much do you think their jewels were worth? Who is worth more, a man who has high earning power, or a poor professor devoted to higher education, a social butterfly or a social worker?

The spiritual application is rather obvious. It is not what we have but what we are that makes life worthwhile. All the riches in the world cannot gild poverty of character. The worth of a person is determined by the way he relates to his responsibilities in life. We should measure worth not in financial terms but in spiritual terms, in all major areas of personal responsibility. Thus, it becomes meaningful to ask:

What are you worth to your community?
What are you worth to your family?
What are you worth to yourself?
What are you worth to God?

The ideal of man is to be a revelation himself, clearly to recognize himself as a manifestation of God.

BAAL SHEM TOV

The Hope Of Israel

One of the greatest men in contemporary Jewish history was Theodor Herzl, the founder of modern political Zionism. The hope of this man's life for a Jewish State mirrored the larger hope of the Jewish people for a return to their homeland. It is unbelievable what the Jews suffered during the time of their exile, from the year 70 until the birth of the State of Israel in 1948. Hounded and harassed, persecuted and pilloried, never once did they abandon hope for the return to Zion.

In fact, the national anthem of Zionist aspirations became "Hatikvah," a word which means literally, "The Hope." Because ancient and medieval Jews never surrendered their trust in the future, we modern Jews have seen the dream fulfilled in our time. Hope is the hallmark of Judaism.

The Jew is noted for his unbelievable sense of historic optimism. Jewish literature is filled with thousands of illustrations and quotations emphasizing our hope for the future. Because we have faith, we have a future.

While within a Jewish breast beats the heart of a Jew,
Then our hope — it is not dead, our ancient hope and true.
                                                              HATIKVAH

A Sense Of Reverence

Life is precious and life is sacred. When we move about in God's world, we must walk and work with reverence for creation.

A story about one of our great atomic physicists illustrates this concern for all living things. This man, one of the chief architects of the atomic bomb, was out wandering in the woods one day with a friend when he came upon a small tortoise. Overcome with pleasurable excitement, he took up the tortoise and started home, thinking to surprise his children with it. After a few steps, he paused and surveyed the tortoise doubtfully. "What's the matter?" his friend asked.

Without responding, the great scientist slowly retraced his steps as precisely as possible and gently set the turtle down upon the exact spot from which he had taken him up. Then he solemnly faced his friend and said, "It just struck me that for one man, perhaps I have tampered enough with the universe." He turned and left the turtle to wander on its way.

This is not a denial or a fear of the world, but rather a recognition that we must have a sense of reverence for the life of the world.

Take your sandals off your feet, for the place on which you stand is holy. EXODUS 3:5

Your Neighbor's Keeper

Some time ago a leading magazine published a cartoon in which two boys were quarreling and obviously ready to fight. Underneath was the following caption. One of them is saying, "My father could lick your father — if we weren't all brothers."

If we really accepted the Fatherhood of God and the resultant brotherhood of man and lived it as a truth, then war would disappear from the face of the earth.

Ultimately, it is not diplomats or politicians or nations that determine the conduct of life, but the individual. Groups are only composed of individuals, and the sum total of what each person thinks or does is the directive force in living.

It therefore comes down to this. If each person develops a sensitive conscience and listens to its whisperings, then the world will become a better place in which to live. In dealing with people, we are relating to children of God — to souls. This one vital distinction may spell the difference between disaster and deliverance.

The love of people is at the same time a love for God. For when we love one, we necessarily love one's handiwork.

JUDAH LOEW

Precept And Example

One of the first strong influences that helps to shape the inner world of the child is the father. The father, as the symbol of justice and right conduct, is the first pattern upon which the design of the child's life is fashioned.

There used to be an old joke about the father who warned his son not to go to the burlesque show because he would see dreadful sights. Naturally, the youngster sneaked off at the first opportunity and went to the show, where sure enough, he saw a dreadful sight — his father.

There is wisdom hidden in this bit of humor. The youngster who went to the burlesque show was literally following in his father's footsteps. Only in this instance, they led him in the wrong direction. The story is a commentary upon the relationship between a father and a son, and upon the fact that precept — what you tell the child — is less important than example — what you actually do.

A father can discourage his son's undesirable friends, but if he turns around and associates with people of poor manners and foul language, can he really expect his son to be much different?

A father can enroll his son in Sunday School and grow hoarse begging him to attend the synagogue, but if that son never sees his father in prayer, can he take his father's urgings seriously?

How can it ever be otherwise? For what you do speaks louder than what you say.

The father to the children shall make known Thy truth.

ISAIAH 38:19

The Rewards Of Relaxation

The mind is a vast collection of beautiful, stimulating and significant ideas. Yet interestingly enough, our best ideas frequently emerge not when we are tense with concentration, but rather when we are relaxed and apparently thinking of minor things.

Thus, Archimedes was sitting in his bath one day, idling away the time, when he discovered that his body displaced an amount of water equal to it in weight. As a result, the whole system of density and measurements — the foundation of the science of physics — was born.

Isaac Newton was sitting under a tree daydreaming when an apple fell right on his head. Seeing the apple attracted with such force to the earth began a chain of thoughts which led to Newton's discovery of the law of gravity, which is the basis of our understanding of the universe.

James Watt was sitting in the kitchen one day and passing the time by watching his wife make tea. As he watched the steam coming out of the spout of the teakettle, he realized how steam power could be harnessed in a steam-driven engine. This discovery led to the industrial era, in which the power of steam was applied to the turbine.

All these great discoveries, like lesser ones, were drawn from the fully-stocked minds of curious and hardworking men. But the finest ideas generally come only when the mind momentarily relaxes.

The wisdom of a learned man comes through relaxation.
                                          BEN SIRA 38:24

Without Measure

At Fort Custer in Michigan, a young soldier of Protestant faith was in emergency need of a chaplain. Since the Protestant chaplain was on leave, the Catholic chaplain went to see the boy. The soldier was somewhat anxious and apprehensive and said, "Father, I appreciate your coming to see me, but I want you to understand that I am a Protestant. I hope you won't try to change my faith."

The Roman Catholic chaplain said with a gentle smile, "My son, I don't want to change your faith. I want your faith to change you."

By having the right kind of faith in God and in man, we can change the destiny of mankind. The ultimate in human tragedy is not suffering or even death, but despair. This is the true meaning of damnation. Men have been known to suffer all manner of torments and to maintain through them all a deep and abiding interest in life, a sense that life is worth living. Martyrs, like Akiba and Socrates, have gone to their deaths with serenity, because they believed that their death was not the final verdict on all they lived for.

All religious faiths require us to believe unequivocally that we can change the course of our personal lives and thus the lives of all humanity.

The recognition of man's innate dignity as God's co-worker is basic to a proper understanding of his nature, as manifested in his creative ability, his moral responsibility, and his untapped potentialities.   ROBERT GORDIS

A Sermon From The Sea

There are two seas in Israel connected by the river Jordan. One is the *Yam Kineret*, the Sea of Galilee, and the other is the *Yam Hamelah*, the Salt or Dead Sea. The Sea of Galilee, on the northern end, is fresh. Fish swim in it and splashes of green adorn its banks. Men build their homes near it and every kind of life is happier because it is there. On the southern end of the Jordan is the Dead Sea. There are no fish in it and few people live there. Neither man nor beast will drink its poisoned waters.

What is the great difference between these two seas, since they are both watered by the Jordan, which sends the same water into both? The difference is that the Sea of Galilee receives but does not keep the Jordan. For every drop that flows into it, another drop flows out. The giving and receiving is in equal measure. The Dead Sea, on the other hand, is greedy and hoards its income jealously. It cannot be tempted into any kind of hospitality or any generous impulse. Every drop it gets, it keeps.

The Sea of Galilee gives and lives. This other sea gives nothing. It is called dead.

There are two kinds of seas in Israel. There are also two kinds of people in this world. Which kind are you?

He who performs good deeds extends the boundaries of heaven.   ZOHAR 3:113 a

How To Be Remembered

A man should choose with a careful eye
The things to be remembered by.

If you could choose the things to be remembered by, what would you choose — fame, wealth, power? How would you wish to be known — as a hero, a saint, a sage?

Perhaps the greatest choice would be to be remembered simply as a man, for the above mentioned terms are essentially mythical or superhuman terms. And what are fame and power and wealth if you are not happy with yourself? Can the title hero, saint, or sage be even a partial substitute for a happy family and many friends?

Basically, we are charged with a single responsibility in life and that is to attain maturity. If one happens to be male, then his task is to try to be a mature man; and if one happens to be female, then her constant endeavor must be to be a mature woman. The real fulfillment in life is to be the best you have it in you to be — and not a cheap imitation of someone else. If we live each moment carefully, each hour wisely and each day honestly, we can be worthy of the names of "man" and "woman." Nothing in life really happens by chance; all is planned. A good character is the result of a life well lived. A good memory is the flower of love and firmness, faith and fairness.

The memory of the righteous is for a blessing.

PROVERBS 10:7

The Eleventh Commandment

A clever little girl noticed that when her father came home every day, he made life miserable for the whole family. He continually nagged his wife and shouted at his children. Every morning he came to breakfast in an ugly mood. One day he found under his plate a note written in the unmistakable hand of his child. It read: "If you would be kinder to your children, your wife and children would be kinder to you." And it was signed, "God."

Any real progress in the tangled world of emotions must be made by the individual. Each of us must hold the mirror to our own soul and gaze intently at what we see there. To change the metaphor, each man's life is a block of marble. He himself is the sculptor; his ideas and ideals are the tools; his soul is the workshop. He can carve any statue he wills.

Too often in normal day-to-day living we refuse to realize our ability in shaping our lives. Instead, we let our emotions govern us; they run riot and become our masters and we their slaves. Our lack of self-understanding leads us to great harm; it actually ruins our lives.

What self-torment and needless strife we would avoid if only we would have the bravery and honesty to recognize our feelings, so that we might learn to control them.

Thou shalt not be afraid of thy hidden impulses.

JOSHUA LOTH LIEBMAN

Deeds And Doers

In a home for disturbed children, one child whined and cried continually. The members of the staff tried very hard to work with him, but they were unsuccessful. Meanwhile, the child had become very fond of the cook in the home and began to spend his free time in the kitchen. One day, the cook became very annoyed with the boy's incessant whimpering and finally said to him, "Look, Jimmy, you can stay, but your whining has to go." The boy understood and at last began to improve.

The cook in the story realized an important truth: We must learn to express our disapproval of certain kinds of behavior without disapproving of the person himself. Or to put it another way, we should always be willing to accept a person, but we are not obliged to accept every single one of that person's traits or acts.

We hear much about the need for toleration. But certain things we are not required to tolerate: We should not permit rudeness, ignorance and immorality. On the contrary we must learn to be *intolerant* of behavior which tends to destroy our society and the well-being of mankind. In condemning such behavior, however, it must be perfectly clear that we reject the deed but not the doer.

Reject the sin but not the sinner.   BERAKHOT 9 b

The Purpose Of Pain

Several years ago a little girl was born without the proper development of the pain apparatus in her nervous system. Her inability to feel pain was discovered by the fact that she never cried. Although some parents might welcome a child that never shed a tear, the child's father explained that this was a terrible danger. The child would be hungry, and the parents had no way of knowing it. The youngster's body was a mass of burns and bruises, for she had no system to warn her to withdraw from fire or cold or sharp objects. The father concluded, "I wish my child would feel pain so that she could learn how to live to help herself."

Although pain is regarded as a bad thing by most people, it actually serves a very important purpose in our lives. The pains of the body teach us how to live in a safe and sensible way; and the pains of the spirit impel us to seek more creative modes of thought and action. Thus pain need not always be deplored; it can be the first step toward learning the lessons of life.

God said to David: If life is what you seek, meditate in suffering, for "the pains of discipline are the ways of life."
    YALKUT PSALMS 67, QUOTING PROVERBS 6:23

A Sense Of Community

A noteworthy study on assimilation was published in Yiddish by Bezalel Sherman, one of the most astute sociologists of our generation. In this work, entitled *Yidn Un Andere Etnishe Gruppen in Amerika* (Jews and Other Ethnic Groups in America) Sherman argues with great forcefulness, that assimilation in the United States is far less widespread among Jews than among other ethnic groups. He credits this commendable resistance to assimilation largely to our profound loyalties to Jewish organizations and institutions.

We support these communal Jewish organizations because, instinctively, we know that they are our best means for self-preservation. A loyal Jew must of necessity support the network of Jewish community organizations, for they preserve, protect and maintain our identity as a people.

The vitality of Jewish living will ultimately depend upon the voluntary association of all Jewish men, women and children who are ready to accept and implement the viewpoint: "I am a Jew, and nothing Jewish is alien to me." Only those Jews who intuitively sympathize with this position can truly share in the benefits of the Jewish way of life.

Join a community, by which alone your work can be made universal and eternal in results.

SAMSON RAPHAEL HIRSCH

Drink As Deep As You Can

Several months ago the story appeared of a little boy in Korea whose family was so poor that they had only one glass of milk a day for all of them to share. Each child was taught how deep he should drink in the glass so he could have his share and still leave some for the others. One day disaster suddenly struck in the community. The little lad was separated from his family and was taken to the Red Cross feeding station. One of the nurses gave him a glass of milk. It was the first one he had ever had all to himself. He did not quite know what to do, so he looked up and asked, "Ma'am, how deep shall I drink?"

With a tear in her eye and understanding in her heart she said, "Son, drink as deep as you can."

The depth of our understanding in a situation marks exactly the depth of our lives. The real test is not whether we have understanding for the happy wife, but for the divorced wife; not for the bright child, but for the retarded child; not for the kind relative, but for the cantankerous cousin; not for the insider, but for the outsider; not for our fellow Jews, but for those who are of another faith; not for our fellow countrymen, but for the foreigners who reject our national policies. If we are to have genuine understanding, then it must not be reserved just for our friends, but for our foes alike. To really achieve understanding that can be worthwhile and useful we must be prepared to drink as deeply as we can from the cup of experience.

"Ho, everyone who thirsts, come ye for water" (*Isaiah 55:1*). *Water here means understanding.*   TAANIT 7 a

Where The Centuries Meet

Just outside of Chicago there is a place where two train tracks run parallel to one another. Two trains pass each other regularly going in opposite directions — one headed east and the other west. One train is called "The Century" and the other, "The Century Limited." Once a curious traveler asked a porter where they were when the trains met. The porter smiled and said, "We're standing where the Centuries meet."

Today, as Jews we stand at the crossroads of history, where the centuries meet. Behind us is the vast past molded by the centuries. We have lived in every century upon this earth and we have been faced with the challenge of all the great civilizations, both hostile and congenial. We have learned through them, but we have remained essentially true to ourselves as Jews.

We now face the coming century. The vital question is whether we have the stamina and the strength to maintain our uniqueness as Jews. Do we have the courage to continue what centuries have preserved? We will have the opportunity to answer in the coming century.

In its journey through the desert of life, for eighteen centuries the Jewish people carried along the Ark of the Covenant, which breathed into its heart ideal aspirations. Such a people, which disdains its present but has its eye fixed on its future is on that very account eternal.

MOSES GASTER

Time Out For God

You are a very busy man, but are you too busy to take time out for God?

Benjamin Franklin was a busy man, but he took time out to help the Hebrew Society in its campaign to build a synagogue, and he himself contributed $25.00 to the building fund.

Abraham Lincoln was a busy man, but he took time out to read the Bible for a half-hour daily.

Franklin D. Roosevelt was a busy man, but he took time out to serve as a church vestryman and to write in the summation of his philosophy of life: "We are inspired by a faith which goes back through all the years to the first chapter of the Book of Genesis."

Arthur Goldberg and Abraham Ribicoff lead active and busy political lives, but take time out to identify with congregations and with the Jewish community.

You, too, are a busy person, but you can find the time to help preserve what the past has worked so hard to build — faith in God and man, loyalty to religious principles and the cultivation of moral values. You may be a very busy person, but you are never too busy to take time out for God.

The Holy One, blessed be He, says: If a man occupies himself with the study of the Torah and with the works of charity and prays with the congregation, I account it to him as if he had redeemed Me and My children.

BERAKHOT 8 a

Operation Survival

Several years ago, a large airplane was forced to land in the Canadian wilderness. The passengers were badly shaken from the forced landing, and they realized that unless help came soon they would surely die from hunger or freeze to death. Panic stricken, they rushed first in one direction and then in another, looking for help, but to no avail. In all of this turmoil and confusion only one passenger remained calm; he was a devout Jew, who simply prayed. The next day the captain of the plane took charge. He divided the crew and the passengers into little groups and sent them into four opposite directions to look for help. As they were being assigned, one of the passengers said to his friend, "Let's go with this elderly Jew."

His friend looked at him with amazement and asked, "Why do you want to go with him? He'll only be a hindrance."

The first man lifted his finger and pointed to the Jew, who was wrapped in his *talit* and *tefilin,* and replied, "He's got connections."

You see, *der velt vayst,* the world knows, that to be a Jew is to be connected with something greater than one's own self. To be a Jew is to be bound up with a magnificent heritage with unlimited resources for survival. Therefore, when one is an authentic Jew, he is never really lost.

We Jews preserved our unity through ideas and because of them we have survived to this day.   SIGMUND FREUD

Choose Life

Karl Menninger, in his marvelous book, *Man Against Himself*, develops an interesting thesis in the first chapter, entitled, "Eros and Thanatos." He points out that man is torn by the urge to conflict and the temptation to cooperate. Man has the impulse to generate suffering and the instinct to create service. How will he choose to express himself?

Jewish lore illustrates this tension with a telling anecdote: The disciple of a Hasidic rebbe once became angered at his teacher and wished to embarrass him. He caught a little bird, cupped it in his hands and approached the rabbi when he was surrounded by his disciples. He placed himself belligerently in front of the teacher and demanded, "Tell me, wise one, what do I have in my hands?" The rabbi, noticing the fluttering motions, quickly apprehended that it was a bird and told him so.

Then the angry disciple continued, "Now tell me, is the bird living or dead?" If the rebbe were to say "living," the disciple planned to crush the bird quickly and prove him wrong. On the other hand, if he were to say "dead," he would simply open his hands and let the bird fly away. In either case, he would prove the leader wrong before his pupils and thereby embarrass him.

The determined disciple once more demanded, "Tell me, is the bird dead or alive?"

The rebbe paused for a moment and said, "That, my son, is in your hands."

I have set before you life and death, blessing and curse. Therefore, choose life that you and your children may live to love the Lord your God and to cleave unto Him.

DEUTERONOMY 30:19-20

Mountains And Men

A young reporter was once talking to the great educator, John Dewey, shortly before Dewey's ninetieth birthday. "What is the good of all your thinking?" the reporter asked Dewey. "Where does it get you?"

Mr. Dewey quietly answered, "The good is that you climb mountains."

"Climb mountains?" questioned the youth. "What is the good of doing that?"

"You see other mountains," was the reply. Then Dewey put his hand on the young man's shoulders and said, "When you are no longer interested in climbing mountains to see other mountains to climb, then life is over."

Our great patriarch, Abraham, crossed the Lebanese mountains to come to Canaan to found a religion. Our great ancestor, Moses, ascended the heights of Sinai to secure a great moral code for mankind. Our parents and grandparents traversed the seven seas to found a community in a new world. Our kin in Israel are at this very moment forcing a stubborn desert to do their will.

It is this continual urge for the finer and more satisfying life that leads us onward. The best of men will never blunt their curiosity in the effort to discover what we may be. For the bounds of possibility reach from the mountains of heaven to the abysses of hell.

God, the Lord, is my strength,
He maketh me to walk upon my high places.

HABAKKUK 3:19

The Best Of Everything

Life is so confusing that we are daily bewildered by the range of choices before us. Often, we seem to be at the threshold of great and new ideas and at the same time, we are warned to retreat to ancient and safe thought. What's to be done?

Strange as it may seem, our predicament is not unique in history. Consider for example, the classic novel about the French Revolution, Dickens' *A Tale of Two Cities*. It begins by saying that times were as always, "the best of times, the worst of times." Indeed, every age of crisis has been woven out of the threads of extreme and often seemingly conflicting opinions.

This same problem of the clash of extremes was experienced during the flowering of the rabbinic mind in the second century, when Hellenistic thought assaulted the fortress of the Jewish faith. Rabbi Meir, the brilliant leader of his time, was accused of borrowing excessively from Greek thought. He answered the charge in a symbolic manner.

"I have found a pomegranate. I ate the best part and then I discarded the seeds and threw away the shell."

This was his way of teaching that in a new situation or in any new conflict one must choose that which is worthwhile and then discard that which is worthless. Any new idea or development has consequences for growth or regression, development or destruction. We must learn to separate the essence from the shell.

Accept truth from whatever quarter it may come.
Whoever calls logic into disrepute is wrongful.

IMMANUEL OF ROME

A Family Affair

In a Cincinnati classroom the children were asked to introduce themselves. One child, granddaughter of the late Senator Robert A. Taft, rose and spoke as follows:

My name is Martha Bowers Taft.

My great-grandfather was President of the
United States.

My grandfather was a United States Senator.

My daddy is Ambassador to Ireland.

And I am a Brownie.

Despite the crashing anticlimax, we are reminded that this young lady comes from a family distinguished for public service. We can expect this child to grow in her family's tradition. The concept of family responsibility is fundamental to society, for our great need today is not necessarily guided missiles, but guided morals.

Family responsibility has traditionally played a crucial role in the Jewish community. In biblical times it was the father-son chain of Abraham, Isaac and Jacob. In rabbinic times it was the Hillel and Gamaliel families. In the medieval era the Kalonymos family produced generations of leaders. In our own time almost every Jewish community boasts of a family whose name recurs on communal records. This continuity of family service is the real mark of Jewish aristocracy, an aristocracy only of responsibility and service.

For I have known him, that he may charge his children and his household after him to keep the way of the Lord by doing righteousness and justice.   GENESIS 18:19

87

The Abiding Miracle

Hanukkah, recalling the rededication of the ancient Temple in Jerusalem, following the victory of the Maccabees over the Syrians, is celebrated for eight days. According to the ancient legend, this is because only one clean jar of oil was found for the Eternal Light and it was sufficient for only one day. But by a miracle it lasted eight days. An old Yiddish jest, based upon this explanation asks, "For such a little bit of oil, such a big festival is celebrated?"

The reason that so much emphasis is placed upon the Hanukkah festival is that it commemorates the first successful revolt in history on behalf of religious liberty. The abiding miracle of this festival as stamped in Jewish observance reminds us of the value of religious freedom in our lives. The spirit of Hanukkah animates the Magna Carta, and the Declaration of the Rights of Man, and there is parallel to the Maccabean revolt in the Declaration of Independence. For without the willingness of early Jews to fight for their religious rights and the inspiration of Hanukkah, these great movements on behalf of human freedom might never have been born.

Not only Jews, therefore, but all mankind must be grateful for the abiding miracle of Hanukkah.

Yours the message cheering that the time is nearing
Which will see all men free, tyrants disappearing.

              ROCK OF AGES (HANUKKAH HYMN)

A Spark Of The Divine

On Hanukkah, the lights of the Menorah are kindled by the *shamash,* the lead or service light. Every Menorah has such a special light, whose sole purpose is to provide the spark for the others.

The importance of the spark can be seen in the following story:

A young man who had become an apprentice to a blacksmith, learned during the course of his training how to hold the tongs, how to lift the hammer, how to smite the anvil, and how to blow the fire with the bellows. Having finished his apprenticeship, he was chosen to be employed at the royal smithery. But the young man's delight at his appointment soon turned to despair when he discovered that he had failed to learn how to kindle a spark. All of his skill and knowledge in handling the tools were of no avail because he had not learned the most elementary principle — to light the fire.

Unless we are fired with the conviction of what we do, then what we do will be essentially meaningless. Unless we find that we are warmed by enthusiasm any project in which we engage will eventually cool off. The spark that kindles a world, a people, or a person, illuminates the causes in which we are involved and fires us with the energy to carry through. The Maccabees of old proved that men who possess a spark of the divine will leave their brand on history.

For centuries the Menorah burned constantly.
In its light a nation walked,
By its inspiration a people lived.   PAUL ROMANOFF

Not Power Nor Might

During Hanukkah in 1960, the American Jewish Committee presented a Menorah to the King and Queen of Denmark in appreciation for the Danish king's efforts to save the Jews of his country from Hitler's death camps. At a time when Adolph Eichmann and his wickedness were at the center of world attention, the heroism and Maccabean love of justice of the Christian leader of Denmark were fittingly recalled in gratitude and reverence.

This is the reason for the gift. When the Germans invaded Denmark, they tried to turn the Danish people against their Jewish neighbors. They were singularly unsuccessful. In 1943 the Nazis decreed that every Jew had to wear a yellow Star of David. King Christian X heard this and immediately went on the radio and said, "The Jews are a part of the Danish nation. We have no 'Jewish problem' in our country because we never had an inferiority complex in relation to the Jews. If the Jews are forced to wear the yellow star, I and my whole family shall wear it as a badge of honor." Needless to say, the badge was never introduced in Denmark. In fact, when the Germans did press for deportation of Jews, the Danes retaliated by scuttling the Danish fleet; and many Danish officers and soldiers lost their lives shielding their Jewish friends.

This is the spirit of Hanukkah — that men and women will voluntarily expose their lives for what they believe. It is the inspiring story of self-sacrifice that lies at the basis of every great humanitarian achievement.

Not by power, nor by might, but by My spirit, saith the Lord of hosts.   ZECHARIAH 4:6

The True Test Of Time

Our way of measuring time is highly inaccurate. Days, months and years are not the precise tools for measuring time. Birthdays and anniversaries are artificialities that we impose on the calendar, but they are not the ultimate, most precise instruments with which to record living. This thought may be illustrated by the following story.

A firm was interested in hiring a man for a top executive position that was suddenly vacated. The firm bypassed the man next in line and selected an outsider to fill the job. The man who had seniority was so upset he went to talk to the president. In very hurt tones he said, "But I have had fifteen years of experience with this firm." The president replied, "That is not so. You have had one year of experience fifteen times."

The point is that we do not measure experience by years, but rather by something else. That something else is the goodness we have created through living. The truest measure of time is not the number of years we have seen, but the vision of goodness that we have held before us; not the number of days we have existed, but the number of good deeds we have performed.

Only he who has been a force for human goodness, and abides in hearts and souls made better by his presence during his pilgrimage on earth can be said to have lived.
                                                    JOSEPH H. HERTZ

The Source Of Light

Jacques Lipschitz, the sculptor, spent his youth in Paris, where he was a close friend of Soutine, Modigliani and Chagall. One day another painter complained that he was dissatisfied with the light he painted on his canvasses. He went off to Morocco, seeking a change in light. He found that the light in his Moroccan canvasses was no different. Lipschitz then told him, "An artist's light comes from within, not from without."

Even as we are all artists in life, we must strive to kindle the light within. All that we see about us, all that we touch and feel only serves as a stimulus. The true creative spark is that which lies within the heart and soul of all of us.

We must learn to kindle our inner spiritual light and to keep its glow warm and strong. We can do this by developing the ability to trust ourselves and our own judgments. The light within must be shielded from the cold blasts of callousness and indifference. The nurturing of the inner spiritual fire is a lifetime enterprise. We must follow that light wherever it leads us.

The light of a candle is serviceable only when it precedes Man on his way, useless when it trails behind him.

BAHYA BEN ASHER

Deep Are The Roots

Many years ago, two of the most famous New Englanders, Henry David Thoreau and Ralph Waldo Emerson, both Harvard men, were discussing higher education. Emerson was especially impressed that Harvard offered courses in all branches of learning. Thoreau quietly answered, "Yes, in all of the branches, but in none of the roots."

Thoreau meant that learning itself does not suffice unless it is anchored in fundamental convictions about using it for the proper purposes. Learning itself, without applying it to the enhancement of one's spiritual life and the betterment of society, can be vain and useless. Furthermore, we need roots to give us that kind of support that will anchor our wisdom to meaning and worth. Life is not an aimless pursuit of distraction; it has very definite purposes. These purposes are revealed by the articles of faith which give us a continuing source from which to draw inspiration and strength.

Unless we have the roots that give us the proper hold on life, we become like the tumbleweed, which drifts and wanders aimlessly, driven by every wind.

Let not your wisdom exceed your deeds
Lest you be like a tree with many branches and few roots.
AVOT 3:22

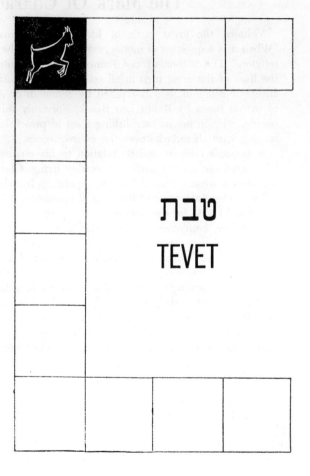

טבת

TEVET

The Mark Of Character

Voltaire, the great cynic of history, once remarked, "When it is a question of money, everybody is of the same religion." This statement can immediately be refuted by the lives of the great men in all religions. In Judaism the authentic religious man is typified by Jeremiah or Akiba, or in our times by Rabbi Leo Baeck. For truly religious people, religion means establishing a set of principles and staying with them, whatever the consequences.

A person's religion and its relation to his character is hammered out on the anvil of everyday living. Character is made by what we stand for, and reputation by what we fall for. These are some of the tests of character:

Shall I vote for the man or for the party?

Did my employee deserve better terms?

Do I give an honest day's work for my pay?

Shall I be faithful to my family name and ideals?

Did I consider my employer's side of the question?

Am I pressuring my parents for my own selfish desires?

Only a sense of deep personal faith and a life pledged to integrity of character can help us to give the right answers to these questions. It is this value of personal honor that religion respects and treasures most highly.

He who walks in paths of integrity honors God.

NUMBERS RABBAH 8

Learning Laughter

A story about a famous clown carries with it a deep message. A British doctor once examined a patient who was very sad and depressed. After performing a thorough physical and mental examination the doctor said, "There is nothing wrong with you. Go hear Grumaldi, the great clown, and laugh; then you will be cured."

The patient looked at the doctor, lowered his eyes and said sadly, "But *I* am Grumaldi."

The incident illustrates that joy and laughter are indispensable to emotional and spiritual well-being. To make others laugh is a talent, but to be able to laugh ourselves is as necessary to living as air is to breathing.

Humor, when properly used, is a means of lessening personal hostility and of dispelling our own self-hatred. Moreover, laughter is often a very effective instrument in expressing the truth. We can often say in jest the things we would not dare to express directly. In situations of emotional tension between people, humor frequently helps those involved to gain the perspective they need in order to look at the situation realistically.

The person who can laugh with life has developed deep roots within the soil of faith. The conviction that one's personal existence has meaning gives one the deep serenity that makes living a real joy. From this joy comes the strength to meet and resolve life's problems.

In laughter the pain of the heart is eased. PROVERBS 14:13

Hidden Treasures

Several years ago the following story appeared in the newspapers. A Spanish businessman bought a painting for the equivalent of $37.50. He engaged a restorer to clean it. Upon examination, the restorer made a discovery so startling that he called in an expert to confirm it. The expert agreed that it was a work of Murillo, a 17th century Spanish master, and therefore worth about eleven thousand dollars.

Perhaps in our daily experiences we are exposed to masterpieces of which we are unaware because we do not take the time to study their value properly.

Thus, we often turn the pages of the Prayer Book but do not appreciate that parts of this masterpiece are over two thousand years old. We do not sufficiently realize that the people who wrote these prayers faced the same problems that confront us, and what they thought and felt has validity for us.

Or we may listen to a popular tune and only find out later that it was lifted from the heart of a great classical symphony. When we are inspired to listen to the original, we often find we respond to it much more fully and deeply than we did to the popularized version.

These are but a few of the spiritual treasures that lay hidden, just below the topsoil of our lives, awaiting our discovery of them to enrich our living.

If a man says, "I have not searched but I have found," do not believe him. But if a man says, "I have searched and I have found," believe him.   MEGILLAH 6 b

Shared Suffering

A woman once came to see her rabbi about some complicated problems at home. She said, "I wouldn't come to bother you, but I have such a splitting headache I couldn't stand it any more. I just have to talk to you."

The rabbi assured the congregant that he would be happy to listen to her problems and try to help, whereupon the woman, detail by detail, spilled out her tale of woe. After twenty minutes of steady talk she sat back relaxed and smiled with delight. "Rabbi," she exclaimed, "it's wonderful! Since talking to you, my headache just disappeared!"

The rabbi sighed and answered wearily, "No, my dear, your headache didn't disappear. Now *I* have it."

All of us can share suffering and thus help lighten the loads of other people. Every time we warmly shake the hand of a bereaved friend, when we withdraw our hand, we take a little of the suffering back with us. Whenever we visit a sick friend, we bring a smile to the face where a tear or a frown had been forming. Every time we make a contribution to a charitable fund upon an occasion of distress, we help by advancing the institutions founded to relieve suffering. These are but a few of the many concrete and practical ways in which we can share and lessen suffering.

Shared suffering is a partial comfort.   MOSES GENTILI

What Do You Know?

Most of us seem to want continually to drag down the image of God instead of coming up to His level. We lift our eyes upward to the sky and think He is at the end of the farthermost horizon, when actually that is only His beginning. We think He is squeezed into the limits of our lifetime, when truly our generation is but a sliver of time in eternity. We think we have probed His secrets fully with the discovery of atomic energy, when verily we are only freshmen when it comes to attendance at the University of the Universe.

This brings to mind the marvelous story of the boy who failed his entrance exams at Princeton University. Before heading home he stopped off to see President Robert Goheen and thanked him, saying, "I've learned a lot here."

President Goheen asked in amazement, "But you were never enrolled here. What could you possibly have learned from us?"

The young man replied, "How little I know!"

Goheen answered, "Son, we will take you in. You are already two years ahead of the freshman class."

This is also true of our knowledge of the grandeur of God. One drop of water is a teeming world. One handful of earth is a million possibilities. One human life is a mystery beyond all comprehension. How much more so must be our knowledge of God!

The beginning of wisdom is reverence for the Lord.
                                                    PSALMS 110:11

What's In A Name?

Most children have read *Alice in Wonderland*. On the surface a simple fantasy, it often reveals flashes of deeper meaning. In the scene where Humpty-Dumpty meets Alice for the first time, he asks her name. When Alice tells him he says, "It's a stupid enough name. What does it mean?"

"Must a name mean something?" Alice asks.

"Of course it must," Humpty-Dumpty replies with a giggle. "My name means the shape I am — and a good handsome shape, too. With a name like yours, you might be any shape, almost."

Every name has a deep meaning and traditionally is an expression of the hopes and aspirations of the parents. A name also speaks the essence of the person. For this reason Jews observe the custom of bestowing a Hebrew name upon a child. The Hebrew name of the Jew has always linked him with the destinies of his culture.

A child bearing the name of Moses is related to the first lawgiver and to Moses Maimonides, the philosopher. A child who carries the name Abraham is linked with the first Jew and with Abraham Lincoln, a giant in American history. Have you considered the meaning of your name?

You can't be frightened — when you know your name.
You can't get lost — when you know your name.
You're somebody — when you know your name.

HAROLD FRIEDMAN

Is This Trip Necessary?

There is the amusing story of the two ladies who went on a very costly Mediterranean cruise. Upon their return home they gathered their friends about them to tell all about the trip. In the course of conversation, one woman quite forgot that she had been to Rome until her companion reminded her with, "Don't you remember, my dear, that's where we fed the pigeons."

Travel is more than feeding the pigeons; it is also feeding the mind. It is important for us to understand that as one travels, one must always be alert to seek out the spiritual treasures of nations rather than their trivia. Travel is broadening only if people are eager to *learn* and to grow.

Growing through travel means making an effort to understand the differences among people. It implies a receptiveness to new thoughts and values, to new ways of living.

Ultimately, travel should broaden our sympathy for the common good of people everywhere, and in this way should deepen our service of God.

I am setting out today on this journey, which I pray may be to the service of God and to our common good.

MENASHEH BEN ISRAEL

The Mother Of Invention

The child's imagination plays a key role in the development of his inner world. Imagination is basically the precious gift of the mother. If the mother encourages the child, then he fills his mind with visions that beautify and dreams that enliven his whole existence.

One of the rabbis of the Talmud records that when he was a child his mother used to take him to play on the lawns of a great academy. The spirit of this academy captured his youthful imagination, and he later became a famous scholar himself.

Caruso said that his earliest childhood memory was that of his mother's beautiful voice. His first sounds were harmonious mainly because his ear had heard only music.

Maurice Utrillo, the great French painter, learned to play with paint brushes and paint tubes as other children play with rattles.

Thomas Wolfe, the noted American writer, records that his mother actually guided his hand to write his first full sentence.

Or as one preacher recently said, "My mother practices what I preach." And the good mother can add, "And I encourage what my child imagines."

God could not be everywhere, so He created mothers.

MOSES HESS

A Sense Of Rumor

Thoughtful individuals have observed that there is a basic distinction between a sincere interest in people and the irresponsible chatter that is known as gossip. It is one thing to be concerned when a person is ill and to try to be helpful; it is quite another thing to broadcast that he is dying and that his business will soon fail. It is healthy to be interested in improving the moral tone of our teen-age community; but it is unhealthy to spread stories about vandalism and delinquency when the informer and the hearer are in no position to know the absolute truth. And what difference does it make who is dating whom, who got a police ticket, or who flunked a course? If only we knew how many lives have been smashed by needlessly maligned reputations.

There is a bitter irony in the quip about the woman who had a nice sense of rumor. All was fine — until people began to talk about *her* family.

An old rhyme could well sum up the religious attitude toward gossip:

> There is so much good in most of us,
> And so much bad in the rest of us,
> That it ill behooves any of us
> To find fault with the rest of us.

As ye speak no scandal, so listen to none, for if there were no receivers there would be no bearers of slanderous tales; therefore the reception and credit of slander is as serious as the originating of it.

ETHICAL WILL OF ELEAZAR OF MAYENCE

Remnants

The oldest Jewish congregation in the United States is Shearith Israel in New York City. It was established when a small group of Jews came to the New World during the colonization of New York, which was then called New Amsterdam. The name Shearith Israel means, literally, "the remnant of Israel." These Jews chose this name because they thought they were the only Jews remaining in their area of the world. Through the years, this handful of Jews has grown into a mighty American Jewish community of almost six million souls.

During its early years, the American Jewish community had to fight for its rights. In time, however, Jews not only reversed the ban against their form of worship, but sought and obtained the full responsibilities and privileges of citizenship. Because of their insistent demand to be treated fairly and to be allowed to accept the full burden of their obligations, their strength and numbers continued to increase.

It is important for us as Jews, as we now begin the early years of our fourth century as a Jewish community in these United States, to keep this lesson firmly fixed in our minds. We must continually seek our equal rights with dignity, but with firmness; and we must at the same time eagerly seek to take on our share of community and national responsibility. What was only a remnant has now become an ever-growing force on the American scene. This force was the reservoir of strength that established the state of Israel, that helped our needy brethren in all parts of the world, that is now becoming the fount of Jewish learning.

Though your beginnings were small, your latter end shall indeed be great.   JOB 8:7

The Humble Heart

Hasidic literature contains the story of a king who once wanted to learn the secret of humility. To achieve humility he wore old clothes on his body, ate very little food, left his beautiful palace to live in a hovel, and employed men to revile him. All this did not help, for he felt more proud than ever before. A wise man then showed him the path to true humility when he told the king: "Dress like a king, live like a king, act like a king; but inside, let your heart be humble."

Being humble does not mean avoiding people, being silent or wearing shabby clothes. On the contrary it implies accepting ourselves precisely as we are, but being fully aware of our potential as well as of our limitations. It means living with integrity on the outside and humility on the inside. For whatever you may be:

> Rich man, poor man,
> Beggar man — no matter your belief;
> Doctor, lawyer,
> Or Indian chief:
> Be what you want;
> But inside, let your heart be humble.

Everything heroic in man is insignificant and perishable unless it be the fruit of humility.   HERMANN COHEN

The Immovable Force

The largest commercial American ship afloat is the SS *United States*. A truly magnificent ship, it is several blocks long and has its own facilities, shops, a gym, and even a swimming pool. It is actually a self-contained floating city. To watch the *United States* dock is a fascinating experience. First, ropes as thick as the span of a man's hand are thrown ashore and secured. Then great motors go to work and, using cables, the ship draws itself to the pier. Because the dock is strong and stationary, the ship literally pulls itself into the harbor. The ship moves because the dock is immovable.

In a similar manner does man draw himself to God through the rope of prayer. God as the symbol of our values is strong and stationary; we never pull Him down to us, but we are pulled up to Him. We move in the right direction precisely because He is immovable.

Whenever we read our prayers, we affirm the principle of the greatness of God. Whenever we chant our liturgy, we repledge our trust in the supreme meaning of love. If uttered sincerely — whether aloud or in the silence of our hearts — our prayers keep us moving in the right direction

God says to Israel: "I asked you to pray in the synagogue of your own city. If this is not possible for you, then pray in your open field. If this is not possible, then pray in your own house. If this presents difficulty, then pray while resting in bed. If this, too, is difficult, then it is enough to reflect in your heart, silently."   MIDRASH TEHILIM 4:69

107

Man In The Making

One of our greatest errors is our real failure to teach our children kindness toward other people. In our hurry to get ahead, in our eagerness to make our mark, we sometimes give them the impression that one must be hard and tough to get the most out of life. Such a view just does not square with a full and wholesome life.

In the beautiful and sensitive play, *Tea and Sympathy,* the emotional growth of a teen-ager is examined. At the end Laura, the heroine, turns to the young boy, who is on the threshold of manhood, and says, "Manliness is not all swagger and swearing. Manliness is also tenderness, gentleness and consideration."

Manliness is understanding poetry, feeling the pain of the world, listening to the music of great composers and responding sympathetically. Manliness does not mean rejecting emotion, but rather feeling it to its very core. Strong emotion that calls forth strong sympathy is the essence of manhood. To be able to carry forth this quality from childhood into old age is to have a kind of strength that will never yield in the face of adversity.

Where there are no men, try to be a man.   AVOT 2:5

The Joy Of Learning

In some Jewish communities in Eastern Europe it was customary for a child starting Hebrew School to have a dab of honey placed on his learning slate. The child touched the honey with his finger and then tasted it, and the sweetness of the honey was intended to be a symbolic foretaste of the sweetness and pleasantness of the study of the Torah.

The custom expresses the traditional Jewish love for the Torah. Study of sacred literature is not only inspirational, comforting and an act of faith, but it is regarded as a delight in itself. The Jew traditionally has found study not an act of compulsion but rather a source of deep pleasure.

This traditional Jewish attitude recalls the delightful story of the rabbi who spent almost an entire month on the same page of the Talmud. Day after day, he meditated upon its contents. After a while his disciples, puzzled by his behavior, approached him and inquired why he never continued beyond the same page. The rabbi answered, "I feel so good here, why should I turn elsewhere?"

There is sheer pleasure in flexing the mind and untold delight in discovering new insights. There is the finest satisfaction in being able to master a passage thoroughly and deep gratification in being able to push a thought to its furthest reaches. In short, there is a great joy in learning.

Wisdom's ways are ways of pleasantness,
And all her paths are peace.   PROVERBS 3:17

The Presence Of God

When Helen Keller was a little girl her parents brought a minister to her to teach her something about God. Since the child could not see or hear or talk, this was an almost impossible task. For weeks, the minister using the language of touch by pressing on her palm, tried to describe the presence of the unseen spirit. It did not seem to penetrate her silent self. But one time as the minister was "talking" to her in this way, her body suddenly began to shake with excitement; her face lighted up, and she signaled back indicating that she had always known there was a God, but had never before known his name.

Each of us in his own way knows there is a God, and it is unimportant whether we know his name or not. Man's spirit cannot be deceived, his own inner feelings are his surest guide toward great spiritual truths.

We stand in God's presence and we know He is here as we live in the world He created — the world of nature and the world of man. We experience God's presence when we view the soaring majesty of the heavens or a bird in flight, appreciate the fragrance of a flower or the warmth of a friend's hand, gaze up at a distant mountain or down at a smiling infant, feel the cool breeze of a summer night and the warm love of one's beloved. All the beauty and goodness and grandeur of the world — all this expresses the reality of God which is a link between us and the universe through the bond of faith.

Religious experience is an attitude of oneness not only in oneself, not only with one's fellow men, but with all life and, beyond that, with the universe.   ERICH FROMM

Do You Understand?

On a crowded train one day a little girl was sobbing wildly, disturbing the other passengers who were reading or napping. She was accompanied by an older girl who seemed to have difficulty in managing the child. After an hour of uninterrupted crying, one of the passengers said sharply, "Where is the child's mother?"

"She is in the next car," replied the older girl, "in her coffin." The passengers immediately poured out warm concern and sympathy for the little girl, because now they understood her feelings.

Think for a moment how understanding might change your feelings.

Look at your boss and try to see what makes him act the way he does. Or study your employees and ask what makes them behave as they do. Observe children at play. What do they do and say? What are they trying to tell us?

Consider carefully a person who is tense. What produces tension in our lives? What relieves it?

Open your newspaper and ask yourself why people hate and kill when they seem to have everything. But do they have everything? What is "everything?" What do they lack?

Understanding does not come easily. Yet it is the only passkey to the mysteries of the world. Do you understand?

I shall light a candle of understanding in your heart which shall not be put out.   II ESDRAS 14:25

Man On A Pendulum

One of the things that many of us miss in our modern homes is the old grandfather clock. This tall and stately object, with its chimes rhythmically marking the hours, was a wonderful thing to behold. Especially fascinating was the long pendulum that swung to and fro in a graceful arc. And if you watched it closely you noticed that as the pendulum moved back and forth, it never swung out of range. Its arc was limited, and its speed could be adjusted by a special mechanism which enabled the clock to keep perfect time.

We can apply the analogy of the pendulum to man's daily living. Man is on a pendulum and he swings back and forth between moods. Our challenge is how to limit our moods so that we can gently and gracefully swing through life.

Religion helps us meet this challenge of balance on the highest possible level for it is a fundamental control that keeps the pendulum of life from moving wildly in either direction. Through the round of holy days the yearly calendar is given a certain pattern; through sacred literature we are given the goals for living, and through rituals and ceremonies we learn to express and control our feelings. Religion is the mechanism that makes the pendulum of our lives glide evenly.

To everything there is a season, and a time to every purpose under the heaven. ECCLESIASTES 3:1

By Precept And Example

There is an intriguing story of a woman who used to place her child every morning in a large outdoor play pen. As soon as she closed the gate, the child would begin to howl bitterly at being enclosed in a confined area. The daily morning clamor soon began to irritate the neighbors.

One morning, one of the neighbors asked the woman if *he* could put the child into the play area. As he closed the gate, he leaned down and whispered something into the tot's ear. As if by magic, the child remained perfectly calm and quiet. Later, the neighbors asked how he had achieved this miracle. He answered that he had merely told the child he was locking the gate to keep the mother out!

This incident illustrates the truth that every child has a secret world of his own — a world which, unfortunately, we adults often fail to appreciate and understand. All too often we do not give the child's point of view the respect that we demand for our own. Perhaps the way to begin to teach our children consideration for the rights of others is to begin by setting an example ourselves of respecting them.

Bless our children, O God, and help us to fashion their souls by precept and example. UNION PRAYER BOOK

Priest And Prophet

One of the most important Hebrew essayists of the twentieth century was Asher Ginzberg. Under the pseudonym Ahad Ha'am, which means "one of the people," Ginzberg wrote a number of essays about current Jewish problems. In one of these essays, "Kohayn Venavi" (Priest and Prophet), he discusses the contrast between priest and prophet, between the man of action and the man of vision. His particular insight is that they both served different but complementary functions in civilization.

For example, he points out that without Aaron, Moses' mission would have failed. Although Moses was the idealist and dreamer, Aaron helped to cast these ideals and dreams in a practical form. Without Aaron, the dreams of Moses, like most dreams, would have perished like smoke in the wind. It was Aaron who dealt with people and brought the moral teachings down from the heights of Sinai into the hard valley of decision. The tradition of Aaron stands for translating morality into reality.

Each of us contains in himself a little of the visionary and a little of the practical man. We must have high goals before us to inspire us, but we must also be prepared to embody them in practical means. It is insufficient to give lip service to moral values; we must find ways to give concrete expression to our convictions. We must take the supreme values of peace, integrity, and humanity and make them operative in our daily experiences and relationships.

Be of the disciples of Aaron, loving peace, pursuing integrity, and bringing humanity closer to the principles of the Torah.   AVOT 1:12

Follow The Leader

The eagerness of our young people to be admitted to college in these times of intense competition for enrollment brings to mind the following story:

A young girl, applying to an exclusive women's college, received a personality questionnaire to fill out. One of the questions was, "Are you a leader or a follower?" She hesitated in answering it. Finally, she decided to tell the truth even if it cost her the admission, and wrote that, in her judgment, she was a follower. She received a prompt reply from the Office of Admissions congratulating her on her acceptance. The letter went on to say, "We are especially happy to have you, since in next year's class we will have 400 students: 399 leaders and 1 follower."

This story points up, in a humorous way, our tendency to overvalue leadership when we should be equally concerned with followership. Followership is the ability to participate without having to dominate. This is the whole basis of democracy, that once the majority decision is made, whether it is right or wrong and whether we agree or disagree, we accept the decision graciously and follow the leader wholeheartedly.

Woe to the city where all are leaders.

DAVID ROQUEMARTINE

At The End Of The Block

Charles Lamb once remarked, "I don't want to meet the man who lives at the end of the block."

"Well, why not?" asked a friend.

"Because if I knew him," Lamb replied, "I would be robbed of the luxury of hating him."

This is essentially the problem of some of our organized interfaith activity. Because we are often asked to relate to people on a large and impersonal scale, we may be left with a nagging doubt about the effectiveness of the experience.

As a result, many have come to the conclusion that what we do in institutional ways must be supplemented by what we do in our daily relationships. We have learned the importance of:

• Becoming friendly with business associates of different faiths,

• Visiting various houses of worship in small groups,

• Working in small committees in P.T.A. and the Little League,

• Quietly taking responsibility as human beings — not as Catholics, Protestants or Jews — in cancer drives, heart funds, and civic affairs.

Just visiting over the back fence or having a casual cup of coffee with one's neighbor is more valuable than a hundred sermons or a ton of goodwill literature.

Thou shalt love thy neighbor as thyself.   LEVITICUS 19:18

So Big

We ought never to have a static and stationary concept of God. If we are religiously mature, our view of God is constantly expanding and growing. Let me express this by a simple analogy from our everyday life:

When you ask a youngster, "How big is the baby?" the child smiles, stretches his tiny arms and says, "So big." His arms are small and so is his comprehension. We hope that as he grows, so will his understanding spread.

It is also this way when it comes to thinking about God. When we are children, our idea of God is "so big" — small and limited by our dearth of experience. As we advance into adolescence, our view of God is "so big" — somewhat wider, but yet restricted by our not having experienced the fullness of life. Then as we reach maturity, in our adulthood our concept of God should be high, wide and deep, unlimited in its scope and expanse. Our experience in living should enable us to stretch our arms and our minds to their farthermost reaches.

This thought was expressed in a poem by Edna St. Vincent Millay:

> The world stands out on either side
> No wider than the heart is wide;
> Above the world is stretched the sky —
> No higher than the soul is high.
>
> The heart can push the sea and land
> Farther away on either hand;
> The soul can split the sky in two,
> And let the face of God shine through.

I have set the Lord always before me.   PSALMS 16:8

An Affair Of The Heart

Contrary to what many a modern man thinks, he needs the deep emotional understanding and commitment of religion, a commitment that goes beyond the utmost limits of reason. This is not to say that religion is unreasonable, for surely it must be intelligible, but rather to emphasize that the core of a religious life is an irrevocable emotional commitment. Religion is, in a very real sense, an affair of the heart.

When Sir Walter Raleigh had laid his head upon the block, the executioner asked whether it lay right. "It matters little, my friend," Sir Walter said, "how the head lies, provided the *heart* be right."

The heart controls the direction and the movement of the total personality. This important teaching was expressed beautifully in an ancient Chinese verse:

> If there is righteousness in the heart,
> There will be beauty in the character.
> If there is beauty in the character,
> There will be harmony in the home.
> If there is harmony in the home,
> There will be order in the nation.
> If there is order in the nation,
> There will be peace in the world.

Say all that you have to say in calmness. Bow your head and turn your eyes down to the earth, but raise your heart up to the heavens.   MOSES BEN NAHMAN

The Golden Door

Dr. Mordecai Johnson, the noted Negro educator, was a passenger on a train in the South. He noticed that his fellow passenger was a Negro boy who seemed very nervous. When Dr. Johnson asked what was causing the agitation, the worried boy answered, "I am the first Negro to be admitted to the University of Arkansas, and I'm scared. I feel that I will have a most unpleasant experience, but all my relations and friends insist that it's my duty to go there."

The boy's anxiety increased as the train drew closer to the University. As he looked out the window, he saw thirty-five white boys waiting on the platform. He looked pleadingly at Dr. Johnson, who urged him to gather his bags and face the group. As the Negro boy stepped off the train, the leader of the group walked up to him and said, "Last night a group of us were talking about you and how you would feel upon coming to the University. We decided to come here and offer you our friendship."

This group of college students displayed a rare sensitivity to the feelings of another. What they did has started a chain reaction in their lives — a chain reaction of good deeds. This occurrence and hundreds like it will have its own repercussions long after present passions have subsided. The moral strength of these students broke the lock of prejudice and forced open the golden door of friendship.

Give me your tired, your poor,
Your huddled masses yearning to breathe free.
I lift my lamp beside the golden door.   EMMA LAZARUS

Hangover

The day after a party often leaves us with a hangover and a let-down feeling. The climax of the celebration is frequently followed by the headache of the morning after. Inevitably, the high points of our lives leave an empty place in the days that follow.

One day, the house is full of noise, childish laughter, excitement. The next day — or so it seems — the children, now growing men and women, are off to college, the army, marriage, pursuits of their own, and we are left with loneliness. One day we are hearty and hale, ready to lick the world, and the next day at the first sign of illness, we feel let down. One day the business is succeeding beyond our wildest dreams, and the next day the market falls. For all of us, at one time or another, the party of life will be over and we will experience an emotional hangover.

What will we do — sit around and mope and seek sympathy? Or will we push on to get the most out of the least and the best out of the worst? If we lose a loved one, will we sink into a swamp of suffering or will we take that love and use it to help others? Will we let financial reverses cause us to reel or will we resolve to make the most out of what is left? Will family problems perplex us and force us to become mentally immobile or will they challenge us to solve them and to solidify our relationships? How we answer these questions will determine the outcome of our "emotional hangover."

The art of living lies less in eliminating our troubles than in growing with them.   BERNARD BARUCH

Fathers And Sons

When Quentin Roosevelt was in the 94th Air Squadron on the western front during World War I, an observer came up to him and said, "I am a friend of your father's. I have come here especially to tell you how millions of Americans back home appreciate the splendid ways in which the sons of Theodore Roosevelt are acquitting themselves in this conflict."

"Well, you see," Quentin replied, "it's up to us to follow the teachings of our father. I'm a Roosevelt. It's up to me to live like a Roosevelt."

The point is that "society" does not produce a Roosevelt; only a Roosevelt produces a Roosevelt. A log cabin does not create a Lincoln; only a Lincoln creates a Lincoln. And in the most important era of Biblical history, the descendant line of great men from father to son went: Abraham, Isaac, Jacob, and Joseph. And out of this lineage came the man regarded in Jewish tradition as the greatest of all human beings — Moses.

Society may bring forth great *programs,* but only a family can produce great *people.*

And he will turn the hearts of the fathers unto their children and the hearts of the children unto their fathers.
MALACHI 4:6

121

Beneath The Skin

In all times, men have used their differences with a small defenseless minority as an excuse to justify their own inadequacies, relieve their tensions, and discharge their fears.

The Roman historian Tertullian, who lived in the third century, records, "If the river Tiber rose to the wall or if the Nile inundation failed to give the fields enough water, if the heavens did not send rain, if an earthquake occurred, if a famine threatened, if pestilence raged, then the cry resounded: 'Throw the Christians to the lions!' "

In our own country, in 1656 two Quaker women were put in a dungeon because they read books. Everybody knew that only women who were witches read books. Three years later, in New England two Quakers were executed because Quakerism was considered a form of devil worship.

In our own times, on March 6, 1960, some men carved the initials KKK into the chest of a Negro. Truly, each of us carries a tiger beneath his skin — the hate that lurks in all of us.

What is beneath your skin?

If you must hate, if hatred is the leaven of your life, which alone can give flavor, then hate what should be hated: falsehood, violence, selfishness.   LUDWIG BORNE

The Doll House

A little girl was once showing off her collection of dolls. Although she had many fine and expensive ones, her favorite doll was the oldest one. It was tattered and dilapidated, its hair was off, its nose chipped, and its cheeks scratched. When she was asked why she liked this one best, the little girl said, "I love her most because if I didn't love her, no one else would."

The greatest human achievement is to love, and love can be expressed in many ways, large and small:

Open your business to the handicapped and give him a chance.

Be a baby-sitter when your neighbor has to run an errand.

Defend a person when all are against him.

Take the initiative in keeping your family together.

Urge your children to invite the new child down the block to join their playing circle.

Work in the kitchen, help with picnics and decorate for the dance.

These acts of love, even the smallest of them, can help us to understand why at times the hands that help are at times holier than the lips that pray. For life does not always require us to do extraordinary things, but rather it most often demands that we do the ordinary things extraordinarily well.

Every man should perceive himself as being half good and half evil. By performing one more good act, he becomes a Zaddik; by performing one more evil act, he becomes a man of wickedness.   KIDDUSHIN 40 b

Giving Life A Jolt

At the Massachusetts Institute of Technology, the well-known mathematician, Dr. Norbert Wiener, was once examining a machine designed for the highly complex job of computing variations in the patterns of brain waves.

As he was talking, he told a visitor that the machine had gone haywire in the morning, but that it was fine now. The visitor asked, "What did you do?"

"Simple," said Dr. Wiener, "I just shook it, and it worked. You see I've often noticed that when a machine becomes too rigid, it begins to function poorly."

This is a fundamental truth. When controls become too rigid, then a machine gives signs of mechanical failure and a person shows symptoms of nervous upset. Every so often, patterns must be changed, pace must be varied and routines revised. This is not only important; it is a basic necessity of normal functioning and living.

Now is the time to shake up the mold of your life, the time to change the pace with a dinner out, a new book, singing or dancing lessons, an art course or even a few days out of town. Ask yourself, "What have I done lately that is different?" If you can't think of anything, then it's time to give *your* life a jolt.

A change of outlook or scenery may sometimes preserve a person.   JER. SHABBAT 6:9

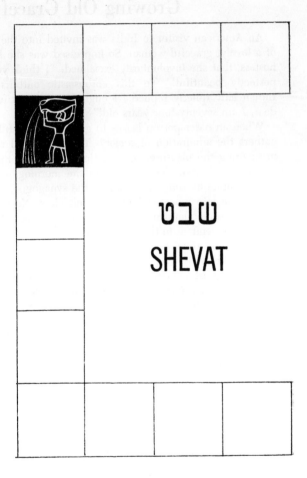

שבט

SHEVAT

Growing Old Gracefully

An American visitor to India was invited into the home of a lovely, graceful woman. So impressed was she by her hostess, that she involuntarily exclaimed: "I think you are perfectly beautiful!" To this enthusiastic outburst, the Indian lady quietly replied, "I ought to be beautiful, my dear, I am seventy-four years old!"

When an older person learns to grow old gracefully, he gathers the admiration of society. There is a real reward in savoring the pleasures of a lifetime of service. Spoiling the grandchildren, sleeping late in the morning, cooking for a community dinner, coming to the synagogue, staying up for the late movie, taking an adult class. No need to worry about spoiling make-up, no need to chase after the dollar, independent in thought and action. What a wonderful time to be alive! Because when you are young, you live to learn and when you are older, you learn to live.

But we must not only add years to life, we must also add life to years. Older people must keep their interests in business and life. They must also give the next generation an opportunity to prove itself. Old age is for wisdom, middle age is for maturity, and young adulthood is for vision and ambition. Each is good in its time. Each must make room for the other.

To know how to grow old is the master work of wisdom, and one of the most difficult chapters in the great art of living.   HENRI FREDERIC AMIEL

Brothers All

Not long ago, the magazine section of *The New York Times* published an article in which ten outstanding figures in various fields answered the question, "What is the world's greatest need?" The most interesting reply was that of C. P. Snow, the British novelist and scientist. He said, "If we can't feel that all individual human beings, whatever they believe, whatever they look like, whatever economic system they are living under, are in essence like ourselves — then, whatever we say, we don't believe in individual human beings and we are headed straight for horrors."

We are all a part of humanity and have like emotions, fears and hopes, anxieties and aspirations, despondencies and dreams. When we are cut, we bleed; when we are pinched, we jump; when we are hurt, we cry. None of us likes to be the target of discrimination, oppression or insult. All of us have the right to equal respect and equal treatment — not for any other reason except that we are human beings. Surely, if God is the Father and we are all His children, is it not an insult to Him to accept one child and then to reject his brother?

We must understand that we are not complete until we belong to the whole family of man. All humanity is joined together with a common awareness of its mutual dependence and its unlimited possibilities for human achievement and growth.

Have we not all one father? Has not one God created us? Why then do we deal treacherously a man against his brother?   MALACHI 2:10

Your Secret Life

Once in a small town there was a very hardened and cruel criminal. Finally, the townspeople could not stand him any more and in a moment of anger they decided to do away with him by lynching him. As they took hold of him and prepared to tie him to the tree, a local priest shouted for them to halt, and said, "There is nothing this man has done that all of us have not felt in our hearts at one time or another. It's only that he has not been able to control himself." Thereupon, they set the criminal free.

The main difference between the criminal and ourselves is that the criminal "acts out" his hostile, antisocial feelings. If thoughts could kill, then we would all be murderers; if all wishes could be realized, then we would all be criminals as well as kings.

Every human being has an inner life, a secret life. It is his own, his right, his sacred privilege. The forces that operate within a man and the dreams that churn within his brain provide the energy that moves his life. Remember to look objectively at your innermost thoughts before condemning others.

Know from where you have come and where you are going and you will not come to sin.   AVOT 3:1

Men And Machines

In the third century, Rabbi Joshua the son of Levi, took a trip to Rome. He was astounded to behold the magnificence of the buildings. He was especially struck by the care lavished upon statues, which were covered with exquisite cloth to protect them from the summer heat and the winter cold. As he was admiring the beauty of Roman art, a beggar plucked at his sleeve and asked for a crust of bread. The sage looked at the statues and turning to the man in rags, he observed, "Here are statues of stone covered with expensive clothes. Here is a man, created in the image of God, covered with rags. A civilization that pays more attention to statues than to men shall surely perish." He was correct, for the decline and fall of Rome had already begun.

This story should make us reconsider the goals of education today. We seem to think that to survive we must create better machines rather than better men. We make our heaviest investments in technology; we place more emphasis on producing engineers than on creating teachers. This is an error, for the solution to living in a peaceful world will not come about through better space ships, but through finer spiritual structures.

Reverence for human personality — that can be our religion. That can be, for us, the meaning of God.

ABRAHAM CRONBACH

A Point Of View

A poor Jewish farmer once came to a rabbi complaining bitterly that his life was intolerable because his wife, his children, and his mother-in-law were all forced to live in one room. Because they were constantly getting in each other's way, quarrels inevitably followed.

The rabbi thought for a moment and then advised, "Bring your cow into your room." Although he thought this suggestion was peculiar, the farmer nonetheless complied with the rabbi's request. The very next day, however, he returned complaining more bitterly than ever.

Upon hearing his words, the rabbi advised him to bring in his two goats. The farmer did as he was told, but soon returned to protest again.

The rabbi then suggested he add his chickens to his home. Needless to say, a bare hour had elapsed when the farmer returned in utter desperation. At that point, the rabbi counselled him to send all the animals outside. He was completely bewildered by this last bit of advice, but he followed it faithfully.

The next day, the farmer met the rabbi on the street and observed, "Ah, rabbi, it is so roomy and pleasant in our home. I never appreciated what I had before."

Whether we can appreciate what we have, rather than be anxious for what we do not have, depends on our point of view.

Who is wealthy? He who is content with his portion.

AVOT 4:1

Man Is Not Alone

When a modern airplane approaches a landing, the pilot finds he is not alone. A signalling device on his instrument panel indicates when the plane is too high or low or too distant from the mark. This automatic signalling device is an indispensable aid in the safe navigation of the airship and also gives the pilot a great deal of confidence.

This is also true of our approach to God. We have within us the instrument of conscience that flashes in our minds when we are wide of the mark of morality. The effort to arrive safely on the runway of right living during our internal storms requires skillful navigation. We must remember in any period of stress that man is never alone in his flight of the soul.

Elijah heard the still, small voice amid the loneliness of the desert. Socrates at his final moments admitted that all that was worthwhile in his life was due to the guidance of an inner angel. Epictetus, the stoic, gave expression to the position of all religions when he said, "When you have shut your doors and darkened your room, remember never to say you are alone, for you are not alone, but God is within."

It is the God within that becomes our surest guide on the highway of life. If a man but try, he will find the correct words, the right direction, and the help from within.

Longing, I sought Thy presence
Lord, with my whole heart did I call and pray,
And going out toward Thee,
I found Thee coming to me on the way.

YEHUDAH HALEVI

Hooray For Books

You cannot ignore books. Their very number and mass is a partial indication of their importance. In the United States alone, there are several billion volumes. Assembled in one spot, they would cover a space larger than the city of Chicago. Put them end to end, and they would reach to Mars and back, and still leave enough to make steps to the moon.

The impact of individual books upon our lives has been equally staggering. Every religion has been founded on a text, on a book. In fact, the word Bible itself comes from the Latin *biblia* and means book — The Book. The role of the book in religion and life is indispensable. Great books, classical books, are the lighthouses erected in the sea of time.

If clothes make the outer man, books make his inner world. The lawyer, the doctor, the minister, the engineer, the teacher all use the book as their main tool of learning, teaching, and building. Songs from books and nursery stories lulled us to sleep in our childhood. Books were the companions of our school days, the most intimate friends of our mature years at college and at home. They filled up hours of waiting and sleepless hours of the night, or days of pain in the hospital. In our old age, they will be our companions, and at our graveside, someone will read consoling words from an immortal book as our bodies go down in the dust and our spirits return to the Author of life.

Make books thy companions; let thy cases of books be thy pleasure gardens and grounds. Bask in their paradise.

JUDAH IBN TIBBON

Modernity And Eternity

One day, Dr. Louis Finkelstein, President of the Jewish Theological Seminary of America, told of an interesting incident which had taken place during a visit to Boston. He had been invited to have tea with Serge Koussevitsky, then the esteemed conductor of the Boston Symphony Orchestra. Dr. Finkelstein drank the tea, but politely refused the cookies. Koussevitsky asked why he would not eat the cookies. Because, Dr. Finkelstein answered, they were not kosher.

Koussevitsky said, "But surely, a theologian, a humanitarian, a scholar, a modern man like you does not believe in this old-fashioned nonsense. Why all the fuss over three little cookies?"

Dr. Finkelstein said, "In that case, would you please play a Beethoven symphony and leave out the last three notes?"

"Why, of course not," protested Koussevitsky. "That would be unfaithful to its total composition."

Then Dr. Finkelstein replied, "Judaism is a religious symphony and when any part of it is deleted, it is not only an act of unfaithfulness, but it spoils the beauty of its total composition."

If we desire to preserve the beauty of the Jewish way of life, we must include all sections of the Jewish orchestration in the daily composition of living.

There is but one thing greater than modernity and that is eternity.   SOLOMON SCHECHTER

Leftover Turkey

The real test of a good housewife is not what she serves on Thanksgiving Day, but how she handles leftover turkey. It is no feat to please a family with fresh turkey, broiled steak, or rib roast every night and then to throw away the leftovers. All *that* takes is money and a certain minimum culinary skill. But the test of a real housewife is to take the leftovers and turn them into appetizing, attractive and tasty dishes. We Jews call such a woman by a term indicating real love and respect; we call her a "balabusta," which means a creative cook and imaginative housewife.

This test of how we handle life's leftovers is one we all must face. It is no feat to enjoy life's Thanksgiving days. Everyone enjoys opening gifts on birthdays; everyone takes pleasure in the family all about him; everyone delights in business success. But the real test comes when life strips us bare as a Thanksgiving bird. How do we act on the day after? How de we conduct ourselves and what do we do with the leftovers?

Each of us will someday be handed leftovers in life. There will be weeks of illness, days of grief, and moments of loneliness. Will we take what we have left over from the experiences of good times to help us live through difficult times? This all depends on whether you know the recipe for leftover turkey.

Grant me the serenity to accept the things I cannot change, courage to change the things I can and wisdom to know the difference. REINHOLD NIEBUHR

The Prophet Motive

An individual once walked into an office building, where by chance he entered a large room. He was struck by the silent and reverential attitude of the people who were in the room. He noticed that everyone wore dark suits and dark ties. All were enveloped in intense concentration as they gazed at the front of the room. The visitor concluded that these men were worshipping, and he looked to the front of the room expecting to see a preacher. To his shock and amazement, what he saw was a stock market official in a short white jacket, chalking up the latest price quotations. Instead of a verse from Isaiah, he saw a quotation from United States Steel. In the place of a selection from Jeremiah, he saw a quotation from American Telephone and Telegraph. As he turned and observed these men he could almost read the prayer on their lips: "O profit, O wealth, thou art what I want to get out of life."

There comes a time when we must choose between values and forms of worship. The choice may very well be simply between the prophet of the ancient times and the profit motive of our society. The decision we make determines whether we want from life gain and greed or grace and godliness.

Judaism can, in our time, make a significant contribution through its unrivaled tradition of the pre-eminence of Torah, the character-building, soul-cultivating emphasis in learning, calling on man to develop ethical alertness, to master himself rather than to rule over others.

MAX ARZT

135

Your Serve

Many seek salvation far away, not knowing that it is near at hand. Men need not run off to the Congo to find salvation; a man does not have to become a medical missionary in outer Mongolia to serve God. As noble as such men are, we need not reject our own society in order to practice virtue and goodness.

Do you want to be a good American? Don't limit yourself to hanging out the flag on the Fourth of July or denouncing the Russians. Rather, follow the legislature closely; express yourself; make good government your real interest every day of the week.

Do you want to be a good Jew? Then forget your foolish fears of anti-Semitism. Others will worry for you. Instead, read your Bible; learn your Torah, your history; worship in your way. If you want to be a Jew, then simply, but quietly, be a Jew every day of your life.

Do you want to be a humanitarian? Drop the daydreams of being a nurse in the jungle. Instead, do volunteer hospital work and then come home, cook dinner and spend the evening with your family. The truth is the people of your community are a part of humanity and they are ready to be served — here and now.

Seek the Lord while He may be found;
Call upon Him while He is near.   ISAIAH 55:6

Consider The Umpire

A minor classic in the annals of baseball is the story of two umpires who, some years ago, "called 'em as they saw 'em" in the Texas League. One afternoon, all through the first game of a double header, they were viciously harangued by the local partisan crowd. The umpires were pelted with paper wrappings and even dodged a few pop bottles.

After the intermission, when the second game was about to start, the two umpires had disappeared from the field. A quick search found both of them sitting in the grandstand.

As the fans gathered about them, one of the most critical of the grandstanders asked, "Aren't you going to umpire this game?"

"Sure we will, but right from here in the grandstand," the two umpires chorused. "It seems you folks can see better from here than we can out there right next to the bases."

This not-so-subtle story carries over into life itself. It is often amazing the way people make judgments about situations, without being close to the events and without knowing all the facts. How can we ever be sure in passing judgment about family incidents, business arrangements, or community problems without a close and careful view of all the issues. We must remember that what looks like a foul in the bleachers, may actually be a clean hit at first base.

In righteousness judge your neighbor.   LEVITICUS 19:15

The Mutual Network

If you were to analyze the contents of your meal this evening, you would find that the ingredients came from twenty-one countries in the world.

Look at your garment carefully — your suit or your dress. Think for a moment of all who had a share in making it. The wool was shorn, the cotton was grown, the chemicals were blended by many unknown hands. The designer, the factory, the transportation system, the clothing store, the tailor — all of them had a share in your garment.

Where would you be right this moment without your doctor and your dentist, your post office and your bank, your library and your community organizations, your school and your synagogue?

Our world is one vast network of mutuality. We are deeply beholden to one another — committed to one another. If only we had the wisdom to understand this truth and fully accept it, we would lead happier and healthier lives. We would be also willing to assume our rightful responsibilities.

How much we owe to the labors of our brothers! Day by day they dig far from the sun that we may be warm, enlist in outposts of peril that we may be secure, and brave the terrors of the unknown for truths that shed light on our way. Numberless gifts and blessings have been laid in our cradles as our birthright.   UNION PRAYER BOOK

Yours For The Asking

It seems that just a few minutes before a service the cantor suddenly took ill. The poor rabbi was frantic, trying to find someone to take the cantor's place at the last moment. In desperation, he asked one of the board members who had a rather pleasant speaking voice to chant the liturgy. To everyone's great surprise — and particularly the rabbi's — the man did exceedingly well, singing with obvious skill and deep conviction.

Following services, the rabbi could hardly wait to congratulate his newly-found treasure. He asked the layman how it was that he could sing the liturgy so well at a moment's notice. The man replied that he prayed every day and that one of his hobbies was listening to Jewish music. The amazed rabbi then questioned, "But why didn't you tell me?" And the layman replied, "Well, you never asked me."

Is it not possible that we have not asked enough of ourselves or of others in terms of participation in life? We often embrace the tried and true and we neglect to develop new talents and to cultivate latent skills. We know that we will never learn until we inquire into new ways; we understand that we will never progress unless we investigate new ideas; we perceive that we can never advance until we try new paths. Then why can we not also ask the person who has not prayed, to pray; the one who has not studied, to study; and the one who has not given, to give?

The bashful person will never learn.   AVOT 2:6

A Tree Is A Teacher

On Tu Be'Shevat, Jewish Arbor Day, the following story is most appropriate.

When James A. Garfield, later president of the United States, was head of an Eastern college, a man brought his son to be entered as a student. "My son doesn't have time to take all the required subjects," said the father. "He wants to get through more quickly. Can't you arrange it for him?"

"Oh, yes," said Mr. Garfield. "He can take a short course. But that all depends on what you want to make of him. When God wants to make an oak, He takes a hundred years, but He only takes two months to make a squash."

It takes time and patience for an acorn to grow into an oak, for a boy to develop into a mature man and for a girl to become a wise woman. Moreover, a tree has not fulfilled itself until it can provide shade, give fruit or be of value to others. In fact, the tree attains a measure of immortality when it can scatter its seeds throughout the world and thus make sure that what it has created will be implanted and in time continue to produce.

In a similar manner, human fulfillment occurs when we can so live as to be of value to others. We also find a portion of immortality by scattering seeds of kindness and making sure that the course in which we are interested will continue to produce the results for which we have planned and worked.

Happy is the man whose delight is in the law of the Lord; He shall be like a tree planted by streams of water.

PSALMS 1:1-3

The Will To Live

A young boy liked to walk with his grandfather, who spoke only Yiddish. One day as they were walking, they came upon a rock through which a small flower was growing. It amazed the child that such a tiny plant should possess the power to split a rock. The child turned to his grandfather and asked for an explanation. The elderly gentleman replied in simple wisdom, *"Es vill leben, mein kind,"* — "It wants to live, my child."

This very thought was given more sophisticated expression by Sigmund Freud, when he advanced the theory that life in every form is a basic struggle between two forces — Eros and Thanatos. Eros is the will to love and to live; Thanatos is the desire to destroy and to die. Within every person and every culture these two instincts are locked in a titanic struggle.

What one wills is all important. If a person is convinced he is sick, then he is fated to be a hypochondriac, and even miracle drugs and skilled doctors cannot save him.

If mankind believes the world is doomed, then it *is* doomed, no matter what the United Nations says or does.

But on the other hand, when the indomitable will to live is present, then a hypochondriac becomes a Hercules, a coward becomes a conqueror, and perdition becomes peace.

I shall not die, but I shall live,
And declare the works of the Lord.   PSALMS 118:17

Passing Judgment

The mastery of the emotions is the greatest challenge faced by man. The study of this whole new area begins with the premise that we must accept people for what they are and not judge others by our own self-centered standards. In the past we have gone astray because we were deluded into thinking that our own lives were pure but that those of others were suspect. As the old Quaker said to his wife, "All the world is queer but me and thee, and sometimes I wonder about thee."

We have been able to apply this new knowledge especially to those who are mentally disturbed. We once believed that people who suffered some breakdown in personality did so because of a moral wrong or because of a family taint. We treated them as the Brahmin in India treats the Untouchable, as though we were defiled by their contact. Our false sense of shame prevented us from helping these unfortunates. In our own confusion and in our secret terror we were lost and unable to give them what they needed. We shunned them and turned our backs on them when they needed us most desperately. We did not try to sympathize with their pain and suffering when in all humility we should have said, "There, but for the grace of God, go I."

The new discoveries in psychiatry and psychology are already beginning to reshape our lives for the better. What we can be and what we can do for ourselves have opened our eyes to the fact that wonders are many, but none is more wondrous than man.

Do not judge your fellow until you have sat in his place.
AVOT 2:5

I Am A Hebrew

Israel Zangwill tells the story of an old Jew who, during the darkest days of the First World War, sought admission to the presence of the British Prime Minister, David Lloyd George. Asked his purpose, the would-be visitor answered, "I want to talk to the Prime Minister about God." The incident reveals the special character of the Jew, his concern with preserving a direct relationship with God that stands as the focal point of all existence.

Consider, for example, the names of the dominant faiths of our time. Every other faith has its name compounded with its founder or savior: Mohammedanism is the faith of the prophet Mohammed; Buddhism is the religion of Prince Gautama Buddha; Christianity is based on the name of the founder of that faith. But the term "Judaism" refers simply to the religion of the Jew. The Jew fervently maintains that between man and God there is no need for an intercessor or a go-between. The relation between the moral world, the natural world, God, and man is one. There is but one God, and He is the God of all men and all creation. It makes no difference whether a man be white or brown, blond or dark-haired; all men were created by one and the same God.

Thus, according to Judaism, all men need not adopt the Jewish *talit* for worship or the Mohammedan prayer rug or the Catholic rosary. What is fundamental is the goal, the reverence for the Creator of the universe and the sense of responsibility toward all His children.

I am a Hebrew; and I fear the Lord, the God of heaven, who hath made the sea and the dry land.   JONAH 1:9

To Tell The Truth

Among the seventy Hebrew names for God, one of the most significant is *emet,* which is also the classic Hebrew term for truth. In effect, it tells us literally in a word that "God is truth, and truth is God."

The word *emet* begins with an *aleph,* which is the first letter of the Hebrew alphabet. The middle letter is *mem,* which is the middle letter of the alphabet and the last letter is *tav,* which is the last letter of the alphabet. It is the Hebrew way of saying that truth is the beginning, the center and the end of all existence.

Most of us would take this, and rightly, as solemn warning not to utter a falsehood. But if we are to handle truth responsibly, we must realize that at times a full truth suddenly revealed can be harmful. For example, to tell a child the complete truth about sex before he is ready can be damaging; to inform someone that he has an incurable illness is not always the better part of wisdom; to indicate to a woman that her dress is unbecoming or to a man that his suit is wrinkled may be a thoughtless cruelty. Truth is a tremendous power and it must be handled with the disciplines of conscience, consideration and wisdom.

Open Thou my heart, O Lord,
Unto Thy sacred Law,
That Thy statutes I may know
And all Thy truths pursue.   MAR BAR RAVINA

Not Good If Detached

The next time you purchase a ticket which has a perforation in it, look at the small print. Usually you will find the words: "Not good if detached." You have probably seen this phrase many times, have you ever thought about its implications? When something is cut off from its source, it often becomes quite worthless. Something detached from that which gives it life and spirit is apt to shrivel up and die.

A branch, as long as it is part of the main trunk of the tree, grows and produces leaves and fruit; but the moment it is cut off, it begins to decay. When a brook is part of the mainstream, it is always fresh and clear because it is constantly replenished with flowing waters; but the instant it is cut off from its source, it begins to dry up.

When a person feels himself part of his family and joins in the celebration of family events, he draws strength from the family circle. It is important to meet periodically for family events, occasions other than illness or death must bring us together, for it is not good to become detached.

The human being cannot generate his own spiritual energy. He must receive it from a source beyond himself, greater than himself. Rituals and ceremonies are the strings that tie us to our source of faith. They become a form of permanent attachment to God. When we loose them, we find that we are "not good if detached."

All forms of existence are linked and connected with each other, but derived from God's existence and essence.

LEON OF MODENA

The Right Mixture

Degas, the great French artist and master of the subtle tones of grey and pink, was once asked, "What do you mix your colors with?" and he replied, "With brains."

In blending the colors of life we must also mix them "with brains." There are pink days in our life when we experience bright joys and brilliant hopes. There are also grey days in our life when we suffer sad sorrows and dark disappointments. Life that is painted with only one color is dull; life that is multicolored is exciting. Our hopes, fears, interests provide the color.

This idea of harmonious mixture may be applied particularly to our emotions. When we give unrestrained expression to our raw emotions, we jar the senses of the onlooker, just as the use of raw color shocks the sensibilities of the critic. But when emotions are controlled and tempered, we create a beautiful personality — and our entire life becomes a work of art.

It is man's duty to forge a oneness out of the manifoldness of his soul.   HANS KOHN

The Broad Way Of Life

There is a delightful story of a New York tailor who took his little boy on a picnic. The child, who was raised on the sidewalks and saw for the most part only cement and steel, was enthralled with the beauty of the country-side and rattled off question after question.

"What is this, Papa?" "Grass, my son," was the answer. "And those bright happy things along the fence?" The reply was, "Flowers, my son." "But what kind of flowers, Papa?" And the man sadly said, "How should I know, son? I'm a tailor, not a milliner."

We are becoming increasingly specialized in our society to a point where we narrow our interests into non-concern for all else. We place blinders on ourselves which narrow our intellectual field of vision. We shrug off new ideas and possible opportunities for innovation by saying, "It's not in my field" or "I was not hired to do that!"

But, the fact is that we will see and feel to the extent that we can enlarge our interests. When we widen our areas of concern we ourselves become bigger. It is only broadmindedness that can give us the desire to add new rooms to the mansion of living.

Man is wise only while in search of wisdom; when he imagines he has attained it, he is a fool.

SOLOMON IBN GABIROL

Partners

A little boy was on his way outside, when his mother stopped him and asked him where he was going. The little boy replied, "I am going to play ball with God."

"How do you do that?" his mother asked.

"It's simple," explained the boy. "I throw the ball up into the air, and God throws it back."

There is a fundamental relationship between God and man in the management of the world. This relationship is one of cooperation. That is to say that man literally co-operates or jointly takes action with God.

The laws of the universe were created for the fulfillment of man's function and destiny. When we begin to look upon life from this perspective, we learn to make full use of natural and moral resources for our own welfare. The law of gravity, like all such laws, can serve us when we discover its true function and learn to obey it. In their obedience comes our cooperation with the divine scheme for the universe.

Judaism has a central, unique and tremendous idea that is utterly original — the idea that God and man are partners in the world and that, for the realization of His plan and the complete articulation of this play upon earth, God needs a committed, dedicated group of men and women.

THEODORE GASTER

The Enchanted Cottage

Some years ago a motion picture, *The Enchanted Cottage,* was presented. It told the story of a man and woman whose faces were so twisted and ugly that anyone who looked at them immediately cast down his eyes with pity. In their loneliness they married and hid their shame in a faraway cottage, where no human being could look upon their ugliness.

In the cottage a miracle took place. As the two lived together, they were elated to discover that their ugliness had vanished and in its place was great beauty. They arranged to give their first party, a surprise party for their friends and relatives. To their shock and bewilderment, everyone who saw them cast down his eyes with the same pity as before. They could not understand why their guests saw ugliness when they saw only beauty. This man and woman decided that they must be living in an enchanted cottage.

Of course, there was no enchanted cottage. There was only the enchantment that was in themselves, the enchantment of their feeling for one another. Through their love, they could see only each other's loveliness, because they were lovely in every way to one another.

We are all capable of weaving a spell of enchantment when we love. We do it by the way we talk, the way we look at another person, the way we treat the one we love. The change that occurs through love does not change a person's outward appearance; it happens inside of us — for that is where we manufacture enchantment.

Love one another from the heart.   PATRIARCHS, GAD 6:3

Keep Your Feet On The Ground

Judaism flourishes today because it has met the test of history. If the principle of the survival of the fittest can be applied to religious cultures, then surely Judaism is fit by virtue of its past and by reason of its promise. One of the reasons for Judaism's spiritual strength is that it has been exposed to every philosophical test and has stood its own ground.

Mahatma Gandhi once expressed this truth in a statement which has been engraved above the entrance of the government radio station of Delhi, India, and reads: "I want the cultures of all the lands to be blown about my house as freely as possible, but I refuse to be blown off my feet by any of them."

The modern American Jew, like this great Indian seer, must be conscious of the need to be receptive to all points of view while holding steadfastly to his own faith. We will consider the best thought of the religions about us, but we will stand on our feet as Jews. We must help the many causes in our wider community, but we will first accept our responsibilities to the Jewish community. We will look at the changes wrought by modern life, but we will also look to the wisdom of the ages and to the martyrs of old before we will change our basic devotion to Jewish life.

The greatest honor I can give my children is love for our people, loyalty to self.   THEODOR HERZL

The Eternal Light

In historic Jewish writings we are told that a strict system of supervision was installed in the ancient Temple, known as *mishmarot*. Each week three priests and twenty-one Levites were appointed to be in charge of the Temple, and they had to stay on the premises until they were relieved of duty in a ceremony that was known as the changing of the guard.

The point of all this elaborate procedure was that the Temple should not be left without supervision, not even for a minute. Day and night someone guarded the *ner tamid*, the Eternal Light, so that it was never extinguished. Temple doors were never closed, and there was always someone in attendance.

The ancient rabbis drew an analogy from this procedure. They said that the *mishmarot* were symbolic of life itself. We must never allow the temple of our soul to be left without the priest of our conscience in attendance. We can never afford to live without values, without a conscious control upon our lives.

If we are driving a car and doze for only a few seconds, then the result can very well be disastrous. If we are shaving and daydream for an instant, then even the slight, sudden tensing of the hand can inflict a wound. If we are speaking and forget ourselves for a moment, then the unguarded revelation of a confidence can send a person's reputation to doom.

What the Eternal Light is to the Temple, the conscience is to the soul.

Woe shall it be to that man who through misguided conduct has lost his share in the world to come. In one fleeting moment, he lost eternity.   GLUECKEL OF HAMELN

151

In A Word

The words we say most often are usually the words we think about least. We constantly use words without being aware of their deeper meanings. For example, many a self-proclaimed atheist is not aware that every time he utters a goodbye, he is really saying, "God be with you." Or a teetotaler may use the phrase, "I prefer the real McCoy," which means "bottled in bond liquor." The word "Oscar," which is used for motion picture awards, came about when somebody first saw the academy award statuette and said, "That looks like my Uncle Oscar!"

The one word which is most commonly used throughout the world is truly the least known of all. It is the most popular word in the Christian, Jewish and Mohammedan services: "Amen." We use it so often in our services, but rarely stop to consider what it really means. Literally, "Amen" means something like "It is true" or "I affirm." Its source is the Hebrew word *"emunah,"* which means faith. It is also close to the word *"ne'eman,"* which means firm and trusting. The uttering of this word is, therefore, in itself an act of faith.

He who says "Amen" sincerely is counted as if he had said the entire prayer.

SHULHAN ARUKH, ORAH HAYIM 124:1

Thermometer Or Thermostat?

Among the instruments which help us to live in greater physical comfort are the thermometer and the thermostat. The thermometer records and registers the environment, and its mercury line always adjusts and adapts; it conforms with the temperature of the times. On the other hand, the thermostat controls the temperature of the room. The thermostat determines exactly how many degrees, how high or how low shall be the temperature of the environment.

The basic question is, are you a thermometer or a thermostat? Do you want to conform to the world or transform the world? Do you want to be like your environment or do you want it to be like you? The phrase "keeping up with the times" means only the bland leading the bland.

When a person can trust himself fully, when he dares to become an originator, this man can live fearlessly on his own terms, he can do what he wants, and people will respect him. He can wear green checks instead of a grey flannel suit, drink yogurt instead of martinis, drive a Chevy instead of a Cadillac and vote the straight vegetarian ticket. And it will not make the slightest difference. Ability and achievements are the only valid sources of respect; and no one dares question excellence, no matter how unconventional the man who presents it.

Son of man, stand upon thy feet, and I will speak to thee.
                                        EZEKIEL 2:1

A Profit And Loss Statement

The parents of a young man killed in the Second World War gave their church a check for five hundred dollars. When the presentation was made, another war mother whispered to her husband, "Let's give the same for *our* boy."

"What are you talking about?" asked the father. "Our boy didn't lose his life."

"That's just the point," replied his mother. "Let's give it because he was spared."

People who genuinely appreciate the many goodnesses of God are moved to express their gratitude in positive ways, not merely in smug satisfaction and a fumbling prayer, but by sharing their good fortune with others.

If we reflect upon our lives during the past few months, we can find so much to appreciate. You may remember the few who died, but have you forgotten the thousands of people who walked out of hospitals healthy and healed? You may recall some harrowing accidents, but have you lost sight of all the near misses, the lucky scrapes and good fortunes? For every loss you find, you can tally up ten gains.

To praise Thy name for the myriads of kindnesses and loving care which Thou hast shown to us in every age.

SABBATH AND FESTIVAL PRAYER BOOK

The True Course

Marcus Aurelius, the great Roman emperor and philosopher, in his *Meditations* tells the story of the pilot who for many years steered his royal boat. Once on a very stormy night, when the waves were pounding the boat, in spite of great personal danger the emperor went out on deck to encourage the crew. He came upon the old pilot who had lashed himself to the tiller to prevent himself from being swept overboard by a furious wind and high waves. He heard the pilot praying aloud, "O, seas, you may sink me if you will, but whether you sink me or save, I will hold my tiller true."

There is a profound lesson to be learned from this story: The course of life is set during our earlier years, and how closely we follow its chartings depends upon our skill as pilots. There is never a given assurance as to what can occur next as we sail upon the seas of life. One moment life is calm, and the next it can become stormy and dangerously turbulent. The important thing is to hold the tiller with a firm hand, to keep it true so that we never steer off course.

What is the true course that a man should choose for himself? That which is an honor to him who does it and an honor to him in the sight of men.   AVOT 2:1

אדר

ADAR

The Oneness Of Man

An American woman lived with her husband on an African rubber plantation. One day a native boy came up to her and asked, "When a white person sees God, has God a white face?" It is a question uppermost in the mind of the Africans, so she answered with great care and said, "I would fear to look upon the face of God, but I will tell you what I think . . . I think the side of God's face that is in the sun will be bright, and the side toward the night will be dark so that no one can say that the face of God is any color at all."

Just as the face of God is without tint so is the soul of man without color, and his conscience has no dog-tag. Each person tends to see God in terms of his own race and culture, but the truth is that God is beyond the restrictions of a particular view. And God, in turn, sees man unrestricted by race and unfettered by a particular outlook. This idea which is basic in religious thinking, unites us all as children of the one God.

It is important to make the oneness of man a part of our daily thought, but even more vital to make it a part of our natural way of life.

One man was created the common ancestor of all so that the various families of men should not contend with one another. SANHEDRIN 38 a

Impulse Living

The Romans had a phrase for an approach to living — *Carpe diem* — which can be translated as "seize the day." They believed that each day one must make the most of what life has to offer here and now, and then give something in return to life here and now.

Perhaps, we can make the approach modern by reshaping a contemporary term. In advertising there is the phrase "impulse buying." We might then improve on this by encouraging "impulse living." This should not mean living by whim but rather living with spontaneity. Imagine how we might be able to enrich our lives by permitting our good impulses — our impulses for adventure, for fullness, for goodness to shape our acts. Not to make the very most of our lives is to waste the most precious of all resources — life itself. It is a tragic waste . . .

to see the sun and not bask in it,

to go to a party and not enjoy it,

to feel the spring rain and not walk in it,

to need a vacation and not take it,

to look at a painting and not really see it,

to start a good book and not finish it,

to be inspired by a worthy project and not share in it.

These are but a few rewards of what "impulse living" might help us earn.

This is the day the Lord has made; let us rejoice and be glad therein.   PSALMS 118:24

The Root Of All Good

In Bernard Baruch's autobiography he writes that when he was a very young man he accumulated his first million dollars. Elated, he went to tell his father about it. His father, however, was not impressed and Baruch, upset at his reaction, said, "I am not even thirty and already have made my first million — and you are not even happy?"

"No, my son," replied his father, "I am not impressed. What I want to know is — how will you spend the money you have earned?"

Money itself is neither an evil or a good: the test is what we do with money. When money is used properly and responsibly it can serve community needs by supporting the many institutions that insure the physical and spiritual welfare of humanity.

The possibility of the good and the bad uses of money was expressed in a nineteenth century American poem:

Dug from the mountain side, washed from the glen,
Servant I am or master of men.
Steal me, I curse you; earn me, I bless you;
Grasp me and hoard me, a fiend shall possess you;
Live for me, die for me, covet me, take me —
Angel or devil, I am what you make me.

Money is a liberal's faithful servant and a miser's hard master.   ISRAEL FRIEDMAN

The Purpose Of Prayer

Most of us are more interested in having our prayers answered, than in discovering the real purpose of prayer. In our quest for prayer we are so intensely concerned with our immediate needs that we lose sight of larger, more important goals. Unthinkingly, we often request that the entire process of nature be reversed for our individual pleasure. Let us be honest enough to admit that prayer cannot cure cancer, save a business, or change a personality.

What, then, is the real reason for prayer? Its real purpose is to permit us to see reality directly and to ennoble our own characters.

Prayer cannot cure cancer, but it can help us to endure suffering and it can motivate us to find a cure for that suffering. Prayer cannot change the offensive character of a boss or a relative, but it can teach us to understand, to be more tolerant and more patient. God does answer our prayers by granting us direction when we are in doubt, and by granting us inspiration when we are in pain and anguish.

The real insight was offered by the poet when he observed: He who rises from his worship a better man has had his prayer answered.

A person's prayer is not acceptable unless he puts his heart in his hands.   TAANIT 8 a

Inside And Out

Most critics of contemporary culture attribute the emptiness of much of modern life to the swift tempo, which permits us only to skim the surface of living without ever taking time to appreciate the finer things of life. We forget that some things cannot be hurried but must be slowly tasted, savored, and digested.

This can be well illustrated by an anecdote about an American couple who were touring France. As they came to the great cathedral at Chartres, the lady looked at her watch, and noticing how late it was she said to her husband, "Well, here we are. You take the outside and I'll take the inside."

Some things in life one must truly enjoy from both the inside and the outside. Our life is deepened when we embark upon a course of study or plan of action and refuse to stop until it is thoroughly mastered. This kind of achievement brings us the most satisfying moments of our lives.

This is true whether it means winning an Oscar or a Nobel Prize, or just once going the course in par, or serving a perfect dinner party, or giving a good book review, or learning to read and translate Hebrew, or being so gracious as to win a glowing tribute from your mother-in-law.

These are just a few of the byproducts of a genuine desire to know the approach of life's pleasures from both the inside and the outside.

A student whose inside is not as his outside is not permitted to enter the hall of study.   BERAKHOT 28 a

Falling In Love

Let us explore the word "love." No other culture has used and abused this word and other such terms of endearment as we have. We say "God is love," but we also "love" ice cream, convertibles and a drink before dinner. At parties, it is common to indiscriminately hear words like "Honey," "Darling," and "Doll" used by guests who have met for the first time. Obviously, people don't feel the affection they speak; they only pretend.

Because we have emptied love of its meaning, our children have followed suit. Many people are loveless today because they think in terms of "being loved" rather than "loving." They do not perceive that real love is active and not passive at all.

A picture may be admired for its beauty, but it is still only a picture because it cannot admire others. People may be strikingly beautiful, but they will never be loved until they begin to love others, for as in the old adage, it is "handsome is as handsome does." The emphasis is on doing, on love as a moving, creative force.

Love is a mother cooking a wonderful Shabbat meal for an appreciative family.

Love is a father enduring the daily grind of work to provide for those to whom he is really devoted.

Love is a student studying late hours to acquire knowledge, for its own sake.

Love is two young people who care for each other, but value the future and themselves enough not to take foolish risks with their emotions, their lives.

This is real love.

To love and be loved — this on earth is the highest bliss.
HEINRICH HEINE

How Beautiful Our Heritage!

One day in the British House of Commons Benjamin Disraeli, the renowned Prime Minister under Queen Victoria, was locked in bitter debate with a member of Parliament. His opponent, in the heat of argument, lost his Anglo-Saxon composure and sneered, "We cannot really take seriously what Disraeli says. After all, he is a descendant of Jews."

Disraeli jumped to his feet, surveyed him with icy calm, and said, "My dear sir, while your ancestors were still naked savages grunting about the cliffs of Dover, mine were standing at the foot of Sinai to receive the Ten Commandments."

Truly, there is something unique about being a Jew, and we respect ourselves only when we preserve that uniqueness.

We must continually strive to preserve the uniqueness of Judaism as a way of life and its individuality as a culture. We can only do this when we dedicate ourselves to living a full Jewish life and making the Jewish heritage vital and meaningful in our daily conduct.

The blessing which this inheritance has always bestowed is of yet daily recurrence, and who would madly neglect what is of vital importance to him? ISAAC LEESER

What Is My Circumference?

Once a school boy was asked to draw a circle and found himself without a compass. He could not remember the name of the instrument, and not meaning to be impolite to his teacher, he turned to her and asked, "Mrs. Jones, may I take your circumference?"

Perhaps some of us may be a little sensitive about our physical circumferences, but we would do well to ask ourselves: what is my spiritual circumference? How large is the area of my curiosity? Whom and what do I include in the circle of my interests?

Are you interested in just a fifth of whiskey or are you willing to also sample Beethoven's Fifth? Do you read only today's best sellers, or are you also curious about the best literature of the ages? Do you only notice the color of the paint in your living room and kitchen walls or do you also occupy yourself by looking at paintings in museums? The fact is that he who ceases to grow becomes smaller; he who leaves off, gives up, and the stationary condition is the beginning of the end. If a man does not widen the circumference of his concerns, he will be trapped in the tiny circle of selfhood.

It is good that you should take hold of this and also not withhold your hand from that.   ECCLESIASTES 7:18

Parents Are Not Just Pals

A distinguished psychiatrist recently noted that the role of the parent is badly confused in our society. He added that a child today has a great difficulty in distinguishing between his mother and his father. For the father now does the dishes and the housework and the mother is employed full time and both are just "pals" to the child — thus no one knows who wears the pants in the family. This example is obviously exaggerated, because a father *should* be helpful at home and a mother *can* be economically and socially useful. Nevertheless, there still remains great confusion as to their proper roles in our society.

In answer to this concern, we can make use of the tremendous wisdom of Judaism to help us define these roles in the family. When a father lifts a Kiddush cup on Friday evening, he does not have to define reverence; he *is* reverence. He is not only a friend, but a father.

When a mother lifts her hands to bless the Sabbath candles, she does not define holiness; she *is* holiness. A mother is not merely a comrade, but a carrier of culture.

Judaism defines our roles clearly. A man wears a *talit* and *kipah*; even a Jewish infant knows that. A woman prepares meals in kosher dishes, and even a Jewish girl playing house understands that. A woman identifies with the matriarchs; a man with the patriarchs. In Judaism, our family roles are defined by the experience of tradition.

Hear, my son, the instruction of your father, and forsake not the teaching of your mother.　　PROVERBS 1:8

Tranquility Through Trust

Not long ago, a foreign visitor came to America and when he was asked his impression of our land, he replied, "The very air in your country is filled with tension." He was both right and wrong. He was wrong because if you took a sampling of the air into the laboratory for analysis, you would not find a trace of tension in it. But he was also right, for the truth is that tension is in the emotions of the people who breathe the air in and out. The reason is that we tempt ourselves to be tense rather than to relax.

Consider for a moment one intriguing example of the way we add unnecessary tension to our lives. The next time you are in a store, go to the cosmetic counter and examine the wares. You will find that most of the products have titles that suggest sin and guilt. The implication is that sex is sin, and love to be fulfilling must be lurid. This is totally wrong. For love, to be worthwhile, must evoke our finest feelings of loyalty and loftiest expressions of responsibility.

Perhaps we ought to change the names of our perfumes. Instead of "Taboo," we should have a fragrance called "Tranquility"; instead of "Forbidden," we should have "Forgiven." We must constantly and consistently, in every aspect of our lives call forth the feelings of fulfillment that come with responsibility. We can reduce the level of our tension by being tranquil through trust.

What is trust? Tranquility of soul in the one who trusts.
BAHYA IBN PAKUDA

The Child Is Father Of The Man

Think for a moment how the child acquires his basic values and attitudes toward others. Freedom to be a person is learned with the right of refusing to take a bottle at 1:36 even if the schedule says so, and decision-making is learned with the privilege of turning thumbs down on spinach. The first rays of gratitude are perceived when a child unconsciously mimics his parents and instead of grabbing a gift and shouting, "That's mine!" he politely murmurs, "Thank you." Responsibility is developed when the child puts his toys away at the end of the day and when he takes pride in a clean and orderly closet.

The sum of all these habits adds up to form character; and while we may occasionally break a commandment, one can never destroy character.

Our real challenge is the education of our young — the child and especially the teen-ager. It is wrong to couch our problem in abstract terms such as integrity, honor, or responsibility. Our problem is really *people*. Before men become doctors, lawyers, or businessmen, they are boys. If they are good boys, they will be fine men who will be first-rate citizens who live with integrity, honor, and responsibility. And before women are mothers, nurses, or teachers, they are girls. If they are gentle girls, they will be virtuous women whose excellent characters will serve society.

Who trains his son in good deeds from childhood on, trains him to be a good pilot who knows how to steer his ship to port.   SEFER HASIDIM

The Challenge Of Darkness

The pupils of an eminent rabbi complained about the existence of so much evil in the world, and asked him how they might drive out the forces of darkness. The rabbi said they should take brooms and attempt to sweep the darkness from the cellar of the synagogue. The bewildered pupils went down to the cellar and attempted to sweep out the darkness.

When this failed, they again approached their teacher, and he advised them to take sticks and beat vigorously at the darkness. This, of course, did not help either. Then the rabbi suggested that they descend into the cellar and shout at the darkness and protest loudly against it.

When this likewise failed, he said, "My children, let each of you meet the challenge of darkness by lighting a candle." The students descended to the cellar and kindled their lights. They looked, and behold! The darkness had disappeared.

The evil of the world is great, but the power of good is also great. And the power of good is derived from many, many small deeds of goodness. The more individuals who share in the act of goodness the mightier it becomes. If each person will determine to do the very most he can to create a better world, he will really make it better. For as Goethe aptly put it, "If each person will sweep in front of his door, then the whole world will become clean."

Blessed is the match that is consumed
  in kindling flame.
Blessed is the flame that burns
  in the secret fastness of the heart.
Blessed is the heart with strength to stop
  its beating for honor's sake.   HANNAH SZENESCH

The Power Of A Woman

On the Fast of Esther it is appropriate to relate the following incident:

Not long ago, during a thunderstorm in a midwestern city, the electric power failed in all the houses in one section of the town. In one of the homes, the family was just about to be seated for dinner when the lights went out. The family included a three-year-old girl. Now for all the lights to go out without warning can be a very frightening thing for a child; it may seem to the child, in fact, as though all the lights in the world have suddenly been extinguished.

When this blackout occurred, the quick-thinking father went to the cupboard and got two candles which he set in candlesticks on the table. By chance, the mother had matches in her apron pocket, so she leaned over and lit the candles. At this point, the little girl looked up happily and said, "Good Shabbos."

A stroke of the match had turned her terror into triumph as fear was dissolved by faith. This little girl is taking the first steps on the road to becoming the traditionally respected Jewish woman who identifies with the traditions of her people and, through the strength of faith, becomes a source of strength to others. Every Jewish woman has the capacity to walk in this tradition.

Throughout the ages Thou hast blessed us, O Lord,
With women who tended the altars of our faith.

SABBATH AND FESTIVAL PRAYER BOOK

The Joke Is On You

Purim, which marks the first serious anti-Semitic event in history, is celebrated in an unusual way. Instead of observing the day in seriousness and gravity and contemplating the possible dreadful consequences, we traditionally treat the whole event as a huge joke. In fact, Haman — the archetype of the classic anti-Semite — is portrayed as a clumsy clown. Children masquerade as Haman, musicals and parodies are the order of the day, and even a special cookie has been created bearing the name of Haman.

This kind of observance gives us a great insight into the Jewish mind. It is precisely his ability to accept life with a sense of humor that has helped the Jew to survive. This saving humor comes out of the wellsprings of the Jewish character, which affirms life and enables the Jew in every generation to gain a perspective of Jewish history from his contemporary vantage point.

When it can be shown that the anti-Semites of history have hurled themselves in vain at Jewish existence, then it becomes clear that to try to stamp out Jews and Judaism is an act of supreme folly. It is laughable. And Haman has been treated to the supreme insult of being reduced to a biscuit — the Hamantaschen which we polish off in one mouthful!

Like the ants, the Jews never lose faith in life. Hamans and Hitlers everywhere; yet they live on, and enjoy life.
BERNARD BERENSON

171

A Hand Out

In a border state city, desegregating on a-grade-a-year basis, the opening of the fall semester was the fateful day for the second grade. The parents of one seven-year-old had prepared her for this traumatic experience. With her new notebook, pencils and lunch box she bounced out of the family car, which had brought her to school in the crispness of the morning. At 3 o'clock, in the warming sun, her mother picked her up. Unwilling to force discussion the mother chatted about trivial things on the ride home. Finally, at the kitchen table with cookies and milk spread out, mother asked the important question: "How did it go in school?"

The answer came sharply: "There was a little Negro girl sitting next to me."

The constriction in the mother's throat was like a paralysis. She forced out the next question: "What happened?"

"We were both so scared that we held hands all day."

Mankind must now join hands to learn to live together in happiness. Perhaps even the fright of a horrible all-out nuclear war is exactly what we need to pull us together, to save our bodies and our souls. Only when we feel that we belong to all mankind are we willing to protect the future of humanity.

Out of man's present spiritual chaos may emerge an ordered, pluralistic universe of thought. It will be a universe in which the principle of federalism is applied to the spirit as it has been in the realm of political life. Unity will be achieved with no sacrifice of liberty; cooperation without imposing uniformity.   LOUIS FINKELSTEIN

Echo Valley

In the Yellowstone region there is a natural formation called Echo Valley, which is very narrow and is surrounded by huge cliffs. Because of its structure, this pass echoes and greatly magnifies every sound that is made within it. Here a mere whisper becomes a shout, and a cry sounds like the crash of a falling tree.

The story is told of two hunters who were passing through Echo Valley. One accidentally hit the other's thumb and a mutter of the injured man became a violent "Curse you."

A miser, coming through, greedily hit his pickaxe on the mountain side and a whisper became a booming "I want gold."

A boy running away from home paused to pant a few words and they thundered "I hate you."

An artist stopped to paint the scene and became so enamored with the view that his lips imperceptibly moved in praise; soon the world heard a melodious "I love you."

Similarly in our daily lives whatever we say and do is picked up and amplified many times by others. Our actions, our conduct, and our emotions are observed and repeated by our spouses, by our children, by our friends, by the world we live in. Love expands into greater love just as hate generates more hate. For this reason we must think before we speak and ponder before we do. Life itself is our Echo Valley.

I believe in the innate dignity of the individual and have learned that, in the main, people are as we choose to find them; that reason can overcome prejudice; that knowledge can overcome ignorance; that love can overcome hate; and that goodness can conquer evil.   DORE SCHARY

For Mercy's Sake

During the fall of 1960, when Khrushchev and his fellow Communists arrived here for their propaganda tirades at the United Nations in New York, something occurred that went almost unnoticed. One of his henchmen was Nasser of Egypt. When Nasser came to the U.N., he brought along his personal physician, Dr. Ahmed Sarwat, who had lost the sight of one eye. Nasser and Sarwat enlisted the aid of Dr. Samuel Rosen of Mt. Sinai Hospital, who had lectured in Cairo. Dr. Rosen arranged for the Egyptian doctor to receive a corneal transplant, and the procedure was completely successful.

Let us see what was involved here. A Jewish doctor at a Jewish hospital restored the sight of an Egyptian Arab. This incident represents Jewish compassion at its highest. It is for this that Jews are called in the Talmud *rahamanim benay rahamanim* — "merciful children of merciful elders."

The correct understanding of mercy is that it must not be limited to one race or one people; for its only judgment is that it relieves suffering. Just as the basic concern of medicine is basically the human body and mind, so does the fundamental concern of mercy center upon the human being as such. The universality of mercy is understood and practiced by the believing Jew.

The glory of God is not visible except to those who are profoundly moved by compassion for their fellow men.
MORRIS RAPHAEL COHEN

Did You Ask Any Questions?

Dr. I. I. Rabi is chairman of the Department of Physics at Columbia University and one of the world's outstanding scientists. When asked to explain why he decided to dedicate himself to science, he said, "I couldn't help it." He added, "I was brought to the United States from Austria as an infant. I shall never forget my mother's daily query when I came home from public school on Manhattan's Lower East Side. Every afternoon, she greeted my return home from school with this: 'Did you ask any good questions today?'" Stimulated by his mother's hunger for knowledge, Rabi devoted his life to inquiry.

This illustrates the value of the inquiring mind. Mankind only learns by asking questions. It is not enough to accept the world, unquestioningly — we must always strive to find the how, the why, and the wherefore of experience.

Granted that we cannot hope to penetrate the mysteries of our world, we can still benefit greatly from whatever wisdom and knowledge we accumulate. As men learn more, they are able to make better use of their time and their lives. As men challenge and question, they literally learn how to live easier and longer lives. This process must come through years of training and schooling. The ability to ask questions is the product of a way of life.

Did you ask any good questions today?

Never hesitate to ask where the acquisition of knowledge is concerned.　　　　　　ELIJAH BEN RAPHAEL

The Lantern Of Sincerity

A young rabbi once came to an older colleague and complained, "When I study I feel happy and content, but when I leave the library, the mood disappears."

The older man answered, "It is like a man who journeys through a forest on a dark night and is accompanied part of the way by a companion who carries a lantern. At length they come to the point where their paths divide and they must go on alone. If each carries his own lantern, he need fear no darkness. My son, if you study Talmud with the lantern of sincerity, its light will accompany you even after you leave your books."

In everything we do, we must examine our thoughts and actions closely to make certain that we are being fully honest. If we are merely self-seeking, if we only act to gain advantage, then we are bound to end up frustrated. If what we do is based on deception, then ultimately we will discover that we have not deceived God or our neighbor, but rather ourselves.

Would you find God? Then take the lantern of sincerity and look into your own heart.

Would you find happiness? Then take the lamp of honesty and look into your own home.

Would you find fulfillment? Then take the light of service and look into your own community.

There is a place of light that opens only to him that occupies himself with the light of the Torah.

TIKKUNAY ZOHAR 13 c

Faith Is Fundamental

Franz Rosenzweig was born a Jew in Germany, and in his early years he was tempted to leave his faith. Before his conversion could be consummated, however, he attended services in a little Orthodox synagogue in Berlin one Kol Nidre night. There something happened inside of him and he decided to remain a Jew. He devoted himself to the study of Jewish theology, and in 1922 he was given the chair in Jewish theology at the University of Frankfurt, the highest achievement of a Jewish scholar.

That very year, when he was thirty-six, Rosenzweig was stricken with creeping paralysis, from which he was never to recover. Little by little, it affected his whole body, even his organs of speech. Yet such was the spirit of the man that the next few years were the most productive of his life. He composed articles on Jewish law, translated the Bible into German, wrote a major theological work, and in his leisure hours wrote chapters on musical history.

All of this was done when he could move only his right thumb, which miraculously retained some motion though slow and limited. This thumb he moved — his arm supported by a sling — over a plate containing the letters of the alphabet. His wife, sitting beside him, combined the letters into words, words into sentences and sentences into elaborate articles and books. Although he lost his race with death at the age of forty-three, he won his immortality.

All our seeming contradictions arise between the today that is merely a bridge to tomorrow and the today that is a spring-board to eternity.　　FRANZ ROSENZWEIG

An "H" On Your Dog Tag

Those who have served in the armed forces know that a serviceman must always wear an identification disk, familiarly known as a dog tag, fastened by a chain about his neck. This disk contains a person's name, serial number and a letter: C for Catholic, P for Protestant, or H for Hebrew. The purpose of this is that each individual will be carefully identifiable at all times. For this reason it is a military rule that he must never go without it. In a very similar fashion the identification of the Jew is clearly stamped upon his soul with the letter H for Hebrew. There is no chance to mistake the identity of the Jew. In the midnight of every Jewish soul there is the consciousness of being Jewish. This truth can be proven with three quick observations.

Why were Jews throughout the world shaken by the Eichmann trial? Why did every Jew look upon the Goldberg and Ribicoff appointments with mingled emotions — first with pride and then with anxiety? What if they fail? Why is every Jew filled with pride at achievements of a Jewish athlete, a Jewish artist, or a Jewish scientist? You see, it is proven beyond any doubt that we are involved with one another, deeply committed to one another.

A quiet dignified pride in the creative achievements of Jewish history is no ugly chauvinism. It is the only effective answer to the filth of the agitator.

ABRAM L. SACHAR

Shot To Heaven

A minister was reading a long list of announcements from the pulpit, which included at least one meeting, and sometimes two or three, for every night of the week. When he finished, he observed, "Well, it looks like this week is all shot to heaven."

This turn of a familiar phrase startles us into a basic understanding about life. Life is a process in which we can apply our energies in any direction we choose. We are given a certain amount of time. We can use this time in pursuit of positive or negative interests.

When we expend our energies in meaningless directions, at the end of the week we are bound to experience a feeling of negation and frustration. But on the other hand, when we fill our days with meaningful and creative endeavors we feel a sense of well-being and satisfaction.

Actually, we could say it this way: In one instance we spend our time, and in the other instance we invest our time. If we live correctly, then the week is "shot to heaven" in the deepest meaning of the phrase.

Let all your actions be for the sake of heaven.   AVOT 2:17

All In A Lifetime

The Bible tells us that Methusaleh lived 969 years. Yet of what significance were all those years? All we know of him is that he begot sons and daughters and then died. What a sad commentary on the futility and emptiness of his long life. Compare this life with that of John Keats, who lived but twenty-six years, and in this incredibly brief span of time was able to set the world aflame with his poetry. Or contrast this with an Alexander, who at the age of thirty sat down and wept because there were no more worlds left to conquer. Again, look at Maimonides, who at nineteen had already written a standard treatise on logic. Clearly then, we live not in years, but in deeds.

We are not blessed with the years of a Methusaleh in which to work out our destinies at leisure. Nor do we all have the poetic passion of a Keats, the drive for power of an Alexander or the religious zeal of a Maimonides to make life burn with a feverish intensity. What then does life hold for us "ordinary" people?

Life means basically fulfilling ourselves. That is, filling full our days with deeds and our lives with meaning. It is not how many things we do, but rather what things we do, and how well we do them.

A long life, a short life — what's the difference?
A life of beauty!   MAX NORDAU

The Dilemma Of Diet

Pause for a moment to think through the challenge of *kashrut*. To a civilized, sensitive individual the taking of a life — any life — is an act of barbarism. Reverence for life is the first commandment in any religion. In the preparation of a meat meal, the first act is to kill an animal. When we eat meat, we do so at the expense of a living thing. And we must ask ourselves, who gave us the right to do this?

On the other hand, it is well-nigh impossible to exist without meat. Physically our bodies demand it. The taste buds in our mouths crave it. What shall we do?

To this Judaism gives us a clear and healthy answer. Realize this dilemma and do something constructive about it. Do not hunt for the sport of it. At least limit your foods to those taken from the class of non-predatory animals who are identified by split hooves and the fact that they chew their cud. Let not anyone take a life but a *shohet*, who has the authority to do so. Let him recite a blessing before he does this. Let the slaughtering be done in the most humane manner possible. Upon considering these values we begin to understand that *kashrut* is not an empty symbol; it is part of a sensitive and thoughtful way of life.

We are taught that while it is difficult to fast for the sake of heaven, it is even more difficult to eat for the sake of heaven.   S. Y. AGNON

The Hidden Persuaders

Many of us ask, "How do we know there is a God?" There are many answers to this query, but one of the most sensitive can be found in the following simple analogy:

A man once met a small boy who was flying a kite. The kite was so high that it was out of sight. The man asked the lad, "How do you know there is any kite there at all?" The boy replied, "I feel the pull of it."

One of the ways we can know there is a God is by the pull He has upon our hearts. The very fact that all of us are concerned about our relationship with a Higher Authority is partial evidence of the great strength and drawing power that spiritual concerns have upon us. But basically, it is the "hidden persuaders" — the good ones — within us and among us that testify to the presence of God.

The exquisite simplicity of a perfect blade of grass;

The first cry of a newborn child;

The endless rhythms of the seasons;

The marvelous movements of the mind;

The self-sacrifice of a mother, father, or a child;

The moral grandeur of the Scriptures;

The dedicated lives of the great servants of humanity.

These are some of the hidden persuaders that pull and draw us toward a living God.

Two things fill the mind with ever new
*   and increasing wonder and awe;*
Above me the starry heavens
*   and within me the moral law.*   IMMANUEL KANT

The Ultimate Honesty

There is a beautiful saying that should be engraved on our hearts. The Rebbe of Kotzk once noted that a truly religious man is *lifnim mishurat hadin* — "one who goes beyond the letter of the law." Interpreting this ideal, he pointed out that according to the letter of the law, one should be honest in his dealings with others. But a thoroughly honest man goes beyond the letter of the law, which means that he is not only honest with others, but honest with himself as well.

It is a kind of spiritual dishonesty that makes us scan the faces of a social set cringingly, searching for approval. Does the need for acceptance by others blind us to the fact that God gave us intelligence to think for ourselves?

It is important to a life of honesty to do what is right in the eyes of God and our conscience, and not what is right in the eyes of our neighbors. A life of honesty is achieved by a person who is less concerned with being socially acceptable and more concerned with being spiritually accountable.

And thou shalt do what is good and right in the eyes of the Lord thy God.　　　DEUTERONOMY 12:28

Collision Or Creative?

Dr. Earl Loomis, one of the founders of the Academy of Religion and Mental Health, once shared a marvelous story in a seminar. An eight-year-old boy in a restaurant was accompanied by his mother and older sister who were persistently trying to order for him. The waitress ignored them and began taking the order directly from the boy. As she left, the boy turned in amazement to his mother and said, "Gee, Mom, she thinks I'm real."

Regarding people as *real* means accepting them with their differences, respecting their judgments, learning to live with their tastes, attitudes and feelings. Reality lies at the intersection between one human personality and another. And whether that human encounter is a collision or a creative experience depends entirely upon our respect for the reality of human differences.

In business, we meet an Easterner and right away we think: "slick, sharp and slippery"; but don't the people in the rural areas of America think that way about those of us who live in cities of the West? Some of us hear the word "Pope" and we conjure up the image of an evil old scheming politician; but on the other hand, there are those who feel the same way about Ben-Gurion. If we are children, an adult can seem to be a pretty domineering person; and if we happen to be angry parents, the teenager appears as a monster. Obviously, none of these pictures is true, for when we get to know people, each is an individual, not just a representative of a class, a creed, or a color. Indeed, reality lies at the crossroads of difference.

Whether a man really loves God can be determined by the love he bears toward his fellow man.

LEVI YITZHAK OF BERDITSCHEV

The Constant Miracle

A hundred million miracles
Are happening every day.
And those who do not agree
Are those who do not hear or see.

This refrain from a song in the musical *The Flower Drum Song* provides us with a provocative thought. We usually think of miracles as those instances in which the natural course of events is interrupted and changed for the welfare of a person or a people. Actually, miracles are constantly occurring around us and within us, miracles that give us more cause for inspiration and faith than we ordinarily perceive.

The Talmud tells that the daily healing of the sick is greater than the biblical report that three men passed through a fiery furnace unharmed. The daily miracle of the body's healthy functioning is more wondrous than the unique instances of miraculous recovery.

Every time we experience the smooth working of nature, we see revealed the miraculous providence of God. There is not a drop of rain that is swallowed by the thirsty soil, not a child that lies at his mother's bosom, not a fruit in the supermarket bin that does not testify to abundant goodness of God. In this essential goodness can be apprehended the true miracle of existence.

The essence of Judaism does not lie merely in entertaining a concept of God, but in the ability to articulate the moments of illumination by His presence. Our whole program of Jewish living is to help us to become articulate and express our wonder as we stand in awe before God.

ABRAHAM E. HALPERN

In A Rut

In the wildwoods of Northern Canada once the winter freeze sets in, all the paths become hardened until the spring. Because of this, one of the unpaved backwoods has this sign at its entrance: "Be careful of the rut you choose, for you will be in it for the next ten miles." It is entirely possible that we have chosen a rut in Jewish life and have been in it for too long.

The tremendous demands of Jewish history during the past half century have in turn forced us to create inordinate pressures in the Jewish community to meet the needs of the hour. To save lives, one must use desperate means. Is it not possible that in this process we have neglected to cultivate the more sensitive and nobler instincts within the Jewish community to do good?

Must we always contribute because it is a crisis, or can we not be moved to give because we have a conscience?

Must we cater to the mass mentality; can we not lure with the mind of Maimonides and the magnificence of Moses?

Must we shame people into coming to services; can we not entice them with the sincerity of the spoken word and the tranquility of the timeless flow of ritual?

Must we continually reproach those who break the Sabbath spirit; can we not seduce their souls with a day free of the terrible tension of profit and loss, a day of truce between men and the world?

Are we in a rut?

O sing unto the Lord a new song.   psalms 98:1

נִיסָן

NISAN

Judaism In 3-D

When the new movie process 3-D was first shown, we were impressed by the new image that the third dimension added to viewing. Similarly we may find Judaism to be more meaningful if we look at it in all three of its dimensions.

The first dimension of Judaism is depth. Our culture goes back thousands of years to almost the first page of history and our ancestors have carved their images upon the heart and conscience of mankind.

The second dimension of our religious culture is breadth. Judaism is a world faith whose adherents occupy every part of our globe. American Jewish soldiers observe the Passover in Arctic Thule, Jews read their Hebrew prayers in Central Africa, and others translate our scriptures into Marathi in Bombay, Tamil in Cochin, Arabic in the Near East, or Medieval Spanish in Turkey.

Judaism truly excels in the third dimension — height, for it challenges man to reach the heights of human thought and understanding. From the simple words of our patriarchs through philosophic inquiries of the medieval rabbis down to the youngest Jewish child sitting at his biblical lesson, all have found the Torah a mighty stimulus to intellectual growth. From every vantage point and in every dimension, Judaism offers a magnificent spiritual vista.

Turn it (the Torah) and turn it over again for everything is in it, and contemplate it, and wax grey and old over it, and stir not from it, for thou hast no better rule than this.
AVOT 5:25

The Wisdom Of The Body

Anyone who has ever visited New York City or any other large metropolis cannot help but be amazed by its complicated system of communications. Yet, as a prominent neurologist has pointed out, the nervous system of any human being is more complicated in structure than is the trunk telephone line system of all of New York City. Indeed, the human body functions in an unbelievably complex and amazingly wise manner.

This ought to give us good cause to acknowledge our Creator who gave us a wonderful mind and body to enjoy the world, serve Him and answer to our responsibilities. In so many marvelous ways does our body sing of a great and magnificent God. The continuous and reliable processes of the body are a living tribute to the Divine Sculptor.

If we really respect our bodies as the handiwork of the Creator we must learn to trust the wisdom of the body. We must accept the warnings of fatigue and weariness. We must trust in our ability to summon the extra strength to meet an emotional or physical crisis. We must patiently accept our physical limitations and, at the same time, be alert to tap our resources for energy and satisfying our daily needs. He who learns to heed the wisdom of body is wise indeed.

Blessed art Thou, O Lord our God, King of the Universe, who has fashioned man in wisdom, and has created in him life-sustaining organs.   DAILY LITURGY

The Voice Of The Devil

According to an amusing and instructive tale, Rabbi Misel used to rise every morning at five o'clock to study Torah. One particularly cold day, the alarm clock as usual stirred him into consciousness before sunrise. He looked out of the window through the frosted glass and saw that it was snowing. The good rabbi hated to leave his pleasant and comfortable bed. At that moment, the evil inclination (*yetzer ha-ra*) appeared and whispered into his ear, "Oh, why get up so early and study? After all, who really cares? Why not enjoy another hour's sleep?" The old rabbi agreed and again grew drowsy. Suddenly, Rabbi Misel sat bolt upright in bed and said, "Oh, you devil, you must have awakened before me to entice me to neglect my duty. If *you* can get up early, so can *I*!" And he hopped out of bed.

The truth is that the evil inclination is not a monster, but more nearly the line of least resistance. It offers us every pleasant diversion to escape our responsibilities. It helps us to blunt our consciences and stop up our senses so as to escape the call of duty. But out of leaden instincts we can never fashion golden conduct.

Not to understand that a demand may be part of God's love for man is to misunderstand love as meaning unconditional acceptance without demand, and to sentimentalize love, emptying it of real content.   MAURICE FRIEDMAN

The Worth Of A Man

In a fashionable resort area a man once arrived at an expensive hotel. Wishing to be noticed, he immediately began to tip very lavishly. At luncheon, he tipped a waiter ten dollars, he gave five dollars to the bellboy who brought him a drink, another five dollars to a boy who brought him a telegram. That afternoon he wandered outside and by accident he fell into the pool. He was rescued by the life-guard, and as he was being carried to his room he asked, "Say, what can I tip for a thing like this?"

This is not as bizarre as it sounds for some people are under the impression that everything has a cost and every man his price. Yet, the most important experiences in life are priceless.

What is the value of a magnificent sunset?

How much could we pay for the cooling rain that comes at the end of a hot, humid afternoon?

Can you buy a friend? What would be his price tag?

What is the purchase price of the respect of our community?

How much does it cost to obtain the love of another person?

Your answer is determined by *your* worth, for the greatest values are spiritual.

Not more things but higher values —
This is the historic challenge of religion.　JOSEPH L. BARON

191

You And Your Sacred Cow

Among the special Scripture readings immediately preceding Passover is a description of the ancient rites for the preparation of the *Parah Adumah* — "The Red Heifer." In this special ceremony, a red cow was rendered holy and everyone was forbidden to touch the cow under the penalty of becoming ostracized. Therefore it was literally untouchable.

The tradition of the sacred cow can be seen today in the Bengal province of India. A certain religious sect believes that all cows are sacred. The cows are allowed to roam about and cannot be touched. They may trample food, ruin shops, and even injure human beings, but they are not restrained for they are believed to be holy.

While we believe this to be wrong, we nonetheless accept the principle of the "sacred cow" in our lives. We believe that certain ideas and institutions are holy and untouchable. As long as we maintain this primitive attitude and refuse to expose our thoughts to reality and truth, we distort our way of life and our opportunities for fulfillment.

An intelligent person should never fear the examination of new thoughts and institutions. Nor should he shirk the opportunity to have his own values challenged. That which is good and valuable can stand the glaring beam of truth, and that which proves worthless when examined thoughtfully should be discarded.

Truth is the seal of God;
He who has truth in his heart has God for his guide.

YOMA 69 b

Sharing Our Homes

An old Yiddish story tells of a soul who once went to heaven in a dream in order to observe the procedure of the Heavenly Court. A learned rabbi approached and wished to enter. "Day and night," he said, "I studied the holy Torah." "Wait," said the angel, "we will investigate whether your study was carried on for its own sake or rather for professional gain or acclaim."

A Zaddik, a holy man, next approached. "I fasted much," he said, "I chanted the Psalms every day." "Wait," said the angel, "until we have completed our investigation to learn whether your motives were pure."

Then a tavern-keeper drew near. He said, "I kept an open door and fed without charge every poor man who came to my inn."

No investigation was required and immediately the heavenly gates were opened to him.

This is an expression of the values that Jewish literature and life has placed upon hospitality. The Jew has always emphasized that keeping a home open, warm and inviting is one of the marks of character. When we share our homes with others, we give what is most important of all — a part of ourselves.

The hospitable person is rewarded in both worlds.

SHABBAT 127 a

Universal And Particular

One warm spring day a young mother took her small son on a school picnic. The boy wandered away from the group, and after he had been missing for sometime, his mother began an anxious search for him. Suddenly, she heard a desperate voice crying, "Sarah! Sarah!" When she reached her boy and calmed him, she asked him why he had called her Sarah when he always called her Mother at home. The child wisely explained, "It was no use calling Mother, Mother — the place is full of mothers!"

The world, too, is full of religions, all valid and good. But, the wise person will find expression of the universal values of man in his own particular religion. Values become meaningless, unless they are expressed in a particular time and place and are captured in an historic setting.

A Catholic who is loyal to Catholicism, a Protestant who is devoted to Protestantism, and a Jew who is faithful to Judaism — each will find fulfillment as a child of God. As Jews, we will find our greatest happiness by accepting our own religious traditions and endeavoring to make the most of them. We cannot till every garden in the world, but we can cultivate our *own* garden and make it produce the finest spiritual flowers possible.

Let all the peoples walk each one in the name of God. But we will walk in the name of the Lord our God forever and ever.   MICAH 4:5

The Service Of The Heart

A man was in a hurry to attend a service at the synagogue. He arrived breathless and he inquired of the usher whether he was in time to attend at least the end of the service. The usher replied, "The *prayers* are over, but the *service* is just beginning."

It is important to understand that study and prayer must lead to concrete expression if we desire to be truly religious. One of the fundamental purposes of worship is to inspire us to work for a better world. Through the process of prayer, we expose ourselves to the collective ideals of our people. Through prayer, we translate these values into everyday living.

It is especially important for the synagogue to relate ancient values to contemporary problems. Throughout the ages, the Jewish House of God has symbolized decency and justice. The willingness to speak forth with prophetic insight on the issues in the marketplace — this has made Judaism vital and dynamic. Prayers without deeds make religious belief arid. Action without inwardness leads to a life of misguided impulse. Truly, prayer and service go hand in hand.

Knowledge of the Torah avails much, yet the chief purpose of its study is doing God's will.   KIDDUSHIN 40 b

Crime And Punishment

When a person commits a crime in the state of Israel — whether it be petty theft or murder — he is sent to a Central Classification Unit. Here for six to eight weeks he is tested, and an outline is made of his whole life history. The social workers strive to answer three questions about the criminal. Who is this man? What is his problem? What can we do for him?

As responsible citizens in society, we might help our fellowmen if every time we read a newspaper story describing a crime we would pause and ask these questions.

Who is this man? He is an individual with feelings and sensitivities. He is a father or a son, or if a woman — a mother, a daughter or a sister. This is primarily a person and neither a statistic nor the hero of a lurid tale told to satisfy the prying minds of sensation-seekers.

What is his problem? Every action in human behavior is caused. Every person has needs and drives. Why was this person moved to satisfy his needs in an antisocial act?

What can we do for him? Our prime goal ought not to be punishment, but rather an earnest desire to help this person solve his problem. Merely restraining a person answers only the needs of society. Restraint is not enough unless we help the person rebuild himself. Restraining should go hand in hand with retraining. And, since the attitudes of all of us need retraining, remember when you next see a crime story to ask yourself those three questions.

And the Holy One, blessed be He, said: "When my creations are suffering, how can you think of rejoicing?"

SANHEDRIN 39 b

But The Beauty Remains

Renoir, the great French artist, suffered from rheumatism in his hands during the later years of his life. He painted by being placed in a chair which was moved as he directed. As he applied the paint to the canvas, suffering intensely, perspiration covered his brow. Yet he persisted and continued to paint masterpieces. One day Matisse, his disciple, pleaded, "Why torture yourself to do more?" Gazing at his favorite canvas Renoir replied, "The pain passes, but the beauty remains."

With the true instinct of the artist, Renoir understood that the creation of beauty helps to make life endurable and worthwhile. It is this basic understanding that makes man human. Man's march toward civilization really began when he tried to scrawl pictures on the walls of the cave in which he lived. In this way man tried not only to depict his impressions of the world, but also to give those impressions enduring shape and meaning.

Through this attempt to express our deepest feelings about the world we become more than mere mortals. The creation of beauty makes us feel noble and uplifted, and what is more it endures beyond any one lifetime. Beauty is created only through intense concentration, passionate devotion, and honest expression. As man thinks and feels at his highest level he hallows his life and draws close to the supreme Creator.

Art and religion are the soul of our civilization. Go to them, for there love exists and endures.

FRANK LLOYD WRIGHT

Milk And Honey

The phrase "milk and honey," taken directly from the Bible, is a symbol of hospitality and consideration. In ancient times, when there were no hotels in the desert, if a stranger or a traveler appeared before a tent, milk and honey were placed before him. To the wayfarer coming off a hot and dusty road, what could be more refreshing than cold milk, and what could be more tasty than a bit of honey on homemade bread? Those who were prepared to receive travelers were praised in Jewish literature because of their consideration for others.

This consideration for others is one of the finest developments of any culture or people. It can be expressed in many ways, all of them reflecting a sensitivity to the feelings and the needs of others. In one New England town it was said of a certain boy: "He was the first to volunteer in war — and he danced with all the girls with whom the others did not dance." This boy was held up as a model for the young people in that town.

There is a direct connection between assuming the big responsibilities in life and the daily awareness of the importance of consideration for others. A culture that stresses this value is truly a great culture, for the advancement of a society is measured only by the degree of the obedience of its members not to the enforced laws but to the dictates of conscience.

And God said to Israel: My beloved children, am I in want of anything that I should request it of you? But what I ask of you is that you should love, honor and respect one **another.**   SEDER ELIYAHU RABBAH 26

A Many-Splendored Thing

One Sunday a woman from Kentucky who was visiting England chose to attend services at Westminster Abbey. The lady was a member of a sect which believes that one should freely express enthusiasm in worship. She observed with awe the dignity and solemnity of this great English service. Then the minister rose to preach.

As at home, she showed her appreciation and agreement by periodically shouting, "Amen," "Hallelujah" and "That's right, Brother." Finally, she worked up to such a pitch and created such a racket that two ushers had to lift her out of her seat and carry her out of the service.

As they were walking out, one of the ushers turned to her and asked, "What's the matter with you, madam?" She replied, "I got religion." He then stared at her and said, "Don't you know that you can't have religion here?"

This is an exaggerated but good-humored illustration of the way in which cultural differences are expressed in religious services. Worship, after all, expresses the deepest needs of people, and they worship most meaningfully in their own traditional ways. This does not imply that any one way of observance is best — only that in the words of a nursery rhyme, "Some like it hot and some like it cold." All of this is a confirmation of the fact that religion is a many-splendored thing.

We hold that all religions have a common aim, toward which they tend in different ways. Each employs parables and images, according to the style of its generation and country, and suitable to the intelligence of its followers, but all aim to lead people to justice, truth and bliss.

LEVI BEN ABRAHAM

To Be Yourself

About two hundred years ago Rabbi Moshe Leib made a penetrating insight into the nature of human existence when he said, "A human being who has not a single hour for his own every day is no human being."

If a man works all day and then comes home to spend the evening being a father and a husband, when does he have time to be himself?

If a woman takes on the responsibilities of the household, the children, social obligations, at what point can she find a private time — just to be herself?

If a teen-ager rushes off to school, worries constantly about what his or her friends think, takes on the latest fads, at what point will he or she begin to think as an individual instead of as part of a crowd?

Every day we need at least one sliver of time to think, to meditate, to wonder, to dream, to hope, to do anything we want. Above all, we must have time to be ourselves.

Every generation of parents says that it is living for the next generation of children. If this is true of the cycle of generations, we might well pause to ask, "Who is living for himself?"

Life with others is good, but to live with oneself is better.
                                    BERTHOLD AUERBACH

Passover Is A Perennial

In the *Seder* ceremonial every Jew becomes a contemporary of Moses and re-experiences the lash of oppression. The *maror*, the bitter herb, leaves the bitter taste of slavery in our mouth. The *haroset*, the mixture of apples, nuts, and wine, is reminiscent of the mortar used in the work of slave labor that is always exploited to build state projects. The dipping recalls the crossing of the Red Sea and the escape to freedom. The use of leafy greens is largely a reminder of the pleasures and blessings of freedom itself.

The *Seder* is thus not just past history, but the past re-created. Through the many rituals, we become actively involved in the issue of freedom. Freedom itself is so vital that we must periodically remind ourselves of its importance.

This concern for freedom is illustrated in the story of an American soldier who returned to the United States after a long term as a prisoner of war. He was asked by one of the throng of newsmen who were waiting at the dock, "What did you think about during your imprisonment?" The young man replied, "I spent such time as I had to think, wondering whether I would be worthy of freedom when I received it."

Passover is a perennial reminder of our freedom. It asks us through the *Seder* ceremony whether we are worthy of the freedom which is ours to have and to hold. It is this intense reliving of the past that illuminates and gives meaning to the present.

In every generation it is one's duty to regard himself as if he personally had come out of Egypt.

PASSOVER HAGGADAH

Strangers No More

The one verse in the Bible more than any other, that expresses the mood of Passover is *ki gayrim heyitem be-eretz mitzrayim,* "For you were strangers in the land of Egypt."

The reason for the importance of remembering this historical circumstance is that we are taught that the most terrible human condition is to be a stranger. Even the word "estranged" has a jarring effect upon us. To be a stranger is to be alone, cut off, even near death. On the other hand, the condition of greatest human satisfaction is to belong, to be a part of something, to be accepted. When we are a member of the in-group, we know that nothing can harm us, nothing can touch us, for we are at one with many.

It is no mere accident then that Passover is celebrated through the *Seder* in which we come together as families, as Jews, and as members of the larger fellowship of mankind. Passover means that we are no longer strangers, that we are part of something important, great, indeed eternal. We are united by common experiences, common memories, all of which are joined together forever with the cement of history.

The *Seder* is celebrated in the home because Jews understand that the family and the home give us our greatest sense of belonging. We know that whether in life or in death we are forever a part of our people.

The Seder Service for the night of Passover is probably the oldest of all rituals of the sort at present current among mankind. The most ancient portions of text are at least two thousand five hundred years old. It is the eternal message of hope that saved the Jewish people from despair even in the darkest hours.   CECIL ROTH

How Do You Count?

The period between Passover and Shavuot is known as the *Sefirah* — which means literally "the counting period." Beginning with the second day of Passover, Jews count forty-nine days and on the fiftieth day the festival of Shavuot is proclaimed. The counting ritual is very exact, and it is the obligation of each person to participate in the counting ceremony. This ritual emphasizes the importance of counting each moment and each person as infinitely precious.

Another counting process that drew much attention recently was the census in the United States. Among the more interesting census stories was that of the census-taker who asked a mother the number of children in the family. The mother paused, then ticked them off: "Well, there is Willie and Ethel and . . ." The interviewer rudely interrupted her with, "Never mind the names, I just want the number." The mother protested indignantly, "They haven't got numbers, Mister — everyone of them has a name!"

Just as a name distinguishes a person, so does his personality make him unique. Each individual counts in his own right and is not just a number. This is an important Jewish value, for Judaism believes that man is not a mere cipher in a statistical column, but counts as a soul — precious, irreplaceable, and unique.

It again resolves itself into the impressive statement: "Thou art the man." Upon thee everything depends. Thou canst create a world, thou canst destroy it.   HENRIETTA SZOLD

Just A Scratch

A king once owned a rare and beautiful jewel of which he was very proud, for it had no equal anywhere. One day the gem accidentally was deeply scratched. The king called in the most skillful craftsmen of his realm and offered a great reward if they could remove the imperfection from his treasured jewel. But try as they might, none could repair the damage, and the king was sorely distressed. After some time a very talented artist came to the king and offered to make the rare stone even more beautiful than before the accident. Impressed by his confidence, the king entrusted his precious gem to the artist's care. After several weeks of secluded workmanship, the man returned with the jewel. With superb skill he had engraved a lovely flower around the damaged area, using the deep scratch to make the stem.

The story of the king and the craftsman contains a profound lesson for us. On many occasions in our lifetime we sustain spiritual wounds and emotional bruises. We can let them remain ugly scars upon our lives and characters or we can use the damage and the scratches to create images of beauty that will enhance the meaning of our lives.

Whoever takes his suffering and converts it into good fortune brings salvation to the world.   TAANIT 8 a

Near You

One of the most basic ways a parent can reassure a child is simply by saying, "I am here," or "Mother is here," or "Daddy is here." The very presence of a loving person is the deepest source of reassurance.

The religious equivalent of these sentences is, "God is here," or even, simply, "God is." The idea of God as a presence is the most meaningful concept in the entire galaxy of human feelings. When a person accepts this idea in perfect faith, then his tension, anxiety, and fear are assuaged.

How often have you sat at the bedside of someone in paid or just emerging from the fog of sedation or anesthesia? You instinctively put your hand on the hand of the patient and say simply, "God is near," then you observe that the hand of the patient relaxes and the entire being is at ease.

God is near to us: as close as the whisper of the heart, as omnipresent as the air we breathe. To summon Him, we need not shout; we need only whisper the thought, "God is near."

The Lord is near unto all who call upon Him;
To all who call upon Him in truth.   PSALMS 145:18

Living In Two Worlds

In light of the cold war and current Soviet tactics, the following incident merits further consideration. Several years ago, the MVD (the Russian secret police) arrested the Lubavitcher Rebbe, the leader of a Hasidic sect. In preparation for his imprisonment, the rebbe was packing his belongings. Irritated by the rebbe's deliberate slowness, the Russian agent pointed his gun at him and said, "This little toy has made many a man change his mind."

The rebbe replied, "That little toy can intimidate only the kind of man who has many gods, many greedy ambitions, and only one world — this one — in which to serve them. But I, who have only one God and many worlds in which to serve Him, am unimpressed by your little toy."

It is important to remember that we are inhabitants of many worlds — this world and the next. We must try to make the most of this life, but at the same time, we must be willing, if need be, to risk it totally for that which we believe is its highest value — freedom to serve God.

Only the soul that understands that this world is not the beginning and end of existence can resist tyranny to the end. Only the soul committed to ultimate service of God can freely choose to offer that soul as a willing sacrifice to God.

The righteous servant of God reveres the life of this world merely because it serves as a step-ladder to the next world.

SAADIAH GAON

Hindrance Or Help?

Many of us have seen a cradle gym strung over an infant's crib, but few of us know how it originated. The cradle gym, a device made of gay and attractively colored balls and rings, is designed to encourage the child to stretch and develop his growing muscles. It was invented fifteen years ago by a man who had become a paraplegic patient during World War II.

One day, as he stared at his trapeze-like exercise bar and wondered what life had in store for him, he suddenly had an idea. How about designing a small attractive exercise bar such as this for infants? Out of this idea grew a huge and very successful business.

In many instances, a difficulty, is actually an opportunity in disguise. A problem, a challenge, often summons the best that is in us. With the right attitudes, we find that trouble strengthens our resolve, summons our creative powers, and lifts our vision. Thus we often discover that a hindrance may become a help.

There is no trouble in one direction without profit in another.   GENESIS RABBAH 38:10

Unity In Diversity

Many of us, to satisfy our own needs, tend to squeeze God into our own national boundaries and theological limits. We simply create God in our own image. We really are quite fearful of sharing God with others.

Consider, for example, how in the movies when the cowboy is shot, we are made to believe (to the accompaniment of tearful background music) that a noble soul has been wounded. But when an Indian is killed, it's only another redskin "who bit the dust," and the music swells up triumphantly. Are not redskinned men also created in the image of God?

And think, too, of the way some people order around their domestic help as if they were animals, as if they did not have souls or religious feelings, as if they did not also have ideas about God.

There are also some religious people whose narrow theology denies non-believers their basic humanity. They tend to forget that *all* men were created with souls by the same God.

Once, a mother tried to explain the meaning of the word humanity to her child. She was singularly unsuccessful. Finally, in desperation, she said to the child, "Well, maybe you'll understand if I tell you that all the people we know are humanity." This seemed to make quite an impression. The little girl's face lit up with the beginnings at least of understanding, but then clouded over again as she asked, "But Mother, how about the people we don't know — are they humanity too?"

Theology separates men; religion unites them.

MAX LILIENTHAL

It Is Not Hard To Die

A few years ago, a religious leader was talking about faith. He suddenly sought out the eyes of his wife who was seated in the audience. Upon finding them, he said, "Death is like going through an open door. We shed one garment and put on another. It is not hard to die . . ." He ended his talk quickly and was taken to the hospital, where he died.

This man had courage because he understood that when the soul is released from the cares and anxieties of bodily existence, it returns to find peace in the reunion with its Maker. God, who cares, who is concerned for the individual as well as the group, does not permit life to become a mockery and a folly, nor to end with the body's death. The Almighty wraps each day at its ending in a bow of beautiful sunset colors as if to say what is good deserves to be preserved in beauty. So does he wrap in beauty each life at its ending as he gathers the soul unto Himself — into immortality.

How beautifully has Wordsworth expressed this in the closing stanza of "Ode on Intimations of Immortality":

> We will grieve not, rather find
> Strength in what remains behind;
> In the primal sympathy
> Which having been must ever be;
> In the soothing thoughts that spring
> Out of human suffering;
> In the faith that looks through death,
> In years that bring the philosophic mind.

This is the meaning of death: the ultimate self-dedication to the divine. For the pious man, it is a privilege to die.

ABRAHAM JOSHUA HESCHEL

A Balk

In baseball, when a pitcher with players on base takes his windup, gets ready to pitch, and then fails to deliver the ball, he is charged with a "balk." Because he aroused everyone's interest and brought everyone's abilities to the fore and then failed to carry through, he is penalized according to the rules of baseball.

This is true of life itself. Often we become greatly inspired by a holyday or a religious experience and we summon all our abilities and spiritual resources. We are all wound up, prepared to deliver the pitch, but then at the last moment, we balk. When we do this, we penalize ourselves.

We attend services during a holyday and we are inspired, but we balk on attendance when the next Sabbath comes.

We share in a Bar Mitzvah and are deeply moved, but the next day we balk at donning the *tefilin*.

We read a Jewish book and find it fascinating, but we balk upon starting another.

It is, therefore, important to realize that Jewish life must be lived according to rules or we are penalized. When we balk at the requirements we pay the penalty of failing to grow and to increase our understanding.

Anyone who begins a mitzvah but does not complete it does not have it ascribed to his name.   TANHUMA 13

He Who Rests, Rusts

On a television program one night, Rocky Marciano, the former heavyweight champion, told an interviewer that he had gained twenty pounds since quitting the ring. Of the years during which he fought forty-nine bouts and never lost one, he said, "I was hungry, always hungry."

When Albert Einstein was asked what his goal was in formulating the theory of relativity, he answered, "I challenged the axioms." Einstein went on to say, "To make a goal of comfort or happiness has never appealed to me."

The highest goals of men are not self-satisfaction, or luxury, or ease. The highest goal is continual accomplishment. The real champion does not compete for money, but to be the best in his field. The physicist does not split the atom to add material comforts to an already opulent civilization. Both are driven forward by the challenge of first-rate achievement.

The champion in any area of human endeavor always guards us from cheapening our goals and corroding them beyond recognition. His insistence on being the finest and the best constantly lifts our levels of achievement and advancement. When we are satisfied with our present condition, we inevitably drift backward with the tide instead of going forward with the waves. Or to put it simply, he who rests, rusts.

He who does not increase, decreases.   AVOT 1:13

The Unnecessary Burden

A recent newspaper story about a cab driver carries an important moral. As a passenger handed him the exact fare, the cab driver frowned in disappointment, "That's correct, isn't it?" questioned the passenger. "Yes, it's *correct*," answered the cab driver, "but it isn't right!"

One of the reasons so many of us are not finding satisfaction in our daily activities is that our relationships with others are correct, but they are not right.

And what are these relationships? They are relationships between mother-in-law and daughter-in-law, between a struggling, growing teen-ager and a perplexed parent, between the uncomprehending salesman and the perfectionist customer, between the unwavering committee and the member who has all the answers.

Some of us carry the unnecessary burden of these experiences as a trailer attached to our soul. If you have a trailer attached to your car, you would find it difficult to park in town, difficult to maneuver through traffic, difficult to climb a hill. Many people are similarly hampered by their distorted feelings. They insist on carrying around all of their hurt feelings, the slights, real and imagined, the insults and the scars of quarrels. It is this unnecessary burden that we must cast off to lighten the load of living. We must approach others with a determination that our relationship with them will not be only correct, but right, as well.

For who so forgives is forgiven in turn; hard-heartedness and a temper that will not make up quarrels are a heavy burden of sin, and unworthy of an Israelite.

MOSES OF COUCY

For The Love Of Man

A father noticed that his second-grader had his eyes glued to the television set. He was prompted to ask, "Don't you have any homework tonight?" "No," the little boy replied, "I get all my work done in school."

Not to be put off, the father persisted, "Let's see how you are doing in your religious school work. Now tell me, why did God make you?"

The seven-year-old hesitated, but not for long. He simply said, "God made me, because He likes kids."

This is a simple expression of Jewish thinking about man and his environment that was revolutionary in its first enunciation. The world of primitive man was filled with hatred. Nature was an enemy and the world was permeated with dread and horror. But with the advent of Judaism came the profound declaration of God's love and hope for man. Whereas primitive man had believed in black magic, the Greeks in *moira* or predetermination, the Romans in *fatum* or fate, the Jews taught that man could determine the nature of his existence.

The very foundation of Judaism is cemented with the belief that out of God's love comes man's unlimited capacity to improve his own life and society. Man was delivered into a friendly environment when he was placed in the world. The forces of nature are hostile only when misunderstood and misused, but the correct appreciation and use of the world is ultimately God's greatest gift to man.

Beloved is man in that he was created in the image of God. Even greater love was shown in that it was made known that he was so created.   AVOT 3:18

213

If You Had Three Wishes

We never tire of fairy tales, for they delight us, charm us and instruct us. There is an unusually fine lesson to be learned from a tale entitled, "The Three Wishes."

A poor woodsman was granted three wishes by a fairy. Dazed by this great gift, the man stumbled home. When he arrived, he found that his wife had not yet finished preparing supper and so he said, without thinking, "I wish I had a piece of pudding before me." A bowl of pudding promptly materialized on the table and the man explained to his puzzled wife the secret of the three wishes. His wife, furious at his folly in wasting a wish declared, "You are so foolish, I wish the pudding would stick to your nose," and up it flew to the poor man's nose. He tried to pull it off, but to no avail. They could not remove it. It looked so ridiculous that they had to use the third wish to get the pudding off his nose. One moment they had a remarkable opportunity, and the next moment they had lost it.

This fairy tale is a story of our lives. If we were granted three wishes, would we choose wisely? Are our dreams and desires in life any loftier or less foolish than the woodsman's? Isn't it entirely possible that we already have the wishes that can give us that which we truly need?

We ought to consider our wishes in life to determine which are mere follies and which are truly desirable.

If you had three wishes, what would you choose?

We often mistake a desire of the body for a yearning of the soul.   HARRY A. WOLFSON

The Passport To Heaven

The following incident, recorded in the Talmud, occurred about 2200 years ago, but it could easily have happened yesterday.

Rabbi Beroka was accustomed to visit the market place. One day, Elijah appeared to him. Rabbi Beroka asked the prophet, "Is there anyone in this market who has a share in the world to come?" The prophet looked about and replied, "No."

While they were talking, two men passed by and Elijah suddenly said, "Wait, these men will have a share in heaven." Rabbi Beroka then approached and asked them, "What is your occupation?" They explained, "We are jesters; and our job is to make men laugh, to cheer them up."

From this ancient story we can conclude that one of the ways we can improve the world is by bringing cheer into the lives of others. There are so many simple opportunities to do this:

- Take an invalid for a ride;
- Give an afternoon to the patients in the hospital;
- Accompany children to the circus;
- Speak a cheerful word to the discouraged;
- Show a sense of humor in a moment of crisis.

For to be able to laugh through tears, smile through pain and be cheerful in distress is to live a heavenly life.

When we serve God with joy, He is more approachable.
DOV BAER OF MEZERITZ

Move At Your Own Pace

The University of Iowa recently commissioned a study of various cultural groupings in order to get some information about the cause of stuttering. A major clue came when it was found that a certain tribe of Indians not only had no stutterers — they did not even have a word for stuttering in their language. For them, the problem did not exist. The reason was that this group of Indians let each child talk in his own way and at his own pace.

This is an important consideration in dealing with children. Each child has a pattern of growth which he shares with all children, but upon this pattern are imposed certain variations which are unique. When the child is allowed to develop at his own pace and feels comfortable with his environment, he can express himself freely and easily. But when a child is asked to meet impossible standards, he soon feels himself a failure and is quickly paralyzed by fear and strain.

Every time a youngster meets a new situation he looks upon it as a challenge. If he is taught in his early years to be self-confident, to regard his uniqueness as his strength, then he will be able to meet the unknown with great inner confidence. This can be done by accepting the child as he is, with all of the characteristics peculiar and personal to him, and by encouraging him to develop naturally, in accord with his readiness.

A parent must respect the spiritual person of the child, and approach it with reverence.   GEORGE MACDONALD

What Are The Odds?

According to a recent newspaper story, one of the gate attendants at the Santa Anita racetrack had spent his life's savings to send a former delinquent boy in the community to school. Some of his friends called him a fool to take a chance on an unknown boy. He replied, "Well, so I am a fool. But day after day, I see men and women gamble on horses. I think I would rather take my chances on a child of God."

The placing of trust in a person is a great expression of religious feeling. It is a concrete manifestation of the belief in the unlimited potentiality of human character. This is one way in which we can indicate our willingness to take a chance on character. There are many other ways, for example:

- Offer employment to someone who has served a prison term;
- Extend additional credit to someone who has suffered financial reverses;
- Believe in a person even after he has told an untruth;
- Be willing to forgive and forget after a bitter quarrel.

There are many who are willing to gamble on men, for the odds are always in favor of a child of God.

Whosoever preserves one soul, Scripture ascribes merit to him as though he had preserved a whole world.

SANHEDRIN 4:5

אייר

IYAR

A Thousand Years

About two weeks before a very exciting period in national elections, a group of men went on a fishing trip. One of the men in the party was a research physician, one a geologist and another an astronomer. As they fished, they talked about the ages of the rocks, evolution of higher animals from the creatures of the sea and the fantastic distances between stars.

All the time, the simple backwoods guide was listening. At last his silence broke down and he poured out a flood of questions: Were the rocks really that old? How many millions of years did it take life to evolve? Were the stars actually billions of miles away? Was everything so inconceivably vast and ancient? When at last he digested these ideas, he heaved a sigh of relief. "I guess," he said, "it really won't make a great deal of difference who wins the election."

A religious outlook is not very penetrating until it begins to measure the issues of life against the backdrop of eternity. A religious attitude toward life gives us the serenity that neither worldly success nor failure, love of life nor fear of death can ever distort. True religion gives a person perspective and balance.

For a thousand years in Thy sight are but a day that is past.
PSALMS 90:4

Only Skin Deep

Someone once asked a beauty expert what she considered the years of a woman's greatest attractiveness. She responded without hesitation, "Every year: the glowing youth and vitality of a teen-ager is one kind of beauty; the alert vivaciousness and keen mental interest of the woman in her twenties and thirties is another kind; still another type of beauty — the softness in the face, the gentleness in the voice, and the tolerance, understanding and sympathy — comes only with maturity." Time may wrinkle the skin, but it cannot wrinkle the soul.

Physical changes that may seem distressing in our later years should be seen in perspective. We could live more happy lives if we learned the truth that beauty is many-sided and that each age has its own characteristic delights; this is as true of old-age as of childhood.

If we really learn to love ourselves by recognizing our inner worth, then we begin to act unselfishly and with greater self-assurance and responsibility. We then approach ourselves with honesty and self-acceptance, and along with the knowledge of our potentiality for loving, we develop real spiritual beauty.

Anyone who keeps the ability to see beauty in every age of life really never grows old.   FRANZ KAFKA

The Need To Grow

A disciple once asked the Baal Shem, "Why is it that even one who clings to God and knows he is close to Him sometimes experiences a sense of interruption and remoteness?"

The Baal Shem explained, "When a father sets out to teach his little son to walk, he stands in front of him and holds his two hands on either side of the child so that he cannot fall, and the boy goes toward his father between his father's hands. But the moment he is close, his father moves away a little and holds his hands farther apart; the father does this over and over so that the child may learn to walk."

It is important to understand that our relationship with God is a continually growing one. Although we never fully comprehend the purposes of existence, we approach such understanding through experience in thinking, feeling, living and groping our way toward God.

The significance of this analogy is that God encourages us to walk and that the world welcomes us with open arms. To grow in knowledge and understanding of life is the most rewarding of all experiences, for we never outgrow the need to grow.

God is subtle, but He is not malicious.   ALBERT EINSTEIN

The Witness Of Conscience

Jewish literature contains the beautiful story of a certain rabbi who had a very strict sense of justice. Far and wide he was known as an incorruptible judge. One day his own wife raised an outcry because she believed the maid had stolen an object of great value. The servant, an orphan, tearfully denied the accusation. The mistress of the house was very angry and she declared, "We will let the court settle this!"

When the rabbi saw his wife preparing to go to court, he immediately put on his best suit.

"Why do you do that?" she asked in surprise. "You know it is undignified for a man of your position to come to court with me. I can very well plead my own case."

"I am sure you can," answered the rabbi, "but who will plead the case of your maid, the poor orphan? I must see that full justice is done here."

A person who believes deeply in justice will surely be concerned that it not be limited to any given group. If we accept the principle of a universal God, then we must apply His moral laws to all humanity. The observance of these laws brings us fulfillment. For life is truly lived by those who accept the rules and demands of conscience.

The reward of such as live exactly according to the laws is not silver or gold, not a garland of olive-branches, nor any such public sign of commendation; but every good man is content with the witness that his own conscience bears on him. JOSEPHUS

Israel Is Here To Stay

In Israel they tell the story of an American businessman who came upon an Israeli who was moving huge rocks from the hills of Jerusalem by hand. It was a hot day and the worker's shirt was drenched with sweat. The businessman watched him for several moments, fascinated. Finally, he said, "You know, I wouldn't do that for a million dollars."

The laborer paused from his work and replied, "And neither would I."

This is indicative of the attitude of the Jewish spirit of the last half century in terms of rebuilding the land of Israel. The amount of Jewish vision, energy, and strength and the numbers of Jewish lives that have been poured into the foundation of modern Israel is vast beyond measure. No sacrifice has been too great to help re-establish the land of Israel as a vital, growing nation.

Even more remarkable is the Israeli determination to maintain Israel's economic, cultural and spiritual growth. The Jewish commitment to Israel was purchased at heavy cost of life; the achievements of the land of Israel will be maintained and advanced. That is why Israel is here to stay.

Independence is never given to a people; it has to be earned; and having been earned, it has to be defended.

CHAIM WEIZMANN

A Growing Wonder

Leo Tolstoy was not only a sensitive writer, but also a highly individualistic thinker as well. Although he was a devout believer in the Russian Orthodox faith, he could not bring himself to practice every one of its rituals. Because of Tolstoy's worldwide esteem and influence, the Church tried to induce him in his old age to accept all of the practices of the Orthodox religion. Tolstoy replied firmly, "Even in the valley of the shadow of death, two and two still do not make six."

Religion should not be unreasonable, nor need it ever contradict the laws of logic. Religion itself undergoes evolution and growth and, if it is deeply sensitive, it is always sifting and refining.

Similarly, in our own thinking about God, we must understand that as we grow we must discard our childish notions about God, without discarding God Himself. A mature faith means a growing and expanding vision of God. Some of us still pray to an elderly gentleman in the sky, instead of learning to grow in religious knowledge and accept new concepts and shed useless thoughts.

At every stage of life, we must be willing to learn more about God, because the more we see of Him the greater He appears to us. Faith is, indeed, a growing wonder.

And so they serve the Creator by doing commandments of reason, and by good spiritual conduct; and by these things they add to the known commandments. They also learn the ways of the prophets and the habits of the devout, in order thus to seek the approval of God, and in order to be accepted by Him.   BAHYA IBN PAKUDAH

The Fallacy Of Failure

Have you ever considered that there is a fundamental difference between the individual who says, "I have failed two times" and the person who says, "I am a failure"? There is a basic division between the one who says, "I have sinned three times" and the one who says, "I am a sinner." And there is a strong distinction between the man who says, "I have lost four battles" and the one who says, "I am a loser."

The fallacy of failure can well be illustrated by the life of an unusual American. I wonder if you will recognize him.

This man ran for the state legislature and was soundly trounced. Then he entered business, failed, and spent the next seventeen years of his life paying off the debts of a worthless partner. He fell in love with a beautiful girl to whom he became engaged, and then she died. He re-entered politics, ran for Congress, and was badly defeated. He became a candidate for the United States Senate and was defeated again. He became a candidate for the vice-presidency and was again defeated. Finally, and at long last in 1861, he was elected sixteenth President of the United States by a very slim majority. His name is Abraham Lincoln, the greatest and most moving figure in American history.

Failure has more to do with one's self-concept than one's actual unsuccessful experiences. He who refuses to admit to failure has not failed.

Who persists in knocking will succeed in entering.

MOSES IBN EZRA

For The Birds

Most people picture Jeremiah as the prophet of doom, when actually he is the herald of hope and life. One of the distinguishing characteristics of his writings is his love for nature, his reverence for life. His writings display a human sympathy for animals that is quite unlike anything else in the Bible. He paints beautiful word portraits of colored birds, tawny lions and graceful deer, and he gives an especially vivid and moving picture of wild creatures in time of drought. He is deeply compassionate in his fellow-feeling for these stricken creatures.

This compassion for creatures is an authentic part of Judaism, for Jewish literature has developed the concept of *tzaar baalay hayyim,* "kindness to all living creatures."

The Jewish mind cannot comprehend the sport of fox-hunting in which hounds, horses and men pursue a tiny, terror-stricken fox for mere sport.

The Jewish conscience cannot conceive of thousands of people shouting "Olé!" as a man is pitted against a bull which is teased, tormented, and finally stabbed to death.

The Jewish soul finds it repugnant to aim a gun at a bird in flight or a deer in graceful leap and to find joy in the killing of that beautiful creature.

Yea, the stork in the heaven knoweth her appointed times; and the turtle and the swallow and the crane observe the time of their coming. JEREMIAH 8:7

A Friend Indeed

Sigmund Freud has taught us that what the child experiences and thinks has a profound influence upon his future development. We often forget that this insight can also be applied to thinking and feeling about God; for the thoughts that a child entertains about God are crucial to his religious development.

If a child's view of God is that of a heavenly detective ready to pounce on him for each little sin, to punish him for each naughty thought, then he will grow up in fear and with his trust in himself and the world badly shaken. But if, on the other hand, he sees God as a friend, a benevolent helper, someone who is understanding, then the child's secret world will be bolstered by spiritual strength and self-confidence.

There should be genuine concern for children who are brought up under a religious system where God is used as a bull whip and the devil is a green-eyed monster ready to pitch him into a burning hell at the first sign of devia‧tion. Literature is filled with such childhood memories, where in bitter resentment the adult turns into a confirmed atheist or a violent anti-cleric. Conversely, how fortunate is the child who is taught to see God as a guide, a supporter, a sustainer. No matter what happens, he will believe that God is his friend. How meaningful to this child are the phrases from the twenty-third psalm: "The Lord is *my* shepherd, *I* shall not want . . . Even though *I* walk through the valley of the shadow of death, *I* will fear no evil, for Thou art with *me*."

God draws all men to Himself by His friendship.

ARISTEAS 207

Swim Or Sink

A philosopher once got into a boat to cross a lake. He began to converse pleasantly with the boatman, and did not notice the waves and the wind increase. The philosopher asked, "Boatman, do you know the theory of immortality?"

"No," was the answer.

"Well," said the philosopher, "you have lost half of your existence."

At that moment the wind began to blow more fiercely, setting the boat to rocking dangerously. The boatman turned to the philosopher and said, "Let me ask you a question. Can you swim?"

"No," was the reply.

"Then," said the boatman, "you have lost the *whole* of *your* existence."

There is a time to philosophize about existence, and there is a time to practice existence itself. Jewish life demands active participation in order to maintain its existence.

In the last decade we have concentrated our efforts to save Jews from extermination; now we must center our energies upon saving Judaism from extinction. The only way we can do this is to encourage active participation in Jewish life.

This was Israel's excellence: at Sinai they were of one accord in accepting joyfully the kingdom of God. Moreover, they pledged themselves to one another.

MEKHILTA, EXODUS 20:2

Mind Your Manners

According to recent statistics, every family in the next decade will be touched by the problem of mental illness. As a result of the strain of modern living and by means of improved diagnostic techniques, we will discover more and more cases of mental illness. This kind of trouble is part of everyday living; it has no respect for wealth, education, or old age. It is our common heritage.

This being so, we must try to understand and accept the mentally disturbed person for what he is. If he needs rest and rehabilitation, he must go where he will receive intelligent care and consideration. If there is any hope for his returning to an active career and family life, then we must spare absolutely no effort to help. Let us smash our medieval notions of mental illness.

Let us equally aid the parents of the retarded child to shed their unnecessary guilt by helping share their burden and anguish. Let us help the epileptic whether in the institution or in active society, by giving him every fair chance in industry and business; he deserves a full life as much as we do. And when a person comes back after a period of rest and cure, let him return a conquering hero, deserving every respect and esteem. More than sympathy, we must offer comfort, guidance, understanding and treatment.

A closed mind is a dying mind.   EDNA FERBER

The Real Way

We often wonder about what is the real way to find the meaning of religion. Many times the direction is misguided. Religion is not to be found only in a book or a building, for it is a way of life. True, the book may be a source for thought and the building an inspiration, but both are valueless unless they help people to live better lives. Religion is the response of the soul to that truth. A person who is really religious will think and live and act indicating his belief in God's existence, as if the Ten Commandments were a part of his daily life, as if truth and honesty were more important than life itself. He will have an overpowering yearning and desire to live with the real meaning of religion.

Buddhist scriptures contain the story of a man who once came to Gautama Buddha asking how he could obtain the secret of the meaning of religion. The founder of Buddhism seized the man and held his head under water. When he let the man up gasping for breath, Buddha said to him, "When you want the meaning of religion as much as you wanted air, then you will find it."

This is the real way.

To the question, "Where is God?" the Kotsker rebbe replied simply, "Where He is admitted."   HASIDIC LORE

231

You And Your Community

Let us ask ourselves honestly what we believe about the community and the wider world in which we live. Despite all that we profess, the fact that so few of us take on community responsibilities or wider concerns marks most of us as narrow-minded and narrow-souled. We don't even know what we stand for except, perhaps, selfishness.

Typifying this attitude is the story told about a theater manager who was interviewing a young man for a job as an usher. In the course of the interview, the manager asked the applicant what he would do in case of fire. "Don't worry," said the boy, "I'd get out all right."

Most of us are exactly like this boy and are only concerned with saving our own necks. Nothing is more abhorrent than the people who pretend to be too sophisticated, too bored, too indifferent for the cares and concerns of the community. For this reason, in our times:

No person should consider himself educated until he has visited a public mental hospital.

No one should consider himself enlightened unless he regularly reads one thoughtful magazine in addition to the front page of his daily paper.

No human being should consider himself tolerant until he is willing to become actively involved on behalf of a specific cause and expose himself to the pressures of the battle against prejudice.

Join a community, by which alone your work can be made universal and eternal in its results.

SAMSON RAPHAEL HIRSCH

The Crux Of A Ceremony

The moments of moral commitment must be incorporated into ritual so that they can be constantly renewed in our daily lives. It is not enough to pledge ourselves to great values, but we must also make sure that we be constantly, regularly, reminded of them in the course of daily living. For so often we make promises and high resolves only to forget them on the morrow or the day after. History is filled with illustrations of this truth.

In February of 1497 in the city of Florence, Italy, an amazing thing occurred. Under the influence of Savonarola, the entire city pledged to reform itself. As a token of this, they erected a Pyramid of Vanities. The people piled all their luxuries in the center of the city, and the pile reached a height of fifteen stories. This was set afire amidst sincere vows, pious prayers and devout chanting. Six months later the city forgot its pledge and sank to an even lower point in immorality. How could they have forgotten it so soon?

The truth of life is that as a person or as a people we only achieve a few moments of greatness, and then we strive the rest of our lives to maintain that high standard. We need rituals to help us preserve that greatness by symbolically and systematically reminding us of them. Such formalized and codified moments of greatness help us to see that in many areas of life excellence has already been achieved and cannot be surpassed. As we must not prejudice the past so we must not bias the future.

Abstraction and mere contemplation are not enough. The soul must have experience of sensation and reverence; the idea must clothe itself in a body; else it is lost to man.

ZECHARIAH FRANKEL

233

The Significance Of Sin

Sin has always been an ugly word, but in the last half century, it has been rendered passé. People are no longer sinful; they are only immature or underprivileged or frightened or sick. While some of these concepts help us to understand and heal human behavior, yet certain actions really are sinful and can only be forgiven and righted when they are seen as wicked.

In this vein, Mark Twain once remarked that "Most people are bothered by the passages of the Scriptures they do not understand, but the passages that bother me the most are those I do understand."

We understand when we have acted basely. We know when we have wronged our neighbor. We recognize when we have lusted, been deceitful and hardened our hearts. There can be no doubt about this. The recognition of these facts is the first step in redressing these wrongs, the first step toward forgiveness. We must see that sin is a reality, that a man must recognize his errors in order to repair them. A man must want to be helped in order to improve his life. He who does not want to be helped cannot be cured — not by the doctor, nor by the rabbi, nor by God Himself. Thus, seeing the significance of sin is the first step in its elimination.

I will build me an altar from the broken fragments of my heart.
                                                        JUDAH THE PIOUS

Maturity In Adversity

The Midrash tells us quite correctly, "There is not a man or woman whom God does not try." We are all subjected to frustration and loss. But that which separates the mature from the immature is the strength of character which enables a person to retain his balance and perspective in any situation. It means placing a sense of trust and faith in God under any circumstance.

The famous statue by Rodin, "The Burghers of Calais," marks an event which occurred in the fourteenth century. When the British invaded the French port of Calais, they agreed to spare the city from destruction if six men would step forward and offer their lives. Six men did so, and thus they saved the city. As one looks at this work of art and sees their faces set with resoluteness and conviction, it is impossible not to be impressed by their maturity in the face of adversity. One sees in their faces faith, hope, strength, and real manhood.

In daily life the choices may not be so dramatic, but they are every bit as difficult, and even as heroic. They demand real maturity. When we are faced with any loss — be it loss of life, loss of health, financial loss, or loss of a cherished goal — we must summon deep maturity to accept this loss and to plan realistically and courageously for the future.

If you faint in the face of adversity, your strength is small indeed.   PROVERBS 24:10

Too Much Is Not Too Good

Too much is not always too good. A man who has one watch knows what time it is, but a man who has two watches is never quite sure of the correct time. A man who has one car knows when he is out of gas, but a man who has two cars cannot be certain. A man who has one enterprise knows his profits, but a man who has several enterprises cannot be positive.

Many of us fill our lives with so many things that we do not appreciate what we have. We overburden ourselves with quantity and so we lose sight of quality. The human mind and heart are limited in their scope and comprehension. They cannot contain more than they were meant to have.

One way we can deepen our lives is to increase our awareness of what we have around us. We must learn not to squander our energies and our time and not to be deluded by the prospect of mere increase. We must school ourselves through self-discipline to appreciate to the fullest what we now possess rather than filling our lives with that which we do not need. All too often we clutter our lives with possessions that only weigh us down. Whenever we desire something else, we ought to ask ourselves honestly, "Do we really need more?" For ultimately, too much is not too good.

The more possessions, the more anxiety,
But the more Torah, the more life.   AVOT 2:8

The Way To Honor

A very profound and unusual play is *Becket,* by Jean Anouilh, subtitled *The Honor of God.* It is the story of the conflict between Thomas Becket, the Archbishop of Canterbury, primate of England, and his closest friend, Henry II, King of England. In the climax of the play Becket changes from literally a playboy to a man of God. But in his zeal to serve God he tries to give away all his money, fasts, prays at all hours, and makes himself generally miserable. Then one day he discovers a spiritual truth: the way to honor God is to be what you are, but to be aware of God. He says in a beautiful soliloquy addressed to God:

> Your scheme of things is secret and profound and You plumb poor men's bones as carefully as kings! It has pleased You to set me as a solitary pawn, face to face with the King on the chess board. I shall go back to my place humbly, and let the world accuse me of pride, so that I may do what I believe is my life's work. For the rest, Your will be done.

The world is our chess board. True, we are the pawns; but we are also the players. So we must use our talents and our abilities and we do not reject them. We must accept the task assigned to us and not withdraw for one moment. We do not quit the game of life until the last move. And even that move is made surely, confidently, in the name of man and God. That is truly the way to honor God.

God is honored when His children decorate themselves with good deeds and Torah.   SEDER ELIYAHU RABBAH 2

The Good New Days

When you step outside, look at a piece of earth. To an insensitive person it is but a clod of dirt, but to a perceptive and alert individual it offers endless possibilities. To a biologist it is teeming with life; to a gardener, it is the source of lovely flowers; to a child, it is an endless object of play to shape and reshape; to a potter, it is a bowl; to a poet, it is a song; to a farmer, a source of livelihood. The possibilities are endless. Look, what a spirit of adventure can do to a little piece of earth!

It was once wisely said by Frederick the Great that, "The greatest and noblest pleasure which we have in this world is to discover new truths, and the next is to shake off old prejudices." There is something that keeps us perpetually youthful when we embark on that never-ending quest for knowledge.

There are many people who continually bemoan the fact that our age is not like the good old days, when things were set and fixed, where life was ordered, when everyone in the world knew his place. One must feel sorry for these people, because they are missing the excitement and the enchantment in the best of what we call contemporary. The new sounds in jazz that stimulate the ear, the free forms in art that excite the eye, the discovery of the Dead Sea Scrolls that adds to our knowledge of the past, the new experiments in drugs that add years to our life, the new models and designs in almost every field of human endeavor that add pleasure and efficiency to living. Today's world offers endless possibilities for learning and individual growth.

The road to learning is endless.   JACOB BEN ASHER

Help

Once a boy was taking his girl friend home after a date. She was a nurse and lived in the nurses' home near the hospital. As they were saying goodnight, the boy heard the screaming siren warning of an approaching ambulance as it swung into the hospital emergency driveway. He turned to the nurse and said, "I hate that sound. It always tells me a tragedy has just taken place; it reminds me of suffering, and I just can't bear to hear it."

The nurse replied, "I'm not hard-hearted either, but I like that sound. You see, it really means that someone is being brought from a place where he cannot be cared for properly to a place where he can have the best of care. It means help is on the way; and where there is help there is hope. That is why I like the sound of the ambulance siren."

The sound of alarms should not frighten us, but rather should inspire us, for they indicate people are mobilizing to help. When we hear the sudden noises that are designed to arouse us, they tell us that there is a genuine care and concern for the welfare of those in distress and those exposed to danger. When we know help is coming, we reaffirm our hope in the future, for when there is hope and help, then, indeed, there is surely a future.

Take from me the hope that I can change the future and you will drive me mad.   ISRAEL ZANGWILL

Machines Or Men

A bizarre scene was recently enacted in the garden of the Museum of Modern Art in New York before a selected audience. An artist named Jean Tinguely created a self-destroying work of art entitled, "Homage to New York." It was a complex super-gadget constructed of such elements as old bicycle wheels, a dilapidated piano, a discarded meteorological balloon, several items from junk yards, and fifteen motors. After the starting button was pushed, this little monstrosity hobbled a few steps and then blew itself up. The audience then applauded.

This was not intended as a stunt and was deadly serious. For the implication of this so-called work of art is that the machine culture of the twentieth century contains within it the seeds of its own destruction. The increasing control that machines have over our lives is dangerous and frightening.

The machine's job is to reproduce faithfully, using standardized means to control the elements about it. On the other hand, the purpose of a person is to produce — to produce that which is original, creative and unique. If machines control our lives, we will be crushed into conformity. If personality dominates our living then we can create a culture of unique worth. Are we men or machines?

I would call the personality of man the gland of creativity.
SHOLEM ASCH

Time On Our Hands

The giant sequoia trees to be found in the redwood forests have endured for centuries. This is because they take a great deal of time to reach their full growth and stature. Some take as long as five hundred or even a thousand years to attain their full maturity.

Similarly, we must understand that it takes a certain length of time to develop *our* spiritual strength and to reach *our* maturity. There are certain things in this world that simply cannot be hurried. It takes nine months to develop a healthy baby, and there is no short cut to that. There are twenty-four hours in a day, sixty minutes in an hour and sixty seconds in a minute, and no force on earth can hurry or delay that cycle. It takes *shivah*, a full week, for a mourner to accept the fact of a death; it takes *sheloshim*, a full month, for the mind to accept the loss; and it takes *avaylut*, a full year for the emotions to adjust to the deep pain of the passing of a dear one. And no pill or scheme has ever been invented to shorten these periods.

That is why we should have time on our minds rather than time on our hands.

The Hebrews affirm the reality and importance of time. To them, it was not an illusion, something from which man must escape, but something which must be redeemed.

JAMES PHILLIP HYATT

241

The Necessary Risk

Every so often, an incident occurs which dramatizes the futility of cowardice and the importance of taking risks. A while back, during the first week in December, a group of Jews in Connecticut protested the observance of the Christmas holiday in the public schools. Standing on their rights as Americans, they insisted on the separation of church and state. Shortly thereafter, a local Jewish merchant, fearing a boycott, felt himself obliged to place a full page advertisement in the local newspaper declaring: "I am not the Goldberg who raised any question concerning Christmas in the schools."

Against this craven cowardice and the fear to risk for what we believe, let us ask ourselves: If Moses had been cowardly in facing Pharaoh and afraid to face death, would we be free today?

If our parents and grandparents had not braved the hardships of immigration — stormy seas, foul steerages, and a strange new life — would we be at ease here as American Jews?

If Israel were not willing to risk being surrounded on three sides by hostile Arab countries, would there be any respect for it in the world?

There are times when we must take the necessary risks to insure our safety and our dignity.

We do not beg for a favor. We demand our rights.

DAVID EINHORN

Of The Essence

A wealthy Texan entered a House of God in order to confide his difficulties to God. It appeared that his difficulties included a five per cent decline in the output of his oil wells, an epidemic affecting three per cent of his hundred thousand cattle and a drought afflicting one corner of his half-million acre ranch. In the next pew, an old woman told God that she was starving. Overhearing this, the Texan hastily gave her a hundred dollar bill. "Go get yourself a meal," he mumbled. "This is no place for wasting the Lord's time with insignificant problems."

Of course, the Texan was completely wrong in his judgment of the woman's problem. But he was right in one respect — the synagogue is not the place for the petty or the trivial. In worship, we must not dwell on the insignificant; but rather we must pray and think at our finest and highest levels. This is an occasion for reviewing our values, and scrutinizing our goals and our beliefs. Being religious essentially means examining the meaning of our lives and being willing to receive answers, even if these answers hurt. The passionate life can only be lived by consistent questioning, constant searching, and continual sifting of our most cherished values. This is essential religion.

Ever insurgent let me be,
Make me more daring than devout;
From sleek contentment keep me free
And fill me with buoyant doubt.   LOUIS UNTERMEYER

Healing Through Encounter

In France a doctor in one of the provinces has worked for many years among the poor. He is now a very old man, but continues to serve faithfully. One day one of the elderly women watched him as he skillfully bandaged the wound of her grandchild. After several minutes she said, "Doctor, you have treated three generations of my family and you have perfected the art of healing." The wise old doctor replied, "Thank you, but I only dress the wounds; God does the healing."

There is expressed in these perceptive words the true relationship between man and God. Man's responsibility is to dress the wounds of suffering that exist about him, and through God, healing will be effected.

We have within us the power to help heal the sores of society. We can live and help when we see our responsibilities to give. We can demonstrate to the world that we truly care — care enough to give the very most.

All we need do is dress the wounds, and as they heal, we ourselves will be healed in turn. For there is no prayer without care, no belief without grief, no healing without feeling. The mystery of healing is that he who applies the dressing as well as he who receives the balm is healed.

Heal us, O Lord, and we shall be healed. Grant complete healing for all our ailments for Thou, O God, art our King, our faithful and merciful Healer.   DAILY SERVICE

Prisoners Of Ourselves

Port Arthur in Southern Tasmania includes in its history some of the most gruesome events of modern times. This small peninsula in southernmost Australia was the site of one of the most infamous convict settlements in the early days of that dominion. The visitor to Port Arthur, as part of his tour, is locked for a few minutes into one of the special solitary confinement cells. The cell has great thick walls, and when the door is closed not a glimmer of light can be seen. The darkness is dense and oppressive. In the days when one prisoner at a time was confined in this cell, a few hours were usually sufficient for him to be reduced to raving madness.

Although we now regard this as horrible punishment, we nevertheless inflict this very same kind of punishment upon ourselves. We set up mental walls of darkness and hate. We allow imagined hurts to weigh oppressively on our spirits. We close the door of reason in our minds. We exclude the light of God from our consciences.

If only we would let the light of love and God enter, it would transform our mental prison. If only we were prepared to accept ourselves and others with reasonable charity, we would trample down the barriers that isolate us from each other and from God.

Ten enemies cannot harm a man as much as he can harm himself.   YIDDISH PROVERB

A Reminder

When Rabbi Jonathan Eybeschutz was a child, his father gave him an empty flask and told him to go to the wine shop and get wine for Kiddush so that the Sabbath could be properly sanctified.

"Where's the money for the wine?" the child asked.

"With money, anyone can get wine," the father replied.

Without saying anything more, Jonathan left.

In the evening when the family was gathered around the Sabbath table, the father, noticing the empty wine bottle, asked Jonathan:

"Where's the wine for the Kiddush?"

And Jonathan replied, "With wine, anyone can recite Kiddush."

It takes money to buy wine; it takes wine to recite the Kiddush; it takes Kiddush to sanctify the Sabbath; and it takes the Sabbath to endow our week with a sense of meaning.

We need a regular periodic reminder of the purpose we serve on this earth. This reminder cannot be left to chance, for what is left to chance often does not occur. The meaning of our lives is so important that Jews have embodied it in the ceremonial of the Sabbath, so that we are reminded at least once a week of the purpose of our creation and our existence.

In love and favor Thou hast given us the holy Sabbath as a heritage, a reminder of Thy work of creation, first of our sacred days.   SABBATH KIDDUSH

Easy Does It

One of our great needs today is patience. Among the most often used current phrases are — "Wait a minute," "Hear me out," "Please listen," "Wait till I finish." They all indicate our restlessness and our inability to learn by patient listening.

So often we hear, "If that tragedy had happened in my family, I would have handled it differently." Well, let me tell you, my friend, *"Mi zoll nit geproofed verin* (May God not try you)" — Wait until you hear the whole story.

Or the teen-ager shouts, "You're just old-fashioned!" Patience, young man! Someday you will grow up to be a parent too, and I hope you will be old-fashioned enough to insist on responsibility and standards.

Or the parent answers the little tot's plea of *"I* can do it" with "No, no — you're too slow." Well, parent, if we never give the children understanding and a chance, when and how will they learn to grow up and become men and women?

It is a pity that in today's world we seem to have so little time to try to understand, when patience is not just a virtue but a necessity to happy living.

Patience yields many good things.

PATRIARCHS, JOSEPH 2:7

The Key To Tomorrow

One of the most beautiful words in the English language is the word, "research." This means literally re-search, to study again, to experiment once more, to investigate yet one more time. When we say, "Research is the key to tomorrow," we are saying something profoundly religious. For learning about God's world is the highest form of human endeavor.

In American life, the name that symbolizes applied research is Thomas Edison. The lights, the automobile, the phonograph — many of the things we now enjoy — were developed from his studies.

In Edison's laboratory, one day, a new assistant came up to him and expressed his amazement upon reading the laboratory reports. These reports showed a staggering total of 50,000 experimental failures in working on the storage battery. The young man asked what could possibly be the use of pursuing these experiments which seemed utterly fruitless. Edison replied, "Why, young man, I have gotten a lot of results. I now know 50,000 combinations that won't work." The next day, he discovered the correct formula for the storage battery.

To study with intensity and to persevere with learning — this kind of dedicated research is not only the key to tomorrow, but serves us as a model for useful, challenging living today.

Great is study, for it endows the learner with life.

AVOT 6:7

סיון

SIVAN

The Great Moments

A very inspiring story is told about one of the greatest ladies of our time — Marian Anderson, the Negro contralto. A reporter once asked her a routine question, "What was the greatest moment of your life?" Miss Anderson's answer was not routine; it was as distinctive as her art and the great personality that glows through it.

Miss Anderson did not mention the obvious high points: the acclaim of performing in the White House, receiving the Bok Award, the Spingarn Medal or other honors. Apparently, Miss Anderson did not consider any of these her greatest moments.

Instead, Miss Anderson replied directly, "My greatest moment was the day I went home and told my mother she would not need to take work home anymore."

The great moments of our lives are not moments of receiving, but of giving. Whatever we keep, no matter how much, we can never take with us. On the other hand, whatever we give, that gift, that satisfaction is ours forever.

I always give much away, and so gather happiness instead of pleasure.   RACHEL LEVIN VARNHAGEN

The Face Of Man

Following a hard day of work, a father sat down after dinner to read his evening newspaper. His child came up to him and asked him to play. The father, wanting a few quiet moments of rest with his paper, gave his son a puzzle with a map of the world on it to put together. The father thought this would take the boy an hour or so to assemble and he would have a chance to rest.

In ten minutes the boy was back, the puzzle was completed, and each piece was in its proper place. The father was amazed and he asked the boy how he could do it so quickly. The child answered, "The other side of the puzzle had a picture of a man, and when I put the man together the world fell into place."

The world is made up of individuals; therefore, if we want the world to be a better place in which to live, each of us must become a better person. This idea was eloquently expressed in these words by Confucius: "When the heart is set right, then the personal life is cultivated; when the personal life is cultivated, then the family life is regulated; when the family life is regulated, then the national life is orderly; and when the national life is orderly, then there is peace in the world."

Men are men before they are lawyers or physicians or manufacturers; and if you make them capable and sensible men, they will make themselves capable and sensible lawyers and physicians. JOHN STUART MILL

The Business Of Life

According to Jewish belief, God can be worshipped anywhere and religion must be practiced everywhere. Judaism believes that religion is not sealed up in a Bible or stored in a synagogue; it is a part of life. Religion is everywhere or it is nowhere.

A wonderful Hasidic story makes this lesson vivid. A congregant once told his rabbi that during the Torah reading, the members of the synagogue were secretly discussing their business affairs. The rabbi smiled and answered, "That wouldn't be so bad, my son, if only during their business affairs they would sometimes secretly discuss the Torah reading!"

We must learn to apply our religious values to everyday life situations if we are to make the most of our heritage. The unique quality of the Torah is that its teachings are gleaned from the lives of men and women who have struggled with essentially the same problems and challenges that we must meet. They continually took their hard-earned wisdom and reapplied it to life, with ever greater spiritual benefits. We should understand that the Torah is the source of wisdom, and wisdom, in turn, is distilled experience.

The works of all Jews from the Bible to modern times contain a unifying principle: that literature is life itself; that intellect is the handmaid of conscience; and that the best books are those which best teach men how to live.

ISRAEL ABRAHAMS

The Silent Language

Very often, we mistakenly believe that we can hide ourselves. We may think that we can run into our houses, lock our doors, pull down our shades, close our drapes, and believe the world does not see us. But this is just not so. We reveal ourselves unknowingly in a hundred little ways.

In a very stimulating book entitled *The Silent Language,* Edward T. Hall points out the way in which attitudes and ideas are conveyed by a smile, a gesture, the manner in which we shake hands, and even the position we assume when we are seated. But our clearest disclosures occur in the way we react to a crisis.

Oh, how we reveal ourselves! At a house of mourning, some sit around and moan, but others move to prepare a meal. Seeing the tense days before the wedding, some friends needle the families with sharp reminders of people they forgot to invite, but others offer to go to the airport to pick up out-of-town guests. During a lengthy illness, some people come to call just to commiserate and have an opportunity to tell about their own operations, but others offer to read aloud, to take the children out of the house for a day, to do the shopping, to act like people truly concerned with helping others by finding constructive ways to heal the hurt and soften the sorrow.

Life is short and we have not too much time for gladdening the hearts of those who are travelling the dark way with us. Oh, be swift to love! Make haste to be kind.

HENRI FREDERICK AMIEL

The Harvest Of Our Years

A tester in a glass factory once conducted a very simple test. At a certain stage of the cooling process, he poured water into a line of goblets. Two of the goblets which stood side by side looked exactly alike. But as the water was poured from the same pitcher, one of the goblets broke and the other did not. The tester remarked, "It's what the glass is made of, not what you put into it that counts."

Trouble, pain and anguish are poured into every soul; the way they are held and shaped is determined by the soul. Some people seem to regard themselves as mere animals — and they act like animals; others choose to see themselves as created in the image of God Almighty, and they aspire to great goodness.

It is as John Greenleaf Whittier has said:

> We shape ourselves the joy or fear
> Of which our coming life is made,
> And fill our future atmosphere
> With sunshine and with shade.
> The tissue of the life to be
> We weave with colors all our own,
> And in the field of destiny
> We reap as we have sown.

The years roll on and we reap life just as we sow life, for in time, life becomes the harvest of our years.

God waits long, but pays with interest.

YIDDISH PROVERB

In The Manner Of Moses

The finest literary study of Moses was done by Thomas Mann in a little book that is now out of print. With his keen mind and gifted pen, he penetrates the character of this great man.

In the climax of Moses' life, Mann portrays him standing on the volcanic ash of Mt. Sinai. With powerful arms, Moses rips two huge, irregular pieces from the mountainside. Then he seizes a sharp stone and begins the hard tedious job of carving the 172 Hebrew letters on the two stones. In the primitive setting, this task takes thirty-nine days. On the fortieth day, as he is about to descend with the two tables of law, he pauses to survey the commandments. He examines his work and notices that the impressions on the rock are hardly visible at a distance. But where on this dry, barren area — he asks himself — will he find color to highlight the Hebrew characters?

Then suddenly, he takes a jagged rock and slashes his hand and with his own blood, he traces over the letters. Having accomplished this task, he descends from the mountain to give them through his people to humanity.

This is the crux of the Ten Commandments. They must be written with a person's life blood or they are nothing. A religious person does not worship the Ten Commandments, he *lives* them. He does not pay them lip service, but he gives them service of the mind and the heart.

The Ten Commandments assert that the force in the making of a civilized people is God's will and that without His will there is formlessness and void.

MAURICE SAMUEL

From Sky To Sky

A child once prayed at bedtime, "God bless dad, mother, and my friends," then he paused. After a moment of quiet thought he added, "And please, God, take care of yourself, for if something happens to you then we are all sunk!" This child freely and clearly expressed our universal reliance upon God as the mainspring of life and thought. The creative power of God underlies all existence. Around this hub does our universe turn.

This thought was given beautiful expression in a poem entitled *Akdamut,* written in the eleventh century by Meir ben Isaac Nehorai and recited on Shavuot in the synagogue:

> Could we with ink the ocean fill,
> Were every blade of grass a quill,
> Were the world of parchment made,
> And every man a scribe by trade,
> > To write the love
> > of God above
> Would drain the ocean dry;
> > Nor would the scroll
> > Contain the whole
> Though stretched from sky to sky.

The center and soul of all religion, the belief in a personal God, is the pillar of the religion of Israel. And it fathomed this truth with incomparable and triumphant energy, and expressed it with incomparable poetic power.

CARL H. CORNILL

Vive La Difference

The story is told of two men in an Eastern European village who had a violent disagreement and came to their wise rabbi for judgment. After hearing one side, the learned man nodded his head in agreement and said, "You are right, my son."

The other man immediately interjected, "But wait, Rabbi, until you hear my side."

After he presented his version, the rabbi turned to him and said, "You are right."

When both men had left, his wife, who had overheard the discussion, confronted her husband with the question, "How can they both be right?"

The good rabbi answered, "You, too, my dear, are right."

This story shows — in a humorous and deliberately exaggerated way — that there are many ways to look at an issue, and all of them may contain a measure of validity. Truth is not always black and white, but often more nearly gray. It is only when we examine different opinions that we discern the various nuances. It can be said that the summation of many differences leads to the truth. For this reason, we must constantly value and encourage difference.

Differences are likely to lead to the world's achievement and add to the charms of social intercourse. Nothing leads to boredom more than the uniformity of manners and thoughts.   JOSEPH JACOBS

The Pillars Of Prayer

The heart of prayer is not how many words we say, but rather the spirit in which we say them. Prayer is not a marathon in which he who has said the most is necessarily the one who has done the best. Nor is it a speech contest in which the one who pronounces the words the most clearly is the winner. Prayer is an edifice built on the pillars of sincerity, conviction and trust in God, man and the universe.

This anecdote illustrates exactly this point:

Once during a particularly hot summer, a group of farmers met in their church to pray for rain. After the services a little girl asked her father if the people truly expected that it would rain. "Yes, of course," the father said. "Otherwise we wouldn't be here."

"But Daddy," the child protested, "I didn't see any umbrellas in the church."

Prayer must rest on a faith and a firm conviction in its purpose and its value. We must believe what we say, we must believe what we pray — or our prayer becomes mechanical, if not downright hypocritical.

My words fly up; my thoughts remain below:
Words without thoughts never to heaven go.

WILLIAM SHAKESPEARE

On Being Selfish

One of the most often quoted but most misunderstood phrases in the Bible is the verse from Leviticus: *V'ahavta l'rayakha kamokha,* "And thou shalt love thy neighbor as thyself." We usually focus only on the first part of the phrase, especially during Brotherhood Month. Loving your neighbor is, of course, very important, but at the same time, we should not neglect the rest of the phrase: *kamokha,* "as yourself."

The truth is that unless you have a self, you cannot even begin to love your neighbor. You must have an identity, or you cannot begin to love — a nothing cannot love. When you understand the importance of yourself as a person, then and only then can you be free to love and to give the greatest gift in your possession — your self.

The self of every person is infinitely precious. Therefore, it becomes the duty of every person to discover his uniqueness. Personality is ultimately that which distinguishes one person from another. In this sense every person must be "selfish" — that is, discover his true self, his best self, and respect it.

Every single man is a new thing in the world, and is called upon to fulfill his particularity in this world.

YEHIEL MICHAEL OF ZLOTCHOV

A Fresh Rainbow

One day, after a rain that had lasted for hours, the sun came out and a glorious rainbow appeared in the sky. A little girl ran to her father saying, "Daddy, a beautiful rainbow is stretching from one end of the earth to the other."

The next day it rained again. Once more, the little girl ran shouting to her father, "Look, Daddy, there's another rainbow in the sky. But, Daddy, is that the same rainbow as yesterday?"

The father said, "No indeed, Darling, there is a fresh rainbow for every storm."

This is the great mystery, the chain of living. If our life has enriched other life, then we have forged a link in the golden chain of human existence. For immortality really is the moving of others long after we ourselves have stopped moving. If we have helped a son grow into manhood or a daughter into womanhood, if we have given the right kind of love to a mate, if we have left our own community a better place in which to live, if we have shown others, through personal example, what it means to live with responsibility — then we have created a rainbow that will surely follow the storm of our immediate passing.

Those who have lived with responsibility, even in their death, are called living.　　　BERAKHOT 18 a

Great God

During the stormy period when women were campaigning actively for the right to vote, one woman came to her suffragette leader to report that she had failed to convince her male neighbors to vote for the nineteenth amendment. She was so upset that she began to cry.

Her committee chairwoman gave her a cold stare and said, "Stop your sniveling. Pray to God and She'll answer you."

All of us tend to identify ourselves with God, and we tend to create Him in our image. The old Mexican imagines God looks like an old peon. An African makes his idols look like the Negro. Many European works of art depict God as a biblical patriarch. Many American children probably look upon God as some form of Superman of the comic strip.

The point is that too frequently God is identified with ourselves and our own limited outlook upon life. We must be objective enough to see this and to enlarge our conception of the Almighty. The reality of God is vast and truly imponderable, and that is why all conceptions of Him must begin in humility and end in awe.

One and unique is God's oneness, inconceivable and infinite in His unity.   DANIEL BEN JUDAH

A Thinking Man's Religion

Many of us treat religion as we do the little plastic case on an airplane labelled, "Pull down only in case of emergency." Those of us who seek religious integrity realize that it isn't just an emergency hatch to be used for sudden escape when disaster strikes. To be of real use in time of trouble, prayer must have become a regular and disciplined part of our lives long before there was trouble. Otherwise, it is very likely to be merely an exercise in futility.

There is no such thing as faith at first sight. A faith that comes into being like a butterfly will soon flutter out of our lives; for he who is swift to believe is swift to forget.

For this reason we must earn our faith every day. Religion is not given to us once and for all as something to be preserved in a safe deposit box. Faith is not a commodity to be placed in a deep-freeze to be defrosted in time of need. To be of value religion must be used and not abused. It must be used constantly, all the time. Mitzvot are forms. To fulfill a mitzvah means to fill it full with meaning. It is pitiful to encounter a "cardiac Jew," one who assures us and himself with, "I am a good Jew at heart." This is an emotional cover-up for a lack of thinking. What we really need is a "cerebral Jew," one who can say, "I am a good Jew in my head." We must not be taken in by nostalgia and empty sentimentality. We must develop a religion of thought and intelligence. A Judaism that will offer guidance, inspiration and hope is a thinking man's religion.

A humble man walks on earth, yet his thoughts reach the sky.
SAMUEL HANAGID

My Name Is Legion

The essential conflict within all of us was expressed in a poem entitled, "My Name Is Legion," by Edward Sandford Martin:

Within my earthly temple, there's a crowd;
There's one of us that's humble, one that's proud,
There's one that's broken-hearted for his sins,
There's one that's unrepentant sits and grins;
There's one that loves his neighbor as himself.
And one that cares for naught but fame and pelf.
From much corroding care I should be free
If I could once determine which is me.

This is the story of all of us. We are filled with doubts and confusion, but we can learn from others that the courage to face our doubts is part of the solution. Are you embarrassed because you have a physical impairment? Then look to Moses who had a speech defect and Jacob who limped. Yet, despite their handicaps they became great leaders. Do you have a tendency towards alcoholism? This need not depress you. Noah had this weakness and yet he was able to leave his mark on history. Are you a victim of marital infidelity? Then read the life of the prophet Hosea, whose great love and forgiveness started his family life anew. Were you struck down with grief? Then look to Job whose faith is already legend. It is perfectly clear that all of these individuals mastered their problems because they faced them truthfully and courageously.

Thou desirest truth in the inward parts.   PSALMS 51:8

The New Red Schoolhouse

An American tourist, who was visiting the University of Stockholm in Sweden, came upon a mob of wildly shouting students swarming around a young man. A wreath of green leaves was about his shoulders, he was being pelted with flowers as the campus rang with cries of "Rah, rah, Carl!"

The American turned to his guide and commented, "This must be an exceptional athlete they're honoring."

"No," was the reply. "He's the top student of his graduating class."

"Well," exclaimed the American, "This is the first time I ever saw so much wild excitement over scholarship."

The guide looked puzzled and asked, "Really? Then for what purpose does your country build schools?"

This question is basic to our existence as a society, for a society will embody the values inherent in its educational system. If we seriously determine that the true purpose of our schools is the flowering of the human mind and spirit, then we will create a society of worth. Mediocrity of the mind is born of indifference and low esteem, but excellence in education is achieved through dedication to the highest standards on the part of a society of interested and concerned individuals.

Education should concern itself primarily with the liberation, organization and direction of power and intelligence, with the development of taste, with culture.

ABRAHAM FLEXNER

Hide-And-Seek

Once a little boy was playing hide-and-seek with his friends. For some reason they stopped playing while he was hiding. He began to cry. His grandfather came out of the house to see what was troubling him and said, "Do not weep, my child, because the boys did not come to find you. Perhaps you can learn from this disappointment. In all of life man is not playing the game fairly. God is waiting to be found and men have gone off in search of other things."

Eventually, man will come back to finish the game, for he is so made that his heart is restless until he has found his Maker. Periodically, man wearies of the chase of life and he returns to the attempt to reach out for God. Our yearning for God is motivated by deep inner hunger.

If fish have fins, it is because the water was there first. If birds have wings, it is because the air was there first. If we have eyes, it is because the sun was there first. If we yearn for faith, then it is because God was there first. The reaffirmation of God is truly the discovery of the essence of all existence.

To find God, we must seek Him with our minds in faith. Man's most thrilling achievement is the audacious act of reaching out through infinity to touch God in communication. We begin our entire relationship with God in the historic faith of our fathers, but we end by finding God by and for ourselves.

The perfection of the creatures consists in their union with God, the primary Source.   MOSES CORDOVERO

Needed: More Squares

In popular conversation today, we label someone who does not conform to our way of thinking or acting as a "square." By this we mean to imply that they are not "regular" and do not fit into our general pattern of contemporary living. Actually, it is entirely possible that upon a moment's deeper reflection, we might find that to be called a "square" can be a title of honor.

A ball is round, and therefore, it can be pushed in any direction very easily. At the slightest tap it moves and is carried forth by the whim of any wind. On the other hand, a square represents strength and resistance. To move a square, one must use great force to push it end over end. It is not so easy to move a square because it has strength and staying power.

A square, therefore, is someone who has the courage of his convictions. He is an entity unto himself and will not be pushed about by others. He is willing to think for himself and make up his own mind. Actually, in our society, we need more squares.

Let everyone act according to his convictions, and rest perfectly assured that this will not displease his Creator.

MOSES MENDELSSOHN

Too Marvelous For Words

At Mt. Wilson in California and at Jodrell Bank in Cheshire, England, men are studying the stars tonight. Through great instruments, the minds of men are ranging farther and farther into the depths of space. The hopes of modern men are placed in these marvelous machines. Through them we hope eventually to comprehend more about the great mystery of our universe.

The superficial marvel of these instruments, however, often blinds us to the deeper vision. The superficial marvels are the optical telescope on Mt. Wilson and the radio telescope at Jodrell Bank. The deeper wonder is first, in the inventiveness of the human mind which has created these mechanical devices, second in the immensity of space and the energies in the universe, and third, in the power of the mind behind that creation which has established the order of all things.

The ultimate problem, then, is how shall the mind behind the telescope make contact with the mind behind the universe? The answer is in the verse of the book of Proverbs: "In all Thy ways, know Him."

Persons are known only through many and varied personal encounters. When we seek and find encounter with the ways of the mind which has created the universe, we then may come to understand the ways of the Creator.

Every evidence for evolution is evidence for the existence and work of an Evolver. JOSEPH KRAUSKOPF

The Lost Dimension

One reason for our failure in living today is that we have lost the dimension of depth. We live so fast that we skim the surface of life and do not penetrate into the deeper sources of meaning. We are cause-centered rather than people-conscious. We think in terms of movements rather than trying to understand the feelings of the individual. The quality of the spirituality of the single soul is devoid in our lives. When we scurry about with little packs under our arms, collecting for Red Cross, Mental Health and Heart Fund, we think we are true blue and have done our work for humanity, for God. But as noble as this may be, it is not enough.

When Moses led the Israelites out of Egypt, he was not just another labor leader leading a walkout. He was a spiritually-oriented person fighting for God-given rights of freedom. When Abraham Lincoln called for preserving the Union, he was not just a cheap politician trying to increase his influence. He was religiously concerned with abolishing the immorality of slavery in his beloved land. When we participate in public morality issues, we must not look upon ourselves as a Lady Bountiful or a Mr. Do Gooder. We must see that this is a moral obligation that we have as human beings who have a commitment to our community and to God.

We do not know depth in its full particulars and in its final definition, but one should ponder what a medieval cleric once said: "I would rather be able to feel depth than to define it."

Deep calls unto deep . . . By day the Lord commands His steadfast love and at night His song is with me, a prayer to the God of my life.   PSALMS 42:8, 9

The Wages Of War

The world today lacks peace because basically in our hearts we do not want peace badly enough. Oh, we will offer lip service upon the altar of international friendship, but yet we are not willing to denounce war in all its evil and horror.

How are we ever going to have a lasting peace if our children can go to the corner store and buy scale models of cannons, tanks and atomic weapons? Is war a game to be learned as a child and to play in earnest when we reach adulthood? When grown men bow down to a rifle as if it were an idol, instead of seeing it as an instrument of death, how can we hope to abolish war? And those words "supreme sacrifice" — how easily they trip off our tongues! Do we understand what it means to lose a child in the full bloom of manhood? You go to sleep at night and the pain is in your heart; you awaken in the morning and the wound bleeds anew.

And our boys, who during so-called peace time serve in the armed forces, are they not directly exposed to the mortal danger, the boredom, the tedium, the arrested growth in career — the utter waste of total war?

It may well be that for security we need some form of military defense, but at least let us understand the horror of war preparations. Let us realize fully that, in the classic phrase, "War is Hell!" and every dollar we spend on guns and weapons is robbing someone of bread and God. Only then will we begin the climb on the tortuous and perilous road to peace.

And they shall beat their swords into plowshares,
And their spears into pruning-hooks;
Nation shall not lift up sword against nation,
Neither shall they learn war anymore.   ISAIAH 2:4

A Human Chain Reaction

Several years ago a writer went on a world tour to collect material for his radio program. During his travels, he spoke with a poor worker in his squalid home in Warsaw. When, as usual, the subject of atomic energy came up, the worker said, "I don't think atomic energy is the greatest force on earth."

"No?" asked the writer in surprise. "Then what do you think *is* the greatest force on earth?"

"The human being," the man replied.

The human being has within himself a potential force that is greater than atomic energy. The reason is quite simple. The human being has discovered the secret of atomic energy, and at his discretion he may use it for good or for ill, for self-advancement or for self-destruction. He, therefore, is greater than the forces we know today.

In a very real sense each human being is also caught up in a chain reaction with all of mankind. A beneficent action on his part can set off a chain reaction of good deeds. On the other hand a wicked action can touch off a chain reaction of evil doings. Thus, every person carries within himself the potential of energizing the most powerful forces in the world. Because of this, every person must take care even in the least of his actions.

One human being is worth as much as the whole of creation.
AVOT DE RABBI NATHAN 31

By Way Of Chicago

Just a few months before the Civil War, a group of Chicago ministers went to see President Lincoln in Washington. The ministers were ushered into the President's office and they proceeded to inform him that at a prayer meeting, God had appeared to them and asked them to go to the nation's capital and tell the President to free the slaves. This was God's will. Lincoln listened to them at length and then said politely, "Thank you for coming, my friends. But, if God wished to speak to me, why did He have to go by way of Chicago? He knows my address in Washington."

No one really possesses a pipeline to God and no one faith has a corner on the market of Heaven. To think in these terms is to distort the function of religion.

Religion does not seek the detailed will of God in any given time and place, for the fundamental function of religion is to discover the basic teachings of ethical truth. Religion does not communicate to us the specifics of life, but rather its broad principles from which we derive a way of conduct. The search for moral perfection is not an easy task and there is no absolutely safe and certain path. The paradox of religion is that God is in every man's heart, and yet no man can know Him fully.

Revelation is the silent, imperceptible manifestation of God in history. It is the still small voice.

HERBERT M. LOEWE

An End To Innocence

When a child begins Hebrew school he is curious and excited. Under this stimulation, his learning is at a peak. But as in every other learning process, his interest levels off and he must then learn through hard work and persistence. In all fields of study — medicine, law or science — there comes a time when we must learn by rote memorization.

But, there is one essential difference between Hebrew study and education in medicine, law and science. In professional training a goal is involved — a title, career, prestige. In *Talmud Torah*, study is an end in itself — providing the parents are convinced that religious education is of paramount importance. When this conviction is lacking, the study of Torah ends with Bar Mitzvah.

This is a tremendous error. For although our children may end Jewish studies at the age of thirteen, they do not end their general studies at that time. Hence, when they are at college or beyond, they possess the minds of adults, but their Jewish concepts are those of an adolescent. They have grown emotionally and mentally, but as Jews they have scarcely developed at all. Is it any wonder then that they reject Judaism as infantile? We seem to be raising a generation who will be, as Jews, "eternally adolescent."

It is time to end our innocence in this matter. Our conviction must impel us to provide our children with a far-reaching and continuing Jewish education.

We must grasp and implement more fully than heretofore the implications of the proposition that education is a lifelong process and is not limited to the pre-Bar Mitzvah or pre-Confirmation period.   SIMON GREENBERG

The Tempest Is A Test

Several years ago, a British ship was lying in a harbor in the West Indies when a violent storm arose. The captain ordered out his ship right into the face of the storm. The crew murmured their complaints, but they had to follow the captain's orders. Two days later, when the ship returned, the other ships in the harbor — those which had refused to face the tempest — were all wrecked. Only the ship that braved the storm survived.

We are living in times when we must brave moral storms to survive. Our time calls for speaking out forthrightly for what we believe. It matters not one whit that we are in a minority, or that our views may be highly unpopular. For unless we speak for what we believe today, we will be shackled by the silence of suppression tomorrow, and death the day after.

If you feel strongly that we should pay more taxes to improve education, then say so. If you believe that all men were created equal, then speak against the evils of discrimination. If you are convinced that money does not mean everything, then live as though you meant it. For only those who brave the storm are destined to survive.

The noblest within us is brought forth not in contentment but in discontent, not in truce but in fight.

BARUCH CHARNEY VLADECK

Polished Religion

A woman was once showing her guests a massive piece of silver. As she took it from the cupboard, she apologized and said, "It's dreadfully tarnished. I can't keep it bright unless I use it."

The same is true of religion. Only when we establish a habit pattern of celebrating customs and holidays can religion have real meaning for us. When we observe the time-tested rituals of Judaism we keep open the channels of communication with God. Every time we participate sincerely in a ritual, we renew our faith.

When a young boy ascends the pulpit and reads the Haftorah, he reactivates his faith. When a young woman kindles the Sabbath candles, she reactivates her faith. And when we stand at the graveside of a dear one and, overwhelmed with grief, utter the words, *Yitgadal veyitkadash shemay rabba,* "Sanctified and magnified be His name," we reactivate our faith in God and His world. Experiences like these give us the inspiration to carry on and the strength to endure.

Religion will not come to our aid the moment we call for her; she must be loved and cherished at all times if she is to prove our true friend in need. Much of the present indifference of our young people is directly traceable to the absence of all religious observances in their homes. Piety is the fruit of religious customs.   GUSTAVE GOTTHEIL

The Support Of The Universe

The problems of cosmogony, the origin of the universe, and cosmology, the nature of the universe, have intrigued the minds of men in all ages. What has especially baffled the human curiosity is how the earth and the universe were supported in space. What enabled the earth to stand firm and how did it remain stationary? Almost every culture has offered an answer to the problem.

The Greeks believed the universe was supported by a powerful giant, Atlas. The Babylonians thought the earth floated in a vast, watery mist. The Egyptians assumed that the earth rested on a huge ball. The Hindus believed that the world rested on a giant turtle. Later on, when man became more sophisticated, he said that the world was supported by rays or magnetism.

The answer of the Hebrews was unique among the other interpretations concerning the support of the world. All other explanations have been reduced and disproved in the course of time, but the Jewish answer, which is to be found in *The Ethics of the Fathers*, is both timeless and indispensable. "Rabban Simeon ben Gamaliel said, the world rests on three things: on Truth, on Justice and on Peace."

The Jew looks at everything through eyeglasses focused by ethics and morality. Whatever the Jew has handled, he has left the fingerprints of virtue. Wherever the Jew has walked, he has left the footprints of conscience. That is why the Jew conceived the world to be upheld by the pillars of Truth, Justice and Peace.

The three are really one, for when justice is done, truth prevails and peace is established.　　JER. TAANIT 4:2

275

Need And Greed

During the period when Alexander the Great conquered most of the world, there arose the legend that on one of his military expeditions, he wandered to the very gates of heaven. When he knocked and told the guardian angel his name, the angel asked, "And who is Alexander?" Shocked and angered, the general retorted, "What do you mean, who am I? I am conqueror of the whole world!" And the angel replied, "But this is the Lord's gate and only the righteous may enter."

Alexander then asked for some token to prove that he had at least reached the outskirts of heaven. The angel tossed him a small fragment of a human skull saying, "Weigh it!" Alexander showed it contemptuously to his wise men, who brought a pair of balance scales, placing the bone in one pan while Alexander laid all his silver and gold in the other pan. But the small bone outweighed them all. Alexander then threw in his crown jewels, but they were still unable to outweigh the bone. Then, one of the older wise men tossed a few grains of dust on the bone and up flew that end of the balance. For the bone was that which surrounded the eye, and nothing can ever satisfy the eye until it is covered with the dust of the grave.

That is why men say that there is enough in the world for everybody's need, but not for everybody's greed.

To covet is to violate all the Ten Commandments.

PESIKTA RABBATI 21

A Word To Remember

Compassion . . . that is an interesting word, is it not? Literally, it means "to have passion with." What does a father feel when his son is wounded? His pain. What does a parent experience when his child is frustrated? His anguish. Then what does a compassionate person feel when someone is hurt? He shares his passion with him.

This word — compassion — is in danger of becoming obsolete. For it expresses an ideal that conflicts with catch phrases of today. In the colleges we are told, "Be objective"; in the laboratories we are taught, "Be dispassionate." In industry we are cautioned, "Don't let your feelings get in your way." Our friends warn us, "Don't get involved." It is, then, no wonder that we are called the "cool generation." Our society's large scale inability to feel genuine compassion has become one of our main stumbling blocks. It is time we went beyond a mechanical liberalism to a deeper comprehension of the problems that are troubling our generation.

Many people actually think that we can solve a problem solely by passing a law. They completely miss the deeper aspects of human compassion. What good are housing laws if neighborhoods will not accept Negroes? How will stricter traffic laws save lives if individuals will not obey them? Can anti-recession laws really be effective if everybody is trying to make a fast dollar in the stock market? We cannot pass morality by a majority vote, for the level of morality is in the depth of the compassionate hearts of people and not in laws alone.

Every time that you are compassionate, the Compassionate One shall have compassion upon you.

TOSEFTA BAVA KAMMA 9

What Are You Taken For?

Speech is a form of human communication, yet every country has its own form of language to express its individuality. In a similar manner the purpose of all worship is to discover and follow the will of God, but the ways in which groups seek God differ in terms of religious denominations. Therefore Jews must strive to see themselves clearly and then to be themselves; they must not deceive themselves or to try to ape others. Perhaps the following story will sharpen the point.

A husband noticed that every Tuesday for several weeks his wife had stayed away from home all day. Upon further investigation he discovered some money missing. He was concerned, but he chose to say nothing. Several days later, his wife came to him and said, "Perhaps you've noticed that I haven't been home for the last few Tuesdays. That's because I've been taking a hundred dollar beauty course, and after only three weeks, I have been taken for Marlene Dietrich."

The husband studied her closely for a moment and then said, "My dear, you haven't been taken for Marlene Dietrich; you've been taken for one hundred dollars!"

Jews should be taken for themselves and for nothing else. The best way for a Jew to contribute to world culture and understanding is to cultivate his Jewishness and appreciate his difference.

We shall not abandon the name Jew which has been linked with the purest knowledge of God, the noblest freedom of the spirit and the refinement of morals.

ABRAHAM GEIGER

Not By Bread Alone

Nicolas Berdyaev, one of the great contemporary theologians, who lived in Russia at the time of the Revolution, made the following observation. "The question of bread for myself is a material question, but the question of bread for my neighbor is a spiritual question."

We do not often approach the problem of economics with this basic consideration. Most of us are concerned with the material aspect of living by satisfying our own needs, without giving equal concern to the spiritual phase of helping to answer the needs of others. Woven into the fabric of economic relationships is the thread of human values.

Labor is not just a commodity; it is also people — people with feelings and hopes and aspirations.

Capital is not just money; it is vision and energy and often it represents an entire life's savings.

Bargaining is not just a process to see who can gain the advantage over whom; it is rather an attempt to arrive at a fair compromise through honest payment for work honestly done.

The real concern in economic relationships is to endeavor to find the spiritual dimension. People who are involved in financial dealings must always be aware of the fact that to earn a few extra coins at the cost of a clear conscience is a bitter price indeed. On the other hand, to bring faith into financing is the sum of spirituality.

Man does not live by bread alone, but by everything that proceeds out of the mouth of the Lord does man live.

DEUTERONOMY 8:3

תמוז
TAMMUZ

A Pleasure Book

A woman noted for her gentle and easy manner, when asked how she achieved this state answered that she kept a "Pleasure Book." Then, to illustrate, she brought it out and read some of the entries: "Saw a beautiful garden . . . Talked to a bright, happy girl . . . Received a letter from a friend . . . Enjoyed a beautiful sunset . . . Had a few precious moments of private prayer."

This incident is entirely consistent with the Jewish attitude toward life. The essential point of Judaism is that man is urged to take the time to see and experience the joys of life. We need not feel guilty if we pause to enjoy what God has given us. To the contrary, it restores our interest in life and ultimately permits us to be happier, more creative, and more sensitive.

If we wish to appreciate the goodness of life, we must pause to savor its meaning by:

Having a quiet luncheon with a friend;

Taking a walk before breakfast;

Reading a book in the afternoon;

Contemplating the wonders of a leaf;

Watching cloud formations;

The slow turning of the mind on a simple problem;

Observing children at play.

In the future a person will have to give account for everything that his eye saw and that he did not take the time to appreciate.   JER. KIDDUSHIN 4:12

Faith Is Not A Blindfold

Faith can never be a substitute for the responsibilities of life. Faith can only do so much and the rest must be accomplished by skill, training, work and study which, of course, are based on a faith in a good and provident God.

Faith is not something we believe in spite of the evidence; it is something we do in spite of the consequence. Faith tears the blindfold from our eyes and forces us to see injustice when we would prefer a life of ease rather than action. True faith does not permit us to remain complacent and calm in the face of evil.

Albert Schweitzer, one of the great men of our era, has expressed this simply. "No one," said Schweitzer, "may shut his eyes and think that the pain which is therefore invisible to him is non-existent. No one may escape his own responsibility."

In other words, serving God and mankind, through the inspiration and instrument of faith, forces us to involve ourselves, to give of ourselves, and if need be to offer up our lives.

It is not incumbent upon you to complete the work,
But neither are you free from doing all you possibly can.
                                                    AVOT 2:21

We Live In Glass Houses

A woman once came to a real estate agent with the intention of buying a house. The salesman showed her a variety of houses, but she was not satisfied with any of them. One was too large, another too small; one had the wrong design, and another was in the wrong neighborhood. Finally, in complete exasperation, the agent said, "Madam, why do you need a home? You were born in a hospital, educated in a school building, courted in an automobile, and married in a House of God. You live at hamburger stands and out of freezers and cans. You spend your mornings at the golf course, your afternoons at the bridge table and your evenings at the movies. All you really need is a garage."

Although there is social satire here, there is also the recognition that home as a place of shelter, or a home as a haven of happy living is one of the main concerns of man. Whether it be in a crude cave or under a cantilever roof, live somewhere we must. No matter what our choice of living quarters, we all live in one kind of house — a glass house.

This observation is not at all as modern as we might imagine. Well over 2,000 years ago, the Talmud contained the following imaginative statement in the section dealing with prayers. "A man should always pray in a house that has windows." By this, the Talmud implied that a man is never alone in the world. Whatever emotional feelings we set in motion always create reactions in terms of responses and feelings. Living in spiritual glass houses, we are always seen. If we throw stones, we must be prepared for stones to be hurled back at us.

As you have done shall be done to you.   OBADIAH 1:15

The Golden Life

A Chinese legend tells of a man who dreamed of a great amount of gold as his heart's desire. He rose one day and when the sun was high, he dressed in his finest garments and went to the crowded marketplace. He stepped directly into the booth of a gold dealer, snatched a bag full of gold, and walked calmly away. The officials who arrested him before he even arrived home were puzzled. "Why did you rob the gold dealer in broad daylight?" they asked, "and in the presence of so many people?" The greedy man replied, "I did not see any people; I saw only gold."

This is our very problem: we pant so for plenitude that we do not see people; we are so mad for money that we ignore morality; and we are so obsessed with gain that we forget God. How desperately we need a new set of values if we are to live with wholeness, with integrity.

The truth is that we will not succeed in life until we understand that money buys everything; everything, that is, except love, personality, freedom, and immortality. These virtues are acquired only by a life of long devotion to the committed search for integrity, and this golden life is the only kind of gold worth having.

He who gives when well, his gift is gold;
He who gives only when ill, his gift is silver;
He who gives only in his will, his gift is copper.

MIDRASH

Who Is Independent?

Baseball fans will recall that Lefty Gomez, who pitched for the Yankees in the thirties, held the World Series pitching record of six wins and no losses. One day he was asked by a sports writer for the secret of his success. He replied, "Clean living and a fast outfield." The point is that no pitcher gets a no-hitter without the good fielding and batting of a superb outfield. Similarly, no one has ever achieved anything worthwhile without the help of many others. The self-made man is really a myth.

Each of us is the product of centuries of history and billions of gene combinations. Those of us who are fortunate enough to live in freedom in the United States owe an everlasting debt of gratitude to those others who made the supreme sacrifice.

Even a quick survey of our technological society indicates our complete dependence upon others. When the car, the television set, the washer, or the dryer breaks down and cannot be repaired that very day, that very instant, the howl of calamity that follows would make it appear that we had lost our dearest friend.

And if our dependence is revealed in these trivial and mundane matters, how much more crucial is our dependence on God?

Where would we be without God? Would we have life? Would there be mercy, love and hope? Would there be summer, fall, winter, spring? Perhaps the greatest folly of our age is that we believe about everything that we can literally "do it ourselves."

Self-centeredness is a form of infantilism.   JULIUS GORDON

Knowledge Gives Courage

Consider for a moment the people you have known who have had heart attacks. Someone in your office, perhaps? A man you play golf with? A relative or a close friend? Think how many of them are now back at work and leading active and nearly normal lives.

Yet today many of us still have an unreasoning fear of heart disease. So much progress has been made in research and therapy that there is actually less and less reason for unwarranted fear. We are learning about the healing of the heart faster than ever before. We know that the heart is remarkably strong and resilient. Look at the facts. Highly refined medical and surgical techniques are now available to correct many heart defects. With proper care and with disciplined living habits, people with damaged hearts can now look forward to enjoying long and fruitful lives.

All of this is part of learning to substitute for our irrational fears a real determination to look at them under the floodlight of truth and thus to begin dispelling them. We must learn to have confidence in ourselves so that we can face the future unafraid and help make our lives as long and fulfilling as possible.

Courage is a special kind of knowledge: the knowledge of how to fear what ought to be feared and how not to fear what ought not to be feared.   DAVID BEN-GURION

Love Alone Is Not Enough

During a brief illness, a woman observed the fact that her husband, in addition to his many other obligations, took charge of the household and the children. Pondering the way her husband automatically accepted his new duties, she observed, "I don't just love my husband, I also like him."

Any good marriage is not only based on starry-eyed love, but is also founded on a genuine admiration of a spouse's strength and capacity to give. A successful marriage is not merely drawn together by the pull of beauty, it is held together by the push of duty.

Getting married, like getting born, is largely a matter of chance, but staying married is largely a matter of art. The poet says romantically, "we blunder into bliss," but our concern must always be how we can deepen love through consideration and sympathy.

A husband must be able to look forward to homecoming in the evening with joy and anticipation.

A wife must feel that her contributions to family strength and solidarity are deeply appreciated.

Children need parents as well as presents.

A family is all for one, and one for all.

Through wisdom is a home builded,
And by understanding is it established.   PROVERBS 24:3

I Am A Jew

There is something significant about being a teacher; there is something worthy about being a doctor; and there is something unusual about being an artist. We accept these truths readily. Then why are we not willing to accept the honest truth that there can be something significant, worthy and unusual about a whole people, namely, the Jews?

The Jew has always been in the vanguard of creative thought in the Western world. The heroic history of our 4,000 years of experience demonstrates that we are the dedicated servants of an ideal. We are intimately involved in the search for knowledge and the furtherance of a social order that will be just and righteous.

Many years ago, a Viennese author, Hugo Bettauer, wrote a book called *City Without Jews*. It is still instructive reading because it shows dramatically what an impact a small Jewish minority has on the progress of the larger community. This really is the story of Western civilization. Take a line and draw it clear through the map of the world. One part is without Jews. The other part, the Western world, has Jews. Where no Jews live, there is illiteracy, poverty and backwardness. Where Jews live, there is ferment, scientific progress, higher standards of living and the struggle for freedom. Of course, the Jews are not alone responsible for Western progress. But ask yourself one simple question: Where would civilization be today if there were no Jews? Truly, there is a destiny about being Jewish.

I find myself born — aye, born — into a people and a religion. The preservation of my people must be for a purpose, for God does nothing without a purpose.

CYRUS ADLER

A Changed Man

We are not today what we were yesterday; and what we were yesterday, we were not the day before. Physically, our entire organic structure replaces itself every seven years. In life itself, we are constantly changing our roles. One day we are children, soon we are adolescents, then spouses, parents, and so on up the ladder of life. If there be any fixed rule about life, it is that change and flux is its chief characteristic.

We must understand this basic rule of living and accept the changes within us as individuals and within society as a group. In truth, we are always playing different roles on the stage of life; and we know that the real actor always makes the most of the role assigned to him for the moment.

In a similar vein, we must learn to taste to the fullest and enjoy to the utmost the present role we are enacting. It is a part assigned to us for a limited number of performances. For whatever number of performances we play, we must make sure that our critical notices be of the finest. We can only do this by living our part to the very height of our abilities and with the very fullest of our integrity. What we are today we shall not be tomorrow. And let us seize the moment, before change gives us another role in life.

The main business of a rational society is the business of living with change, comprehending it, and if possible, making it subordinate to the human situation.

NORMAN COUSINS

Turn Off The Dark, Daddy

Sometimes the freshness with which a child looks at things forces us to pause and reconsider our approach to life. A father was carrying his three-year-old into a dark room. Suddenly he felt the tiny arms of the child tightened around his neck. "Turn off the dark, Daddy," he whispered. Not "turn on the light," but "turn off the dark."

All too often we concentrate on brightening our lives, but we neglect the fact that one of the ways we can do this is by ending the dark and evil thoughts in our lives. We must give more time to eliminating the negative influences upon us which yield us only discomfort and pain. It is not enough to accentuate the positive; we must also make an effort to eliminate the negative.

Someone once wrote the secret creed of a child, which also might be the hidden belief of the adult.

> I believe.
> By this I mean
> My mind is open to things yet unseen.
>
> I believe.
> I firmly hold
> To great truths that are yet to be told.
>
> I believe
> Tomorrow's light
> Is always burning round the rim of night.

Turn off the dark, Daddy.

That house is in error whose windows open to the dark.
EXODUS RABBAH 14:2

A Constant Need

One of the teachers of the kindergarten class in a religious school brought a child to the principal because he had a theological problem. The principal remarked in jest to the teacher, "How on earth can a five-year-old have a theological problem?"

The teacher said, "Listen and learn."

The principal asked the youngster what the difficulty was, and he replied almost defiantly, "My teacher said, 'God is anywhere.'" The principal agreed and the child continued, "Well, I don't just want a God anywhere. I want a God somewhere!"

Leaving aside the theological problem for a moment — and there is one — this child spoke for all of us. We all have a need for God somewhere, sometime, and somehow. We all need guidance, direction and faith. We all need understanding, forgiveness and love.

This lifelong process begins within the secret world of the child and ends, if we are fortunate, in the serene world of the man. All of this is part of the religious process of growth. This growth begins with the father and mother, develops with the addition of God and reaches full bloom when we in turn as parents, as friends, as teachers, as workers in the community can help the next generation of children to attain maturity.

Contemplating this vast, on-going process of life in this intimate way makes one aware of the great community of cosmic activities which sustain and promote life. This cosmos becomes a community, near and neighborly. It is, indeed, a vivid awareness of God. BERNARD MELAND

People Are Not Causes

Julia Ward Howe was talking one day with Charles Sumner, the distinguished senator from Massachusetts. She asked him to interest himself in the cause of a person who needed some help. The senator answered, "Julia, I have become so busy, I can no longer concern myself with individuals."

Julia replied, "Charles, that is quite remarkable. Even God has not reached that point yet."

Understanding the selfhood of others is the real secret of survival. We cannot wave away the problems of prejudice and discrimination with the phrase, "That's a minority problem." The "minority" is made up of people like you and me, with families to raise, with children getting sick, with insurance policies to meet, with ambitions to fulfill and goals to realize. They are wise and they are foolish; they are bright and they are dull; they are angry and they are loving. But above all, they are people.

If we learn to see minorities not as groups but as the individuals, then and only then, will we be able to make the kind of life that will be free from fear and filled with dignity.

Every man, no matter how great or small, must be viewed not as a means to an end, but as an end in himself.

HAYIM GREENBERG

First Comes Courage

In Herodotus' history of the Greek wars, there is recorded the story of an Athenian soldier who was lame in one foot. One day, some of his fellow soldiers were laughing at him because of his lameness. After tolerating their derision for a while, he finally could stand it no longer, and he silenced them with the words, "I am here to fight and not to run."

This is basically the philosophy of all those who have the courage of their convictions.

This was a part of the courage of the first surgeon who dared to cut into a heart in order to repair it.

This was the fundamental courage of the first psychiatrist who plunged into the dark pit of the emotions and opened a new door of healing for the emotionally ill.

This was essentially the courage of the first airplane pilot; the first man to let a mosquito bite his arm to test an anti-malaria drug; the first printer to set type for a free press; and all the "firsts" that have helped our lives become more productive and more worthwhile.

Courage is the first lesson in the advancement of life. For all of us are here to fight and not to run.

Have I not commanded you? Be strong and of good courage; be not frightened neither be dismayed; for the Lord your God is with you wherever you go.   JOSHUA 1:9

Make Every Day A Holiday

There was a woman in a certain congregation who was beloved by all. She raised a fine family and in the course of the years had carried many burdens. But, in spite of it all, she was lighthearted and gay, and people found it a pleasure to be in her company. The rabbi of the synagogue could not help but marvel at the way she could be so cheerful in the face of so much difficulty. One day he asked how she was able to do this. She replied, "Rabbi, I have adopted as my motto 'Make every day a holiday.'"

This is a wonderful philosophy. When we make every day a holiday, we are, in the basic meaning of the word, rendering that period of time as a "holy day." We have, in fact, hallowed that day. If we do this every day of our lives, then we will find that our entire lifetime will be endowed with a sense of sanctity.

We make a mistake if we reserve only certain special days for consecrating our lives. To do this is to live at a high level only occasionally. For this reason, we must sanctify each day with a prayer, a kind word, a good deed, and a moment of meditation.

We can do this if we make every day a "holy day."

If you sanctify yourself a little, you are sanctified much.
                                    YOMA 39 a

The Sane Society

In our modern western society, we consistently refuse to face death with sanity. Therefore, unrealistically, we have glorified youth. We all worship at the shrine of youth and in this way hope to stave off the inevitable. We torture ourselves to keep the youthful figure; we burn ourselves to a crisp to keep the youthful skin pigmentation; and we color our hair and paint our faces to convince ourselves we are still young.

Isn't it time to reveal this deceit for what it is? Isn't it time to say that youth is inexperience and age is wisdom? Isn't it time to proclaim the sane truth that we must recognize age not by the infirmity of the body, but by the maturity of the soul? Isn't it time to proclaim the wise words of the Bible: "Thou shalt rise and respect the grey head of experience"?

Most of us miss the point entirely. We think that it is shrewd to concentrate on ourselves to preserve our own health and well-being. This is precisely the wrong approach. For the people who live saner, and therefore longer, are precisely those who forget about themselves in their concern for others. They are the people who lose themselves in the business of life and find themselves in the satisfaction of things well done and days filled with meaning.

There is worse than oppression — there is inward stagnation of the spiritual life.
                                    ISRAEL ZANGWILL

The Expense Of Achievement

In Jewish literature we find the phrase *tzaar gidul banim,* "the anguish of rearing children." This refers to the parental responsibilities not only to feed, clothe, house, and educate children, but also to help them mature and grow. Parents must give a child a set of values and standards. To become a person in his own right, the child must modify and even reject some of these standards. A child who accepts a parent's views completely is a carbon copy and not a free person at all. But when a parent, even the most understanding parent, is partly rejected, he feels hurt and pained. Yet this painful process of creating personal values is part of the child's growth and is in the deeper sense the real importance of the parent as the standard-setting and goal-defining agent for the child. This normal process of growth can never be without anguish.

This insight can be applied to many other areas, large and small. A business can never advance without struggle, the anxiety of risk and push. Learning and thinking in new areas often literally give us headaches. The greatest symbol of growth, the development of a child through the embryonic stage, is accompanied by discomfort and even pain for the mother until the final moment of birth. But anyone who has built a business, earned a degree, or given birth and raised a child knows that the achievement is worth the expense.

According to the pain of the effort is the reward.

AVOT 5:26

A State Of Mind

Recently, the Philadelphia Philharmonic Orchestra gave the premiere performance of the work of an eight-year-old composer, Kenneth Brown. This was most exciting, but what was even more thrilling for Jews was that the composition was entitled, "An Israeli Rhapsody."

The boy's mother knew that he had never been outside of Pennsylvania, so she was curious about the title and subject of his composition. After the concert, she asked him how he knew about Israel. The young musical genius replied,"I just pictured it in my mind." And the mother protested, "But, you have never really been there."

The boy replied, "That is true. But I felt I was there, and that is enough for me."

This illustrates the deep feeling that almost all Jews have for Israel. The feeling is just as strong and intense in the eight-year-old as in the eighty-year-old. The depth of this feeling moves many to creative expression and gives evidence of the strong bond that unites Jews throughout the world on behalf of Israel. It is not important that every Jew should live in the state of Israel, but it is vital that all Jews should have a perpetual and proud affinity for Israel.

No man can bid a fool or sage from feeling to refrain —
For a feeling can glide through stone,
And steel and iron chain.   SUSSKIND VON TRIMBERG

The Jewish Purpose

One man lost his way in the mist upon a mountain top. Another man — a Jew named Moses — met God face to face and gave the world a moral law.

One man heard the noisy tuning of instruments. Another man — a Jew named Leonard Bernstein — turned them into the Jeremiah Symphony.

One man went into the laboratory and found disease incurable. Another man — a Jew named Selman Waksman — uncovered a life-saving drug, streptomycin.

One man saw the First World War lost because the Allies could not devise an efficient way to handle explosives. Another man — a Jew named Chaim Weizmann — after many sleepless nights, gave the world the solution.

One man went to the Dreyfus trial in France and pitied himself for being a Jew. Another man — a Jew named Theodor Herzl — gained the inspiration there to found modern Zionism.

One woman was cynical about the bitter struggles of American immigrants. Another woman — a Jewess named Emma Lazarus — saw America as a haven for the downtrodden and wrote the immortal lines that are engraved on the base of the Statue of Liberty.

Some Jews had dreams and fashioned them into facts. So has it been and so will it always be with the achievements of anything worthwhile and lasting in Jewish experience.

Whether we like it or not, and however inconvenient it may be, the Jewish people have become the personification of the issues involved in the world struggle between right and wrong, between good and evil.　　LORD DAVID DAVIES

Within My House

Hunter's Horn, a fine novel by Harriet Arnow, offers an interesting parable. It tells of a farmer in the hills of Kentucky, who becomes obsessed with hunting down a great red fox nicknamed King Devil, which has managed to eat his prize chickens and to elude him for many years. To capture the fox becomes the farmer's one goal. He buys pedigreed fox-hounds at great expense, while starving his own wife and children. He uses money from the sale of eggs for dog food; the dogs get milk while there is none for the baby; his fence is allowed to rot; loose rocks and soil for which he has no time to care ruin his plowing; his stock and crops wither from neglect. In the end he winds up with empty jars in his kitchen and his life is ruined beyond repair.

What a striking parallel to the way we neglect our homes in pursuit of outside interests! We become obsessed with our careers, our clubs, our community work. We forget our basic responsibilities to our families. While our responsibilities to life are not bounded by our homes, yet we cannot hope to help others until we have first helped ourselves. Love, while not limited by the home, must be born and tended in the home, or it will never be born at all. He who neglects his home does so at his own peril.

I will walk within my house in the integrity of my heart.
PSALMS 101:2

No Comparison

Benjamin Jowett was distinguished for translating the works of the Greek philosophers into readable modern English. In the last generation he was widely respected for his scholarship and his achievements. One day, a very enthusiastic lady rushed up to him and asked, "Oh, Professor Jowett, do tell me, what do you think of God?"

He answered very simply, "That, my dear is very unimportant. The question is: What does God think of *me*."

Whenever we think of God, we must be aware that we are exploring a mystery; and when we have exhausted our thought, we have moved but one small fraction closer to comprehending Him. When we consider our lifetime, we must remember that it is as a split second against the earth's eight billion years. Then we grow humble. When we consider that we stand upon approximately two square feet and then remember that the universe is described by a number with twenty-four ciphers in it, then we begin to perceive that we are but specks of dust.

Such thoughts stir us greatly. How, we wonder, can an individual stand on the hills and gaze at the stars, walk by the seashore and hear the endless pounding of the surf, look at a newborn infant and not understand that there is a God? And what that God thinks of us is far more important than what we think of Him.

To whom will you liken God?
And to what can you compare Him?   ISAIAH 40:18

The Future Lies Ahead

When we calculate the world's chances for peace, we must keep certain values in mind. We must not bow to despair and we must live in hope.

The future of the world today can be expressed in the concept underlying the word, "Esperanto." Esperanto is an international language to be used by all peoples. Interestingly enough, it was created by a Jew, Dr. Louis Zamenhof, who believed if all men spoke the same language, perhaps there would be less misunderstanding.

The term Esperanto itself comes from the word *esperer,* which means to hope. If all men hope together, then there can be a better world. This is really the fundamental belief of all faiths.

In Judaism, hope is the highest act of faith.

In Catholicism, despair is the only sin for which there is no forgiveness.

In Protestantism, the belief in the strength of life is the cornerstone of conviction.

We are one in our belief in the possibilities of the future.

The vital impulse is optimistic. All religions are opposed to a negative approach to life.   HENRI BERGSON

The Sum Is All The Parts

William Carey, a famous Scottish preacher, was also a shoemaker. Even though he was the leader of a great religious movement, he spent the better part of each day practicing his trade. One day someone asked him what his business was and he replied, "Well, my business is to extend the Kingdom of God to men's hearts, but I repair shoes to pay expenses."

His life was an excellent illustration of the principle that religion, if it is to have any value at all, must be practiced every day, hour and minute. When religion is sealed off from involvement in the concerns and affairs of men and the concrete particularity of daily decisions, then it becomes sterile and meaningless. If our faith is to function, we must allow it to grapple with our pressing personal problems.

In truth, every day is a messenger of God. He places choices before man daily so that one can never isolate himself from ethical issues. Those who sit in seclusion or retreat to ivory towers, or stay out of politics, or dodge issues, or think they will find salvation by a few pious words are sadly mistaken.

We cannot rise to God by stepping on the heads of men. We cannot hate men during the week and love God on Saturday or Sunday. Religion is the sum of *all* its parts.

Men must beware of looking upon religion as an ideal to be yearned for; it should be an ideal to be applied.

SIMON DUBNOW

It's Only Money

A couple were quietly conversing at dinner one night about their life together. Suddenly, the wife turned to the husband and remarked, "Some day we will be rich."

He reached over and took her hand and replied, "Darling, we are rich; some day, we may even have money."

Often, without being aware of it, we possess riches that are beyond the grasp of a good portion of mankind.

If we have our health, it is the equivalent of great wealth.

If we have a lovely family, then we are already in possession of a fortune.

If we have a job that gives us a steady income, then we already have a kind of riches.

If we have at our disposal a library, a museum, a symphony, a theater, a study group, then we have access to the unlimited resources of the human spirit.

It is wrong to confuse earthly wealth with spiritual gain, for the former comes and goes, but the latter abides forever.

A good name is rather to be chosen than great riches,
And honor rather than silver or gold.   PROVERBS 22:1

In The Groove

Take a record — an old one — and punch a new hole in it about an inch off center and then play it. After a few turns you will soon stop the record player. The noise will be horrible and you will become tense. Then, once more, place the record on its true center, put the needle in the groove and restart the machine. Soon you will hear the accustomed harmony and you will feel perfectly at ease.

The same thing is true of life itself. When our values are off center then our lives are distorted. We whirl about daily in an inharmonious manner, bringing unnecessary tension into our own lives and needless unpleasantness into the lives of others.

On the other hand, when we place God at the center of our lives and let religious wisdom control our living and thinking, then we can find harmony and happiness. We live without tension and wholly without fear. The tempo of our lives, the musing of our minds are directed into the channels that can yield us the most worthwhile harmonies in living. Only God at the center can enable us to have high fidelity in living.

The ultimate imperative of Jewish ethics is the affirmation of the Living God and repudiation of idolatry. The universe of our existence can have but one source and center.
WILL HERBERG

The Everlasting Bond

During the war, when hate was at its highest, an incident took place involving a Japanese family named Yamamoto of San Francisco. They were pleasant people who spoke English and were interested in politics only to the extent that they had left Japan because they preferred democratic ways. They were like most people — hardworking and honest; they belonged to the P.T.A. and participated in the usual community activities.

Like everyone else during the war years, the Yamamotos cultivated a vegetable garden in their back yard. Then an ugly thing occurred.

One spring night, some vandals broke in and uprooted every plant. The next day, when the neighbors discovered the damage, they were shocked. But there were no public statements, no petitions, no paid protest ads in the newspaper. What happened instead was that people with gardens of their own came hurrying spontaneously to the rescue with plants, with seedlings, with spades for digging and stakes to drive in the ground. By the end of the day, the garden was restored to its beauty. By an act of common love, they wiped out their common shame.

Those who have love in their hearts will always act silently, decisively and humanely with unlimited faith in the future.

Let the time be dark with hatred,
I believe in years beyond —
Love at last shall bind the peoples
In an everlasting bond.

SAUL TSCHERNIHOVSKY

Inventions

A Hasidic teacher once explained to his disciples that every invention contained a spiritual truth. He said, "The train teaches us that everything can be missed in a single moment. The telegraph reminds us that all our words are counted and must be paid for. The telephone suggests that what we say here is heard there."

Everything in life that is of value can be missed in a single moment if we are not careful. It takes the trained eye to watch for signs of affection or anger; neither are to be missed.

Our words are also counted and must be paid for. If we speak in words of love, we are well rewarded; and conversely, if we shout in tones of hate, we also must pay the price. Therefore, we must plan carefully what we wish to say.

Even more than this, we must understand that what we say is heard by many others. There are no secrets in this world, and soon everything we tell is revealed. If we understand this, we can prevent many a wrong. Whatever we say — as a nation or as individuals — eventually is heard around the world.

Everything that was created in this world was created for a purpose.   SHABBAT 78 b

Love's Measure

Once two men were in a tavern. As the evening wore on they became increasingly intoxicated and began professing their undying friendship for each other. One turned to the other and said, "You're my friend. I really love you."

In the moment of insight that sometimes can be found in drink, the other replied, "How can you say you love me, when you don't even know how much I need to support my family?"

We say we love our community, but do we really make the effort to know the basic needs of our community? Do we rid ourselves of our responsibilities by giving token gifts to causes?

We say we love our children, but do we take the time really to learn what bothers them and what their problems are? Or do we just care that they stay out of trouble or at least not embarrass us?

We say we love our mates, but do we really know what gives them satisfaction? Or do we give them what we think ought to satisfy them?

The real measure of love is to be found in our honest concern with the needs and welfare of those whom we love. The depth of our consideration for their security is the measure of our love for them.

When the satisfaction and security of another person becomes as significant as our own satisfaction and security, then the state of love exists. So far as I know, under no other circumstances is a state of love present, regardless of the popular usage of the word.   HARRY STACK SULLIVAN

Hope For The Troubled

The line between health and illness is often thin, especially so in the case of mental illness. One of the key factors in determining whether we need help to be restored to emotional well-being is indicated by instances of failure of emotional control which consequently make life intolerable. It is then that we must have the courage to seek counsel and guidance from competent professional people. When gnawing questions begin to undermine our self-confidence, it is time to turn to others for hope and help.

Problems like these may be the clues to serious difficulty: A person appears to have everything yet lives in miserable discontent. A wife and husband cannot tell each other what they really want. A man drives himself so frantically that he falls ill. A simple act of discipline throws a child into an uncontrollable tantrum.

There is no need today to force ourselves to perish in anguish. If we have the proper guidance and help, our tears do not fall unseen, our words are heard and our reasonable requests can be fulfilled. Family service agencies and others are staffed with qualified personnel, whose ethics require that they keep in strictest confidence whatever is told to them professionally. To them we can turn in our hour of need, for they and others like them have proved that there is truly hope for the troubled.

Trouble is universal, and so must be help.

ELIJAH GUTTMACHER

A Do-It-Yourself Religion

A firm once placed the following advertisement in the morning newspaper: "Wanted immediately young man, college degree, specialist in chemistry." That afternoon, an elderly man appeared in the employment office of the firm and told the manager that he had come to see him about the advertisement. Puzzled, the manager asked how old he was. The reply was 67. The manager protested, "But, we wanted a young man." He continued, "Are you a college graduate?"

"No," was the applicant's answer, "I never went to college."

He further inquired, "Are you a specialist in chemistry?" Again the elderly gentleman replied in the negative. Finally, the manager spoke with irritation. "Well, then, why did you come here?"

Calmly and innocently came the reply. "I just wanted to let you know that on me you should not count."

While most people live on the principle that they should not be counted, Judaism as an historic faith has been built on the axiom that every person must be counted upon, that there are no proxies for religious participation.

No one can study for you; you must do it yourself.

No one can rest on the Sabbath for you; you must do it yourself.

No one can give charity for you; you must do it yourself.

Judaism is a do-it-yourself religion, accepting no substitutes for the self and insisting that nothing really counts except what the individual himself contributes to living.

Everything depends on the way a person measures himself.
                                            KELIM 17:11

אב

AV

The Courage To Care

One of the most moving literary works of our time is Dore Schary's play, *Sunrise at Campobello*. The play is essentially a study of the life of the late Franklin D. Roosevelt from the moment he was stricken with infantile paralysis until he learned to walk again by taking ten painful steps which brought him, metaphorically speaking, into the American political arena.

The play very dramatically points up the element of courage, which was Roosevelt's real strength. Here was a man who had the best of everything: money, position, education, and an adoring family. How easy for him to retire as an invalid, a lazy country squire, and be shielded from the world. But the powerful sense of courage within him, the courage to care about his life forced him to relearn to crawl, to relearn to walk and then to seek political office, culminating in the presidency of the United States.

This man's story, in one form or another, is everyone's potential story. The one factor that makes a difference in our life is the courage to care about making the most of it.

Where a man wishes to go, there he is led.   **MAKKOT 10 b**

The Antidote To Anger

The story is told that Samuel Hanagid, an eleventh century Spanish-Jewish poet who was prime minister to the king of Granada, was once insulted by an enemy in the presence of the king. The king was so angered that he ordered his prime minister to punish the offender by cutting out his tongue. Contrary to the king's mandate, Samuel treated his enemy with the utmost kindness. When the king learned that his order had not been carried out, he was greatly astonished. Samuel was ready with a pleasant answer. He said, "I have carried out your order, Your Majesty, I have cut out his evil tongue and have given him instead a kindly tongue."

Often we are caught in the snare of the old adage that we must fight fire with fire. We retaliate against hate with hate, and we answer anger with anger. All we really succeed in doing is magnifying the problem, for by increasing a fire all we simply do is intensify the heat.

The true way to extinguish a fire is with cool water. Likewise, the effective way to quench a quarrel is with cooling and soothing words. Most arguments are rooted in irrational hate; before reason can be applied to relationships, hate must be dispelled. This can only be done when the voice is soft, the temper is low, and the regard for others is gentle. The real antidote to anger is, obviously, pleasantness.

A soft answer turneth away wrath.　　　PROVERBS 15:1

On Beginning From Within

Martin Buber, the distinguished Jewish theologian and exponent of Hasidism, tells the tale of a man, who found when he got up in the morning that it was hard for him to find his clothes. It reached the stage where at night he almost hesitated to go to bed because of the trouble he would have upon waking. One evening, he finally made a great effort, took paper and pencil and as he undressed, noted down exactly where he put everything he had been wearing. The next morning, very pleased with himself, he took the slip of paper in his hand and read: "trousers-dresser," "shirt-closet." Then he read the last item on the list. It was "self." But opposite the word was a blank space. He paused and in puzzlement he wondered, "That's all very well, but now where am I myself? Where in the world am I?"

And indeed that is how it is with us. Everything is in its place. The sun rises every morning and sets every evening. The moral standards of the Torah are fixed and immutable. Life moves slowly and steadily upon its course. The only question that remains to be answered is "Where in the world am I?" Or in the words of a modern anonymous poet:

> "Your task . . . to build a better world," God said.
> I answered, "How . . . ?
> So complicated now,
> And I so small and useless am.
> There's nothing I can do."
> But God in all His wisdom said,
> "Just build a better you."

First improve yourself, then improve others.

BAVA METZIA 107 b

Limits

Intelligent and responsible people understand that they must establish limits to their actions in all of life and especially in their dealings with nature. We cannot experiment just as we please. We cannot wantonly waste and destroy. We cannot exploit forever our natural resources without a day of reckoning.

All of us have favorite public parks and scenic routes where we enjoy natural beauty in quietness. But occasionally, we see things that sadden us. We see an area strewn with bags of garbage dropped and rusty beer cans flung carelessly from car windows by inconsiderate people. One often wonders if these people would mess up their living rooms the way they mess up God's world. These offenses against nature give us good reason for asking oneself:

Is it right to carve our initials into growing trees?

Is it proper for us to waste food, jam our garbage cans with good food that we never intended eating in the first place?

Do we have the authority to contemplate — much less create — bombs and chemicals that can destroy all or even a part of existence?

We must limit our activities or else our happiness and our very lives may be curtailed completely.

What is contrary to nature is contrary to God.

LEOPOLD KOMPERT

315

Stop, Look, And Listen

The rabbi of Berditchev once saw a man hurrying along the street, looking neither right nor left. "Why are you rushing so?" he asked the man.

"I am pursuing my livelihood," the man replied.

"And how do you know," continued the rabbi, "that your livelihood is running before you, so that you have to rush after it? Perhaps it is behind you, and all you need do to encounter it is to stand still. Yet here you are running away from it. Stand still, my friend."

Stand still. Look at your wife. Love her now; for who knows what tomorrow may bring?

Stand still. Look at your children. Share in their experiences of growth for soon enough they will grow away from you.

Stand still. Look at your friends. Don't take them for granted. To have a friend, you must continue to be a friend.

Stand still. Look at the sunset. Admire it today. Tomorrow it may be cloudy. Or tomorrow the sunset may be here, but you may not.

The great victories of life are oftenest won in a quiet way, and not with alarms and trumpets.   BENJAMIN N. CARDOZO

Money And Conformity

Most of us think the way to make money is to conform to the presumed laws of the business world: "Be a plugger," "Listen to your boss," "Get along with everybody, and you will someday be a smashing success."

J. Paul Getty, the richest American alive, in an article entitled, "Money and Conformity," says just the opposite. He declares that the way to become a millionaire is to be a non-conformist — someone who has the flexibility to think of new ways of doing things. Thus you'll make your mark in the financial world. Business, he tells us, does not need another gray flannel suit, another cringing clerk. These are a dime a dozen. Rather, new developments and new endeavors need creative thinking that can break through into new forms of earning power.

Getty points out that the wealthiest men in America are precisely so because they are basically individuals and care very little for what their competitors and their neighbors will think. For example, John D. Rockefeller made it a habit to give out shiny new dimes wherever he went, and he really didn't care whether you liked it or not. Howard Hughes wears tennis sneakers and sport shirts, and sneers at Ivy League dress and the Continental look. Bernard Baruch holds meetings on park benches and disdains memos, intercoms, and fancy tape recorders. The reason these men are millionaires is because they are not afraid to be themselves — individuals.

Money lost, nothing lost. Courage lost, all is lost.
JUDAH LEIB LAZEROV

The Holy And The Profane

Almost everything around and within us can be made sacred or sacrilegious.

Take a piece of cloth. It can be used as a mask to disguise a robber; or it can be dropped a few inches to adorn the neck of a lovely lady; or it can rest on the shoulders of a Jew to become a *tallit,* an object associated with worship and inspiration.

A man's restless, driving energy can be used aggressively to bully, to push, to hurt others; or it can be directed profitably into constructive business pursuits; or, again, it can be put to communal use to head charity drives and organize for human betterment.

Even knowledge is a neutral force. Learning itself, mere information itself, is no criterion of wisdom. In Hebrew an apt phrase describes this situation: *hamor nosay sefarim,* "a donkey carrying books." This refers to one who has learning but does not use it wisely. When we use our information and our possessions for our selfish ends alone, we rob the world; but when we share our gains with others and give of our knowledge, we enrich the world. This is the difference between the holy and the profane.

He who possesses both learning and piety is like an artist with his tools ready in hand. YOHANAN BEN ZAKKAI

The Base Of The Pyramid

The pyramid of socialized living is based on the family. The greatest guide for humanity still remains the actions of a mother and a father.

When we practice our faith in our homes and our children see us pray and worship and exult in our Jewishness, we are not only doing our religious duty, we are also setting the tone for respect, for *kibbud av v'aym*, the honoring of the mother and father. Ultimately, we get as much abuse from our children as we tolerate; and we receive as much respect and honor as we deserve.

A stroller was walking in a park. It was a warm day, so he sat on a bench to rest. The bench was in front of a beautifully sculptured fountain. He watched the children playing about. Suddenly, one little boy, obviously over-heated and thirsty from the hard play, ran up to his father who was standing near the fountain and said, "Lift me up, Daddy, so I can drink." How lovely! "Life me up, Daddy, so I can drink."

From which source of knowledge will *your* child drink? From whom will he learn the facts of life? By what book will you raise him — the comic book, the bank book, or the Good Book?

What a child says on the street, the parents have said at home.   SUKKAH 56 b

The Wall

There is an ancient rabbinical tale of the high priest who went to the Temple the last night before it was destroyed by the Romans on the ninth of Av. The high priest prayed and wept, and finally he fell asleep exhausted. In his dream he saw the Temple sway, about to fall over. He placed all his weight against the wall from within, but soon the wall started to sway in the opposite direction. He called for help. A man passing outside at that moment saw the Temple shake, and he placed his weight against the outside wall. The combined strength of the high priest from within and the man from without supported the wall and stopped it from swaying.

Israel placing its weight on the inside and American Jewry placing its weight on the outside can cause the wall of creativity and the Temple of Judaism to stand firmly. The strength of world Jewry can accomplish miracles in saving Jewish life from extinction and from the attrition of apathy. We can create. We can build. Our lives can be filled with new life, new strength and new meaning if we but will it.

It was not an ibn Gabirol or a Maimonides, still less a Spinoza who fulfilled the Jewish mission most truly or rendered the greatest service to the Jewish cause. No, it was the many little Jewish communities, persecuted and despised through the ages, who kept alive the flame of purest monotheism and the supremacy of the Moral Law.
CLAUDE G. MONTEFIORE

Leave A Little To God

Very often, we forget the implication of the phrase that the world is a unity. It means simply that there is a purpose and destiny in the world.

Solomon Schechter, the second president of The Jewish Theological Seminary of America, used to say repeatedly, "Leave a little to God." Now note what he did not say: "Leave it all to God," for then man becomes nothing, nor "Leave nothing to God," for then man is doomed to failure. But "Leave a little to God" is the counsel we need. We must do our share and know that God will do His. We must work and wait.

What will eventually emerge in the future will be in accordance with God's purposes for the world — not Russia's nor America's, nor yours nor mine, but something far different, far better than what we or our adversaries possess at present. For mankind was created in the image of God and what He does imagine will be the future. The world is a unity, that is why we must work and wait, and leave a little to God.

He who has created the day has also created sustenance for it.   MEKHILTA, BESHALAH

Touched By Human Hands

Mrs. Horace Havemeyer, whose collection of paintings is today the pride of New York's Metropolitan Museum of Art, was once confronted by a wealthy, bejeweled dowager who asked, rather scornfully, why she spent so much money on dabs of paint on paper and canvas. Mrs. Havemeyer examined the dowager's pearl necklace for a long and studious moment and then answered, "I would rather have something made by a man than have something made by an oyster."

This is a wonderful insight, because really fine things are created by people and not by animals or machines.

A TV dinner may save time, but a home-cooked meal tastes better. A copy of a painting purchased from a decorator may be good, but an original work of art chosen with your own taste is even better. A clever twenty-five cent get well card may provide a chuckle, but a hand-written note of good wishes will go even farther toward healing.

The finest gift we can give to others is a portion of our time, our efforts, our thought — our personality.

Rings and jewels are not gifts; but apologies for gifts. The only true gift is a portion of thyself.

RALPH WALDO EMERSON

Building Bridges

The following case is cited in psychiatric literature. A sick man once dreamed that he was approaching a drawbridge in his car when the two sections lifted and the bridge opened. After the ship had passed, the sections began to descend and the man drove his car toward the one descending. Then, suddenly, the other section for some reason stopped and did not come down to meet its partner. He was going so fast that the application of the brakes had very little effect, and he skidded off the bridge into the water.

In real life as well we must meet our partners in responsibility in order to join our lives to a healthy society.

We do not give to the United Jewish Appeal because it is a handout, but rather because so many Jews in Europe and Israel are dependent upon our mature acceptance of responsibility.

We do not give to the synagogue only because it makes us feel good, but because it is our solemn duty to support our source of goodness.

We do not pay taxes because some people pass laws, but rather because taxes are necessary to the kind of society in which we want to live.

We belong to the United Nations not only because we want to, but also because we have to. For the fact is, if we are not united today, then tomorrow there will be no nations.

Unless we are willing to build bridges, we will surely end up in disaster.

Religion should have not only the sacrament of prayer but also the sacrament of social service. ISRAEL I. MATTUCK

How Do You Feel?

A student in the rabbinical school once came to the rabbi in charge of the seminary and asked to be ordained. The senior rabbi then questioned, "Tell me about your Talmud studies."

The earnest student replied, "I have gone through the Talmud five times."

The rabbi then replied, "That's fine, my son, but how many times has the Talmud gone through you?"

It is one thing to understand a subject intellectually, but it is something quite different to comprehend it emotionally. All too often we think of social problems only in intellectual terms. We do not concern ourselves with them in terms of our deeper feelings. It is one thing to discuss brotherhood abstractly, but it is quite another thing to consider it in terms of your neighbor's being a member of another race, your employee's seeking a raise, or someone very dear to you becoming ill.

The real understanding of a problem occurs not when we go through the problem but rather when the problem goes through us. When we think intellectually we limit the scope of our character, but when we also learn to feel sympathetically we open new vistas.

For you know the heart of the stranger, seeing you were strangers in the land of Egypt.   EXODUS 23:9

No Man Is An Island

Frederick Barbarossa, the Emperor of Prussia, once conducted an interesting experiment. He wanted to know what was the first language of mankind, so he devised an ingenious experiment. He took forty newborn babies and put them in a nursery in which they were isolated from each other and had minimal contact with adults. Nobody was allowed to talk in their presence; the idea was that when these babies began to talk, whatever language they spoke would represent the basic language of the world.

Frederick never found the answer, because, as we know, stimulation by others is essential for speech development. But even more important — for want of human contact, human relations, human understanding — every one of these babies died.

The important conclusion of this and of modern studies among institutionalized children is that unless human beings relate to each other in a positive manner, they will shrivel up and die, destroyed by their own isolation.

Thus, while it is man's right and responsibility to stand on his own feet, he must not forget his responsibilities to society. What, then, is the good life? It is the life of the socialized individual — the person who retains his individuality but develops and extends it to embrace humanity.

DAVID ARONSON

Throwaways

A recent magazine article entitled "Throw-Away Living" describes the extent to which we are living in an age of "disposables." Not only tin cans but almost all kinds of utensils are made to be thrown away after use: napkins, tablecloths, paper dishes. One man suggested solving the parking problem in cities by "disposable cars" which can be thrown away when the parking area is reached.

But there is a different and more serious kind of "throwaway living" in which many people are indulging today. People are throwing away moral convictions and principles which are needed for essential living. We cannot dispose of our religious and moral heritage to suit our particular convenience.

Actually this is the basic distinction between a materialistic and a religious outlook. Materialism seeks satisfactions from living through the world of things and the amassing of material possessions. In the spiritual approach, matters of the spirit are primary. Material acquisitions are valuable only insofar as they advance the life of spirit. Things are to be used and not loved. On the other hand, people and ideals are to be loved and not used.

Be not like servants who serve their master upon the condition of receiving a reward; but be like servants who serve their master without receiving a reward; and let the reverence for Heaven be upon you.   AVOT 1:3

A Slowly-Mastered Art

We are born through love, but we ourselves must learn to love. We do not fall in love; we stand in love. Love is a process of deepening.

It is no great feat of love to adore the pleasant child, but it is real, deep love to want to help the angry child, even when he hurts us. It is no lasting achievement of love to give money for education, but it is real love of learning to enroll in classes and to study, even at the end of a weary day. It is no great effort of love to roll bandages, but it is real love of humanity that makes us willing to read to the blind, bathe the bedridden, and feed those unable to lift their hands.

Or put it this way:

> Did Rubinstein play Chopin
>> The day his hands first touched the keys?
> With his first chisel did Rodin
>> Turn stone into a masterpiece?
> Then why should beginners in love
>> Suppose that from the start
> They must be polished masters of
>> That complex instrument, the heart?
> The finest talent must be trained
>> By time and patience, part or wholly.
> All skill must be attained,
>> And love's an art that's mastered slowly.

People associate love with sentimental feeling alone,
But love includes much more.　　　　ZVI JUDAH KUK

Beliefs Have Consequences

While it is fashionable nowadays to say, "one's creed or system of beliefs really does not matter," this is not true. For what we believe matters a great deal in itself and our relationships with others.

To prove the point, is it important whether or not your employee believes in integrity? If he did not, would you employ him? Is it significant whether or not a teacher believes in fair play and in truth? If not, would you wish him to teach your children? Is it essential whether or not a young man believes in fidelity and faithfulness? If not, would you willingly let him marry your daughter? The conclusion is obvious: What a person believes determines the consequences of his life.

Or let us put it another way. In the enormous missiles and satellites that are now being launched into space, the smallest part is the guidance system, yet this is the most important part because it determines the path in which the object will follow. Without it the missile would wander aimlessly to its destruction.

Similarly, unless we develop a spiritual guidance system, we are destined to travel about life without plan or purpose. We must make every effort to sharpen our spiritual sensitivities and to give the most meaningful direction to our lives.

As a man thinks, so is he.   PROVERBS 23:7

Knock On Any Door

When Lord Halifax was the British ambassador to this country during the Second World War, he made it a regular practice to travel across the United States in order to strengthen the bond of friendship between these two great countries.

Once he visited a small village in the western part of our country. He had to rise early the next day in order to continue on his journey. The bellboy in the small hotel was instructed to knock at the door at 5 A.M. the next morning and announce loudly, "My Lord, this is the boy knocking."

The next morning, he arose early and mounted the stairs to deliver his message. As he approached Lord Halifax's door, he suddenly became very excited about awakening such an important personage. This caused him such confusion that, as he rapped on the door, he called out loudly, "My boy, this is the Lord knocking."

Although the "punch line" is meant to be funny, if we take it seriously we can see that it describes a central observance in Jewish life — the Bar Mitzvah ceremony. This Jewish ceremony of entering manhood stresses the fact that from that day forward the Lord knocks upon the door of the heart of the young men. A Jewish man must know that from his Bar Mitzvah onward, he is expected to answer the summons of his responsibilities.

I will be faithful to my people, to our Torah, our faith and our common hopes. I pray that I may stand the test honorably and well, in a spirit of love and brotherhood for my own people, and in a spirit of truth and justice toward all who are created in the image of God.

BAR MITZVAH PRAYER USED IN THE
GREAT SYNAGOGUE OF TEL AVIV

To Hold With Open Arms

The autobiography of a famous minister, Harry Emerson Fosdick, contains an unusual incident. One day, while walking through the campus of a well-known seminary, he met a theology student who had just finished his examinations. The minister asked him how it all went, and the student replied, "I had no trouble with the questions in philosophy. I had boned up on all the arguments for the existence of God."

The wise and experienced minister then observed, "I'm glad you know all the arguments, but do you really know God?"

Arguments for the existence of God are almost as numerous as the gods men have invented, but really to know and to feel God requires more than definitions of Him. It is an experience and an achievement that is of the intellect but goes beyond it. The knowledge of God may begin in the crystal clarity of reason, but it ends in the stained glass windows of revelation. Ultimately, we cannot define God, but those who experience God know him with a definiteness that transcends all else.

Only with God can we ease the intolerable tension of our existence. For only when He is given, can we hold life at once infinitely precious and yet as a thing lightly to be surrendered. Only because of Him is it made possible for us to clasp the world, but with relaxed hands; to embrace it, but with open arms.   MILTON STEINBERG

The Glory Of Middle Age

King Solomon and King David led very merry lives
With very many concubines and very many wives,
Until middle age came creeping with very many
    qualms —
Then Solomon wrote the Proverbs and David wrote
    the Psalms.

As indicated by this jolly quatrain most people assume
that middle age is a period in which the excitement of
living ends. Actually this age represents the real challenge
of living, for the mind requires about four decades to
learn to master the body. For this reason middle age is
the time to stretch our horizons and to make full use of
our experience and knowledge.

You have always had your eye on a new development
in business, but somehow you were always afraid to risk
it. Perhaps this is the time to give it a whirl. You have
always wanted to take a trip to Europe and Israel, but
you have been afraid to leave the children. Now who is
tied to whose apron strings? You have wanted to take up
dancing, take apart an engine, learn some Hebrew, become
a leader in a community project. Surely no one will issue
an engraved invitation; you must take the first step. When
all you exercise is caution, then you have ceased to grow,
whether you are 15 or 50.

O song as yet unsung!
You glint and glare; you scent the air
And you lure and snare with words yet unsprung. YEHOASH

Inheritance Tax

Once a rabbi tried to reach one of his leading congregants. The man, however, was either "out" or "busy" whenever the rabbi called. After many futile attempts, the rabbi finally, in desperation, left this message with the congregant's secretary: "Please call me. A mutual relative of ours died and left us a large inheritance." No sooner had the rabbi put down the receiver when a call came through from the very excited man, who wanted to know the details.

"Well," explained the rabbi, "our mutual relative is Moses. He left us the Ten Commandments, and I know you want to share in this great inheritance." The congregant was taken aback but readily agreed.

Most of us subconsciously yearn for a large inheritance. We have daydreams of someday being left great wealth. Meantime, we foolishly neglect the great fund of wisdom that is at our fingertips. The wisdom of the Scriptures enables us to live with ourselves and others and to make the best use of our lives, which in turn is the source of happiness.

But we must understand that an inheritance does not pass to us without some sort of tax. The inheritance of the Torah can only be ours when we pay our fair share of the tax by personal participation in order to further Jewish learning and the development of spiritual resources.

The next time you read in the paper of a great inheritance, remember, you already have one.

Moses gave us the Torah as an inheritance to the congregation of Jacob.   DEUTERONOMY 33:4

Sweet Mystery Of Life

A mystic is one who believes that knowledge is not limited by the laws of logic, for there is much more to living than that which meets the mind or the eye. More than a quantity of facts, there is a quality of understanding.

Will one man and one woman make just two people, or do they make a marriage? Is marriage just two, or is it more than we understand? Add together four people at dinner and we have a dinner party. But what if their names happen to be Rabbi Abraham Heschel, the Reverend Reinhold Niebuhr, Dr. Albert Schweitzer, and Francis Cardinal Spellman? Would not the quality of that dinner conversation be more than we realize?

In this sense, the view of the mystic has great validity, for it tells us that contemplation of events and experiences yields rich rewards and that regarding events from various points of view adds to the fullness of experience.

We can see this emphasis in the work of El Greco, the great and advanced Spanish artist of the 17th century who was considered by many the father of modern art. It is told that he used to paint while standing on his toes. One day, a friend summoned enough courage to ask the artist why he worked in this uncomfortable position. El Greco replied, "Standing on my toes gives me a new perspective, and when I stretch myself I see things that other men overlook."

For as long as nature and man are conserved as God's creation, then the quest for the hidden life of new experiences and new interpretations will always be one of the most important preoccupations of the human mind.

GERSHOM G. SCHOLEM

What Is The Give?

Clifton Fadiman, author and lecturer, once recorded an interview with the violinist Yehudi Menuhin to be used during an intermission in a broadcast of the Metropolitan Opera's production of *Carmen*. Fadiman asked Menuhin about his recent decision to give up concert work in order to teach. The violinist explained it in these words: "I think there comes a time in any person's life when he seems ripe to give back a little of what he has taken."

This is a very telling thought. Most of us go around unconsciously bent on what we can take rather than what we can give.

We take so much sunlight, and yet we never pause to think what we can do to give someone else a place in the sun. We take the natural wealth of America and exploit it in every way, but we are rarely concerned with giving some of it to impoverished lands. We take love and security for granted, but we never want to know how we can love those unloved and how we can make secure the insecure.

Unless we learn that to give of ourselves is the secret of living, we shall never attain immortality. For the money stored in our bank accounts, the food we hoard in our cupboards, the love we lock in our hearts — all these die with us. What we share, what we donate, what we truly love is ours forever.

Love that is hoarded moulds at last
Until we know someday
The only thing we ever have
Is what we gave away.   LOUIS GINSBERG

A Large Step Forward

An elderly rabbi, who was celebrating his 50th year in the rabbinate, fell to reminiscing about his naiveté during his first year as a rabbi. The first problem that had been brought to him was advising an alcoholic, who was drunk when his family brought him to the rabbi. The rabbi looked him squarely in the eye and asked if he knew that his drinking was destroying his family. He sniffled and said, "Yes." Was he aware that his wife was almost a nervous wreck because of him? The man began to cry softly. Did he know that his children were ashamed to go out in the street and play? The alcoholic began to weep openly. Then the rabbi concluded in triumph. "Well then, why don't you give up liquor and make everybody happy?"

The poor drunk straightened up, dried his eyes, beamed, and said, "You're right, I will." Then he grasped the rabbi's hand and said, "And to seal the bargain, Rabbi, let's have a drink on it."

Many of us naively believe that emotional problems can be solved with a simple prayer, a pledge to reform. Often, the sources of these problems are extremely complicated and require the specialized guidance of the psychologist or psychiatrist. When this is the case we must be honest enough to recognize it, for only out of such courageous honesty can healing come.

The time has passed when any stigma attaches to those seeking help. To know that something is wrong is to take a large step forward. The most important requisite for rehabilitation is awareness.   ABRAHAM N. FRANZBLAU

For Crying Out Loud

It happened that one of the most devoted students of a great teacher lost a child. The bereaved father did not shed a tear. The teacher noticed that every day the student grew more gaunt and tense and that his hand began to tremble. The master took the saddened man into his study and told him this story. "Once I drove cross-country with three horses. Though they performed their labor, yet not one of them could neigh, and I was greatly afraid for their health. Then I met a peasant coming toward me and he shouted, 'Slacken the reins!' So I slackened the reins. They suddenly all began to neigh and to trot in rhythm. Do you understand, my son?" The student burst into tears. He wept and he understood that sometimes we must learn how to cry.

There are moments in our lives we must freely express the pain that is within our hearts. If we hold back all our anguish we build dangerous pressures. Unless these pressures are released through the normal God-given channels, we risk an internal explosion. It is for this reason that we must avail ourselves of natural expressions of sorrow — primarily through tears.

When the heart is full, the eyes overflow.

SHOLOM ALEICHEM

Live All Your Life

A small boy, just learning to write, ended a birthday greeting to his uncle in this way: "Happy Birthday, Uncle, and I hope you live all your life." What a wonderful insight! Are you prepared to live all your life?

This question is the key to the understanding of the third chapter of the Book of Ecclesiastes:

> For everything there is a season, and a time for every matter under heaven:
> A time to be born and a time to die;
> A time to break and a time to heal;
> A time to tear down and a time to build up;
> A time to rend and a time to sew;
> A time to weep and a time to laugh;
> A time to mourn and a time to dance;
> A time to lose and a time to seek.

Yes, there is a time for everything. And in the words of Philip James Bailey:

> We live in deeds, not years; in thoughts, not breaths;
> In feelings, not in figures on a dial.
> We should count time in heart throbs. He most lives
> Who thinks most — feels the noblest — acts the best.

Years wrinkle the skin, but to give up enthusiasm wrinkles the soul.   SAMUEL ULLMAN

In His Image

Dr. John Rambo, a medical worker in India, told of saying goodbye to an old Indian woman on the steps of his clinic in the hill country, after having successfully operated on her eyes for cataracts. Now as she was leaving, with her sight restored, she bowed low and said, "Goodbye, God; goodbye, God." Dr. Rambo hastily explained that he was not God, but only a poor, weak servant of the Almighty, but the woman would have none of it. As she continued on down the road, she turned every little way and waved gratefully, shouting, "Goodbye, God; goodbye, God."

In one way or another, in this capacity or that, we become the image of God to others. As a visitor to the sick, as a worker for society, as a parent, as a contributor, as a boss, as a supervisor — in a hundred different roles we have the opportunity to revere life, even to create life. In the constant re-creation of life comes the deepest satisfaction of living. When people look at you, whose image do they see?

"Ye shall be holy, for I, your God, am holy." The Talmud explains this to mean the following: "God says if you sanctify yourselves, He will consider it as though you sanctified Him."   COMMENTARY TO LEVITICUS 19:2

AV 28 כח אב

The Only Policy

There was a very fine practice in the ancient world that we might well consider for our own modern age. When workers in Roman times accidentally chipped their statues, they would fill in the damaged places with wax of the same color as the marble and then sell their work as perfectly made. Other statue makers, wishing to sell honest products, stamped their product *sine cera,* which means "without wax." From this custom has come the contemporary word *sincere.*

It is only when we begin to deal with sincerity that we can give honest money for real worth; value given for value received. Sincerity means saying what a thing really is and then accepting the consequences. If we are at all serious about creating a healthy society, we must be deeply concerned with practicing truth and honesty in business, for honesty is not just the best policy to a sincerely religious person; it is the only policy. Honest dealing may not make us richer, but it will enable us to live in comfort with our consciences; it may not be the way of society, but it is the will of God, and no matter what we do today, we will have to face Him some tomorrow.

When a man is summoned to the final judgment, the first question he is asked is, "Did you deal honestly?"

SHABBAT 31 a

339

The Curse Of Conformity

According to an ancient rabbinic legend which has its counterpart in Greek mythology, the people of Sodom had a special bed. Every visitor that arrived was placed in this bed. In order to pass through the city he had to fit the size of the bed. If his legs were too large, they were simply and brutally shortened. Conversely, if they were too small, they were stretched to fit. The stranger had to conform to the measurements of society. For this cruelty — so goes the story — the city of Sodom was destroyed.

The habits of Sodom are not completely different from our own, for we, too, are expected to fit the bed, fit the social norm, or we are cut off. Either we conform to popular thinking or we are isolated from society. If a teen-ager does not conform he is branded a "square"; if as an adult he does not take up the accepted pattern, he is an "oddball," and even if we deviate only slightly from the usual mode of society, we are labelled "maladjusted."

The sin of forcing people into a certain mold not only hurts others but also retards our own possibilities of growth. We owe it to ourselves and to our fellow men to respect individual thoughts and actions and to promote our own individual development as well.

The idea of liberty as evolved by the Anglo-Saxon mind signifies liberty of conscience, the full, untrammeled development of the soul as well as the body.

ISRAEL FRIEDLAENDER

The Orderly Universe

When Napoleon was a child someone approached him and said, "Little boy, I will give you an orange if you tell me where God is." The little genius quickly replied, "And I will give you two oranges if you tell me where God is not."

We do not often pause to contemplate the fact that the order of the universe reveals the presence of God. The solar system is perfect in its arrangement; the sun rises and sets at its appointed hour; and in general nature functions with absolute precision. The ever increasing discovery of the "miracle drugs" is founded on research which in turn is based on fixed mathematical principles of an orderly universe. The precision and the power of the laws and forces of the universe daily declare the reality of an intelligent God.

The sensitive mind does not see a conflict between science and religion, but rather a cooperative effort in which each discipline helps the other; the scientific study of religion and the religious study of science can help men live better lives.

A little science estranges men from God,
Much science leads them back to Him.　　LOUIS PASTEUR

אלול

ELUL

What's Your Hurry?

It is customary to begin High Holyday preparations on the first day of Elul, a month before they actually begin. This is done by sounding the *shofar* at the morning service, reading special prayers and considering the meaning of the coming holydays.

A *hasid* once hurried past his rabbi on the first day of Elul. The rabbi asked him, "Why are you hurrying?"

"Well," he said, "I must look in the *Mahzor* and put my prayers in order."

"The prayer book is the same as it was last year," replied the rabbi. "It would be far better for you to look into your deeds, and put yourself in order."

The moral of this story is that the hardest people to reach with the love of God are the good people, the self-righteous people. We are often so complacent about ourselves that we cannot imagine any flaws in our character. The purpose of reading a prayer book is to evaluate ourselves in light of its contents, rather than using it as an escape from our lives. We must be willing to concentrate on our own selves if religion is to have value in straightening out our lives. This self-scrutiny takes a lifetime, and it is never ending.

In my youth, I thought I would convert the whole world to God. But soon I discovered that it would be enough to convert the people who lived in my town, and I tried that for a time, but did not succeed. Then I realized that my program was still too ambitious, and I concentrated on the persons in my household. But I could not convert them either. Finally it dawned on me: I must work upon myself, so that I may give true service to God. But I did not accomplish even this.   HAYIM HALBERSTAM

Priceless

A missionary to Africa was preparing to return to America for a visit. One of his closest friends was a native named Ivan Madagra, who lived far back in the bush country. On the morning of his scheduled departure, the native appeared with a large and very beautiful shell as his parting gift.

The missionary was delighted and impressed by the fact that the shell had been brought from such a distance. "The shell is wonderful," he said. "Yet, still more wonderful is the fact that you carried it so far." Ivan's face beamed as he asserted, "Long walk part of gift."

Many of us mistakenly believe that the true worth of a gift is measured in terms of monetary value. We think that the more expensive the gift, the more regard or affection it shows. This is a fallacy, for love cannot be bought and friendship cannot be purchased. In time all material things must perish and vanish. What we ourselves do for others — what we give of our thoughts, our energies, our consideration — this truly expresses our devotion.

The expression of personal concern and interest makes the kind of impression on memory that time cannot erase, nor circumstances alter. When we give something of ourselves, we have planted a seed of friendship that will bear fruit continually.

God desires the heart.   SANHEDRIN 106 b

Great Jews

One of the greatest rabbis of contemporary times was Abraham Isaac Kuk, the first chief rabbi of modern times in the land of Israel. In his lifetime he spoke for the eternal verities of Judaism as they apply to our age. He struggled with the issues of translating Jewish uniqueness and the love of the land of Israel into modern terms. He was the first rabbi to return, after a lapse of many centuries, to delivering sermons in Hebrew.

He offered a living example of the way the traditional Jew can relate to the concerns of contemporary living. In light of this it might be appropriate on the third day of Elul to ponder the last phrase he uttered on this earth.

Precisely on the third day of Elul in the year 1935, it became clear that this unusual man was near death. A world-famous physician was called to attend him during his last moments. When the famous scientist, whose adherence to Judaism was very tenuous, bent over the dying Rabbi Kuk, the latter whispered, "I still hope that the day will soon come when the Jews who are great will become great Jews."

The task, then, of the modern Jew is to learn that there is a straight line to be drawn between the point of his greatness and the point of his Jewishness, and that line is called "great Jews."

If today's Jews are not prophets, they are, at least, the sons of prophets.   PESAHIM 66 b

The Way Of Wisdom

In the year 133 of the Common Era an important rabbinical council took place at Lydda, in Palestine. The issue under discussion was: Which is more important — study or action? After long and intense debate, the council decided that, "Study is important when it leads to right action."

The aim of the Torah is to regulate conduct. Therefore, the purpose of all scholarship is to enhance our way of living, help us live responsibly and appreciate the fullness and the depth of life.

That is why an old *baba*, an aged grandmother, can be wiser than a grandson who has a Ph.D. degree. He has knowledge of facts, but she has the wisdom of experience — of living and doing.

That is why a nurse can sometimes be more effective than a doctor. He has a mind, but she has a heart.

That is why a man who builds a *sukkah* can sometimes be greater than a man who builds a space ship. The technician wants to know more about the moon, but the *sukkah* builder wants to know more about his morals. And who shall say which is greater — a man who masters the cosmos or a man who masters his conscience?

Wisdom without action is like a tree without fruit.

JOSEPH KIMHI

347

The Upward Reach

The other day the newspaper carried the story of a man who once found a shiny new dime on the street. From then on, his mind was focused on little things and he never lifted his eyes off the ground. At the end of forty years, he had accumulated 39,000 buttons, 17,000 pins, 73 pennies, 22 more dimes, 6 bus tokens, a bent back, and a bad disposition. In the meantime he had lost the glories of light, the smiles of friends, the beauties of nature, and the opportunity to serve his fellow man by sharing happiness and developing a worthwhile ambition.

Most of us are in fact like this man and we continually focus our minds on little things. We worry about petty ailments, we are irritated by slights and we are absorbed by trivial concerns. By fearing to enlarge our ideas and aspirations, we become blind to the great vistas of living. As one poet put it:

> Who Thou art I know not,
> But this I know:
> Thou hast set the stars
> In a silver row;
> Thou hast sent the trackless winds
> Loose upon their way;
> Thou hast reared a colored wall
> Between Night and Day;
> But chief of all Thy wondrous works,
> Supreme of all Thy plan,
> Thou hast put an upward reach
> In the heart of man.

May it be Thy will, O Eternal My God, to bring me out of darkness into light.   GENESIS RABBAH 68:11

Don't Sneer At Nonsense

Jimmy Durante, the famous comedian, once said, "Don't sneer at nonsense, for sometimes 'nonsense' can teach us a lot."

Have you ever seen a serious dignified grandfather, head of a huge and successful business get down on his knees to play with his grandchild? They roll on the floor together and generally look rather silly, but through that nonsense they are building a basic relationship.

Very often a patient in a hospital will complain about the nonsense of occupational therapy, of having to make an ash tray, a belt, a wallet, or a basket. But it is that kind of simple construction work, seeming so nonsensical, that helps him regain a hold through diversion and accomplishment.

Again, some of us miss a great thrill in life by dismissing all of modern art as child's play, as nonsense. For if you take the time to study a contemporary work of art you see a beautiful design here and a sudden stroke of genius there. You find lines soar, shapes twist and turn; power here and pleasure there. The same may be said for much of modern music or poetry. What seems like nonsense may often turn out to reveal worlds of feeling and meaning.

Nonsense is often the wisest form of allegory.

JOSEPH LEFTWICH

Haves And Have Nots

One day two little girls in a small town in Italy were invited by their neighbor for a snack. The neighbor woman gave them some hot cocoa and cookies, which the children delightedly consumed. Presently, one of the little girls looked up and said, "Are you rich?"

The woman looked around at her worn furniture and replied, "Of course not. We are not rich at all."

"But look!" said the little girl, "Your cup and saucer match."

Periodically, we hear people complain about the lack of possessions. Very often, this is used as a self-protective argument against giving or participating in community. These people do not realize that they possess comforts and luxuries that to three-quarters of the world would seem a Hollywood dream. The world would be an entirely different place if we understood that when our cup and saucer match we ought to thank God. If we could learn to express our gratitude rather than forever voicing our grumbles, we would live more fruitful lives. The next time you complain about what you have not, see first what you have.

Scripture says, "Blessed by the Lord day by day"
(Ps. 68:20). Are we then to bless him by day and not by
night? What it means to tell us is that every day we should
give him the blessing appropriate to the day.

BERAKHOT 40 a

Wrong Problem

It is a characteristic inversion, so typical of our times, to speak of the "problem of God." At stake in any real discussion about God is rather the "problem of man." Man is problem, but God is solution. Trouble occurs whenever we confuse one with the other.

What is the purpose of attending services? It is to find atonement for guilt and inspiration to raise our spiritual standards of living. But we are so wrapped up in ourselves and we see things from so narrowed an angle that we never stop to think of how we might look to God. Let us look at the world from God's end of the telescope.

How would you feel if God gave us the same amount of time and attention as we devote to Him? If God offered as many excuses as we do, and if the excuses were no more justifiable than ours, how would we feel? If God withheld His blessings from us as we withhold our offerings from Him, how would we feel then? The next time you are asked to do something, to give something, suppose you stop to ask yourself, "What would God have me do?"

Make no mistake about it. God is not sitting in heaven and doing nothing. He is pulling us by the ideals of the prophets and pushing us by realistic necessities. He pushes and pulls us to the goals He proposes, and it is we who hold out against Him. In our stubbornness and our pride, we resist Him.

You depend on Him, not He on you.

BAHYA IBN PAKUDAH

The Pressures Of The Herd

A contemporary play entitled *Rhinoceros* has excited a great deal of favorable comment. The work of Eugene Ionesco, a Rumanian who lives in France, it has already been performed in several European capitals. In this remarkable play, right before your eyes as it were, a man turns into a rhinoceros. In fact by the end of the play the characters — all except one — have become a herd of rhinos. Only one man, the hero, is able to resist the pressures of the herd and remain himself. The message of the play is stated in one line, spoken by the heroine as she watches a man turn into an animal: "Just before he became a beast," she says, "his last human words were, 'We must move with the times!' "

Something very important is being said here, because the feeling that we must move with the times and be like everyone else is exactly that which destroys our individual humanity and turns us collectively into a herd. It makes very little difference how we are caught by the current of the times, whether it be thinking like everyone else, acting like everyone else, or living like everyone else. The point is really that to preserve our minds, we must be courageous enough to reject the mass mentality. If you are to survive as a person, you must be exactly that — an individual, a human being capable of feeling and thinking for yourself.

A man who does not understand his essence is like the beasts that perish.   PSALMS 49:21

A Short-Term Loan

In an interesting passage in the *Ethics of the Fathers,* a collection of the sayings of the early rabbis, Rabbi Yohanan ben Zakkai asks his students, "Which is the quality a man should shun most?"

Rabbi Simeon answered, "The quality of borrowing without repaying. It is the same whether one borrows from man or from God."

The thoughtful person considers every new day to be a loan from God — a loan of time, the most precious currency of all. All God expects from us is that we use it wisely and well. All He desires is that we enjoy and appreciate His world where we are guests, that we love our friends, who are His children, that we preserve our integrity of character wherein we are created in His image. The zest for living, the sensitivity to the lives of others and the honor of an individual are the only sure things that can never change.

How can we repay this loan of life with interest? We can repay it by filling our lives with many interests. Life is lent to be spent; a wise investor will use it for its maximum benefits. Let us use our God-given curiosity to discover the half-hidden marvels of God's world. By living every day to the fullest, we will make the most of our short-term loan of life.

The day is short and the work is great.   AVOT 2:20

Bittersweet

A father who had two boys wanted to learn which one was apt to enter community service. One day he summoned the children to the kitchen. He gave one a lemon and told him to bite into it. The boy did as he was told and immediately spit it out with the comment, "It is bitter."

The father thought, "Not him."

Then the second boy took a bite and said, "It's bitter, but still it's good."

Whereupon the father thought, "*He* will enter community service."

Our people have always had a tradition of helping others and an authentic dedication to communal responsibility, despite all of its trials and hardships. This wonderful tradition we must continue to foster and maintain.

In order to prepare properly for the future we must begin to create a conscious community policy today to train our leaders for tomorrow. One of the concrete ways we can begin is to raise the earnings and the esteem for the work of the teacher, the nurse and the social worker. We must be keenly alert to their needs and use every opportunity to advance their welfare and increase their number. In their hands lies the destiny of those who need help, and hence the destiny of all of us.

Who shares in the community's trouble will also share in its consolation.   SEDER ELIYAHU ZUTA 1

To Sublimate Is To Exalt

Fundamentally, how much we can live without is the real determinant of character. Goebbels, the Nazi minister of propaganda, once made the revealing statement: "We can well do without butter, but not without guns." That was his approach. On the other hand, Franklin D. Roosevelt could do without legs and learned to make his mind reach where his legs would not carry him. George Washington Carver, the illustrious Negro scientist, was born of slave parents in indescribable poverty and dirt, yet by sheer perseverance he acquired an education and has gone down in history as one of the greatest agriculturalists produced by the South. Helen Keller could do without sight and hearing and learned enough to say, "I thank God for my handicaps, for through them I found myself, my work, and my God."

This same capacity to transcend shortcomings can be developed in the psychological realm. A neurosis, a distorted view of reality, should not be an excuse for becoming a burden. Many people have emotional problems, but the point is what one does about them. One person turns to poetry, another to bitterness. One expresses himself in social work; another turns to crime. One will build a business of worth; another builds a bomb of destruction. We all have blind spots, problems and troubles, but the test is how we handle them and resolve them. It is no accident that the word "sublimate" comes from "sublime," which means "exalted."

Desires must be purified and idealized, not exterminated.
ELIJAH GAON

The Opiate Of The Masses

The timely story is told of a Russian girl who in her examination for a government position was asked, "What is the inscription on the Sarmian Wall?" She guessed that it might be, "Religion is the opiate of the masses." But she was not sure, so the next day she walked seven miles from Leningrad to the Sarmian Wall to check on her answer. Fearfully, she looked upon the wall, where she found just what she had written, "Religion is the opiate of the masses." Then vastly relieved, she bowed her head and said, "Thank God."

Whether we admit it or not, we are all involved in deep religious feelings. There are times when, because of group or personal rebellion, we find ourselves hostile to the idea of God, but then in our unguarded moments, we let slip through our authentic feelings. There is not one person who does not at some time struggle with his conscience about the mystery of existence. Even those who insist they do not believe in God show by their very vehemence that they are concerned about His existence.

God is an undeniable part of our lives, and ultimately we cannot live in peace with ourselves until we are prepared to accept this. We may scribble anti-religious slogans on the walls, but when we find that a crisis has passed, we will still pause and say humbly, "Thank God."

For He is not the God of would-be-spirits — He is the God of the human heart.   HAYIM NAHMAN BIALIK

Two-Faced Man

There is a classic legend about an artist who wanted to draw both the most beautiful face in the world and the most ugly face in the world. He searched far and wide for a beautiful face that would fit his conception. After years of effort, he finally found it in a little boy with the expression of an angel. As soon as the artist completed his masterpiece, he began to search for a suitable model for the ugliest of faces. Here the task was more difficult. In vain he searched, for he could not find a face without some trace of kindness and some beauty. Finally, after looking for many, many years, he found one day what he was looking for — a man with a face bereft of any beauty. As he began to draw, the face disturbed him; it seemed most familiar. Overcome by curiosity, he asked the model if they had ever met before. And the man replied, "Master, I was the child you once drew."

Each person is an artist in that he paints the portrait of his own personality. His character creates the image that he presents to others. By our own deeds and thoughts, we can make this an image of infinite beauty, or we can daub it with ugliness. What we do, we must do with extreme care, for the portrait of personality is open to all to see, and it is what we ourselves have created.

Man eats, drinks, lives and dies like an animal. But he also stands erect, speaks, thinks and has vision like an angel.
GENESIS RABBAH 14:3

357

Trial By Fate

A Japanese man named Kagawa is well-known to those in religious vocations for his remarkable devotion to helping the poor in Japan. He was imprisoned and tortured by the Japanese during the war years. When he was released (because even they recognized him as a kind of saint) he survived the blast at Hiroshima. As a result of his exposure to poverty and illness, he contracted trachoma and tuberculosis. He has since recovered and is to this day still working hard in the slums of Japan.

Not long ago, a group of ministers was discussing him. They marvelled at his tireless energy and wondered how he was able to survive these incredible things. One minister thought for a moment and then said, "You know, I think Kagawa is so busy that he forgets to die."

The truth really is that those who have deep convictions about living deeply, fully and meaningfully are totally unconcerned about death. They firmly believe that man who has a soul and was created in the image of God has a role and a purpose on this earth. What it is we can never be entirely certain, but one of the ways we can live in faith is to live with fortitude.

As we grow older, we learn that not everything in life can be cured; some things we must learn to endure. To dare is great, but to bear is even greater, for bravery we share with brutes, but fortitude and endurance with saints.

There is no limit to trials, but the wise learn thereby.

SOLOMON IBN GABIROL

Just The Right Amount

Years ago in Lithuania Rabbi Israel Salanter, the father of the modern *musar* (Jewish ethics) movement, found two boys quarreling over which one was the taller. One forced the other to stand in a ditch to settle the argument. Seeing this, Rabbi Israel sadly commented, "Isn't it characteristic of the world, that to prove his superiority man must prove others inferior? After all, the same purpose could have been achieved by standing on a chair."

If we want to experience life to its fullest we must achieve real stature by learning to develop the best within ourselves while at the same time restraining our appetites, desires and energies. Certainly, we can carry our responsibilities, but we can also set an honest limit on them.

We speak of children being weaned from their parents. It is also just as necessary for us to wean ourselves from our children, to extricate ourselves from too great an emotional involvement with them. We go to parties and drink too much and pay with a headache, eat too much and moan all night afterwards, talk too much and have our conscience torment us, wax jealous and become consumed with bitterness. All these excesses prove we have not learned to make the most of our best and the best of our worst. A French phrase sums up this principle of living. "L'élégance est dans la juste mesure" — "Good taste is in just the right amount."

The Torah suggests life is a choice of two paths: one of fire and one of ice. If he turns in either direction he will be harmed. What shall he do? Let him walk in the middle.

JER. HAGIGAH 2:1

First Things First

How deep are your convictions about God? Is your attachment to Him like a rubber band, pulling toward Him under pressure, but then releasing Him when there is lassitude? Is your relationship with God a crutch and a convenience or your deepest commitment and overriding concern?

The owner of a large shoe manufacturing firm in St. Louis has the following motto framed on his office wall: "God first, others second, shoes third." I have often wondered what would really happen if we all adopted this motto with deep personal commitment.

There would be no war, for we would say, "God first, humanity second, and arms third."

Family quarrels would disappear, for we would say, "God first, relatives second, and jealousy third."

Many of our tensions would vanish, for we would say, "God first, others second, and my drives third."

When we truly believe in God, we suddenly turn our values upside down so that we begin to live right side up. When we truly believe in God, we put first things first.

All that the Creator demands is that a man make a beginning in the right direction; thereafter He will aid him to continue on the right path.   REB NOAH LEKHIVITZER

Thirty-Six Just Men

According to an old tradition, there are thirty-six just men for whom the world is maintained. The origin of the legend is the following. After the flood subsided, the Lord promised Noah that He would never attempt to destroy the world again, and He created the rainbow as a sign of His promise. But knowing that mankind would surely again fill the world with wickedness and violence, the Almighty wished to establish a means which would prevent them from doing so. He then created seventy-two just men: thirty-six He placed beside Him in heaven to plead for their erring brethren on earth, and thirty-six He placed on earth. These righteous men are the bulwark for whose sake God spares all mankind.

According to the tradition, the thirty-six who are on earth are completely hidden. They go about performing their good deeds, but they are never discovered. They appear as the lowliest of the lowly, outwardly very humble and often illiterate, but inwardly deeply spiritual and kind. Our sages drew a wonderful conclusion from this: treat with reverence and kindness any poor and uneducated man who has humility and goodness; for that matter, treat every man, poor or rich, illiterate or educated, with respect, especially if he has humility and goodness. Why? He might be one of the thirty-six, for whom the world is preserved.

"Happy are they that wait for Him (Isaiah 30:18)." Upon which the rabbis say, the numerical value of the Hebrew word for Him is exactly thirty-six.   SANHEDRIN 97 b

Labor Day

When Sir Christopher Wren, the noted architect of London's St. Paul's Cathedral, was in the midst of directing the building of this church, he one day decided to walk incognito among his workers. Coming upon one of them who was busy at work, he asked the following question: "My good man, what are you doing?"

The man gave a gruff reply: "Why, I am piling bricks."

Coming upon a second workman, the great architect interrogated him in the same fashion: "My good man, what are you doing?"

The second workman replied, "I'm making five shillings a day."

Sir Christopher Wren went on walking, and when he met a third workman, he again asked, "My good man, what are you doing?"

The eyes of the man lit up, and with reverence in his voice, he said, "I am helping Sir Christopher Wren erect a cathedral to God."

These three workmen typify society. The first laborer epitomizes those who see life as dull, uneventful and prosaic; they go through life piling bricks. The second worker represents those who are only interested in acquiring more goods, they go through life making money. The third workman who replied with reverence to the question, represents the idealists who are dedicated to the improvement of the spirit.

For what and for whom do you work?

Except the Lord build the house,
They labor in vain that build it.   PSALMS 127:1

Either / Or?

Inherit the Wind, a well-received play and more recently a movie, dramatizes a famous incident in American history. In the 1920's the state of Tennessee became the storm center of America when it passed a law outlawing the teaching of the theory of evolution on the grounds that this theory contradicted the Bible. A Tennessee school teacher named John Scopes had the courage to explain the theory of evolution to his students. He was arrested and brought to trial. The case attracted nationwide attention because more than the fate of one man was involved; the supremacy of science or religion was at stake. Representing the prosecution was William Jennings Bryan, who had been a candidate for the presidency of the United States. Representing the defense was one of America's greatest trial lawyers, Clarence Darrow.

The interesting feature of the play is that the author presents both views objectively. All during the play the audience wonders, what does the author believe? Why did he write it?

Then the trial is over. The people have gone, and Darrow is packing his things. As the play ends, he takes a copy of Darwin's *The Origin of the Species* and his copy of the Bible, puts them together in his briefcase, closes the briefcase and walks off the stage. In that last gesture the author passes judgment. He says in effect, both were wrong. It is not a case of either/or. Rather, in order to travel through life, a man must have both reason and faith.

Those who are learned in the principles of religion and are also well versed in science have the wisdom that will yield them much satisfaction.   ABRAHAM IBN DAUD

We're The Answer

During the Sinai Campaign several years ago, when tiny Israel stunned the world with its audacity and prevented the buildup of a Communist Nasser and a possible world war, the following incident took place. In the first wave of attack, the Israeli commanders struck hard and drove the Egyptian troops back almost to the Suez Canal. Then they dug in and awaited a ferocious counterattack. Two grimy and hollow-eyed Israelis remained under fire for several days, but the Egyptians never moved up.

Finally, one Israeli soldier remarked to his friend, "I wonder why the Egyptians have not tried to retake their positions." The other straightened up, looked him in the eye and said, *"anahnu hateshuvah"* — *"We're* the answer."

It is a very valuable insight for the individual to understand that he is a part of the solution instead of the problem, for he is then on the path to positive, helpful action. People must realize their potential in problem-solving and must learn to make the maximum use of that understanding.

I believe that the individual counts — that I count, that what I do as a volunteer in my community counts, that what I say and think count. I believe, therefore, that I cannot afford to be either complacent or uninformed, prejudiced or small, indifferent or aimless. I was born to privilege and therefore, each day, in tasks great and small, I will live up to the hilt of my full responsibilities as a free citizen, with an obligation to mankind that must be repaid in my community and within my lifetime. LEONARD MAYS

The Lost Art

A little girl was saying her evening prayers. After she recited the last line she remained at her bedside for a considerable period of time. Finally, the mother, thinking it was the old trick of trying to stay up a few seconds longer, told her rather harshly to get to bed. "But I was waiting," the child protested.

"For what?" her mother demanded.

And the answer was, "I was waiting to see if God has anything to say to *me!*"

We, too, are so busy talking to God that we cannot hear what He has to say. If we pray merely to talk and not to listen, we miss the meaning of worship. Prayer is dialogue with God; it is conversation with the Almighty. It is common knowledge that the best partner in a conversation is the one who is the best listener.

God is not a cosmic bellhop whom we call in to attend to our needs. He is not a man and He cannot be fooled or deceived. Man scans the face, but only God knows the heart. We must not promise that which we cannot keep. We must not ask for that which cannot be given. We must be cautious in our speech and even more patient in our silence. We must learn the art of listening in order to learn.

Man was endowed with two ears and one tongue that he may listen more than speak.   SHEM TOV FALAQUERA

The ABC's Of Belief

To accept the good of life and the bad of life with equal grace is the mark of the religious person. None of us ever achieves all that we want in life or, indeed, even a tiny fraction of what we wish. To say this is one thing; however, to truly believe it is something else.

A ruler was once pacing back and forth in worry over a problem. He was concerned about certain conditions in his land. An old servant, noticing the anxiety of his master, came up to him and asked, "Sir, may I ask you a question?"

"Surely," replied the ruler.

"Did God govern the world well before you came into it?"

"Undoubtedly," was the answer.

"And will He rule the world well when you have gone out of it?"

"I am certain that He will," was the response.

"Then, Sir," continued the servant, "don't you think you can trust Him to rule it while you are in it?"

If we believe in God then we must be willing to accept His rule and His world. We must have implicit faith, even in the most bitter depth of our sorrow, that His way is just and good. We can achieve this if we are willing to be truly religious, if we live as we believe.

In the day of prosperity be joyful and in the day of trouble consider: God made one as well as the other.

ECCLESIASTES 7:14

The Conscience Of The Rich

A very famous rabbi, Rabbi Abraham Isaac Kuk, once appealed to Nathan Straus, one of America's greatest Jewish philanthropists, for a donation to a certain needy cause. Straus consented to help, but wondered why the rabbi did not turn to other wealthy Jews who did very little for charity.

Rabbi Kuk smilingly said, "There was once a prince who went hunting. He lost his way and noticed an inn in the distance. He hurried toward the inn and ordered eggs. After the modest meal, the prince asked how much he owed for the eggs. 'Twenty-five dollars,' said the innkeeper.

'Are eggs so scarce here that you charge so high a price for them?' asked the prince.

'No,' replied the inkeeper, 'we have plenty of eggs, but few princes.'"

The possession of riches, both material and spiritual, imposes a great responsibility upon us. It gives us the means to advance the causes in which we believe. In fact, the possession of means is an added burden upon our consciences, for it implies that we must be judged for the manner in which we apply our resources.

We can act in indifference, interference or intelligence. The manner in which we apply our riches will indicate whether we are amoral, immoral, or moral.

If you are wise and rich,
Let your good deeds reveal your wisdom and your wealth.
SABBATH AND FESTIVAL PRAYER BOOK

Unmasking At Midnight

On the Sunday before Rosh Hashanah at the stroke of midnight, it is the custom to gather in the synagogue for special *Selihot* services. These are prayers of supplication that move the congregation, inspired by the dramatic mood of midnight, to think soberly about their spiritual natures and the purpose of living.

Another tradition of revelation at midnight is found in masque balls staged by European aristocracy during the eighteenth and nineteenth centuries. Everyone came masqueraded as someone else. At the stroke of midnight, all unmasked. Some who were disguised as kings turned out to be commoners, while others who appeared as peasants were seen as princes. At midnight the face of each was revealed.

There are times when every man and woman alive asks in his heart of hearts what his life signifies. While during the course of the year we may evade the truth, yet there are still moments when we cannot avoid it. "There comes a midnight hour," says a Swedish theologian, "when all men must unmask." From this type of soul-searching no one is exempt. During these instances, we must face the truth about ourselves, for no man wears a mask in the presence of God.

The Selihot prayers strike so universal a note that most of them remain significant as devotional literature, regardless of the flight of time and the change of circumstances.

LOUIS FEINBERG

Body And Soul

The quest for the soul has occupied the greatest minds of all time. From Aristotle and before to William James and after, philosophers have searched for the soul, but in vain, for it has eluded them all. The reason is plain to see. They sought to discover it in the body; they looked for it in the brain, the heart and the nerve endings. It is not there at all because it is imperishable.

Where, then, is the soul? The answer is found in one of the greatest statements of Jewish thought. It was expressed by one of the giants of the Jewish intellect, Rabbi Akiba. "Beloved is man in that he was created in the image of God. Even greater love was shown to him in that it was made known to him that he was created in God's image."

The truth is that the soul is the image of God within us. It is not a thing; it is a concept, a quality. It is mercy and love and truth. It is precisely the qualities within personality that endure in memory even after our earthly bodies have vanished from sight. The soul in man is the Godly in man.

In Thy hand is the soul of every living thing
And the breath of all mankind
For the soul is Thine and the body as well.

SELIHOT LITURGY

369

Faith Through Living

Leo Baeck was a man who will go down in history as a great Jew. He was a rabbi in Berlin during the years when thousands fled Germany, but he chose to remain. Just at his seventieth birthday, he was sent to the Theresienstadt concentration camp. There he was harnessed to a heavy garbage wagon and assigned to labors usually performed by animals. In the evening he held services and comforted people. He endured twenty-seven months of Nazi brutality.

An amazing story about this man is told by Dr. Abraham J. Heschel, one of the great theologians of our age. Just before Dr. Heschel was expelled from Germany in 1939, he sent Leo Baeck an article on prayer, entitled, "Prayer as Expression and Empathy." Then followed the years of Baeck's confinement in Theresienstadt. Shortly after he was released from the camp in June of 1945, he flew to London to meet Dr. Heschel. As they approached each other, Dr. Heschel trembled when he thought of all that had befallen Baeck. But Rabbi Baeck simply stretched out his hand, smiled and said, "Shalom! Now that article on prayer that you sent me, this is my reaction." He went right on, completely ignoring the horrors that had gone on between the time he received the article and the meeting with Heschel.

This is the living demonstration of the Jewish belief that life goes on no matter what happens, that the search for truth is pressed forward no matter what intervenes. The important thing in life as far as the Jew is concerned is to live with honesty, honor and responsibility.

Through faith man experiences the meaning of the world; through action he gives it meaning.   LEO BAECK

A Sense Of Belonging

We Americans are great joiners. We are catapulted out of the womb into a hospital nursery where our cries soon join a chorus of demands. As soon as we are socialized, we participate in youth groups and clubs. We grow into unions, professional organizations and service clubs. Even our private social life is organized about classes, country clubs and the "Saturday night crowd." We do this to evade our loneliness and to achieve a sense of belonging.

But no matter how much we join, we cannot help feeling that our spiritual hunger is not satisfied. The truth is we will never *really* belong until we have a strong sense of connection with the source of our being and existence, our Creator.

There is the instructive story of Henry Thoreau, the great American writer. Shortly before his death, a pious aunt visited him and asked, "Have you made your peace with God, Henry?"

He replied, "Auntie, I don't know that we have ever quarreled."

We must always remember that at the root of our being we are animated, as the word literally means, *given life,* by God. It is only this feeling of being drawn to a living God that gives us the ultimate sense of belonging.

My heart and my flesh sing for joy to the living God.
PSALMS 84:2

At The Gate Of The Year

The end of one experience and the beginning of another — this is study and self-evaluation. Our forefathers termed this process *heshbon hanefesh,* "the accounting of the soul." Every life's balance sheet has both a credit and a debit column. Ultimately, our spiritual accounts are known only to ourselves and God.

This day in the Jewish spiritual calendar marks the closing of the year's books. For each Jew it is a time to reconsider the past and to plan for the future. The tools for moral measurement are prayer, meditation and honest self-appraisal. The past cannot be undone, but it can be understood and forgiven. The future awaits each of us with promise and hope. As we stand at the gate of the year which marks the transition between yesterday and tomorrow, we can find the correct way to live if we walk with God.

This thought was given beautiful expression in a poem by Louise Hawkins, which were the closing words of the last New Year's Eve broadcast by King George VI of England:

> And I said to the man who stood at the gate of
> the year:
> "Give me a light that I may tread safely into the
> unknown!"
> And he replied, "Go out into the darkness, and
> put your hand into the hand of God."
> That shall be to thee better than light
> And safer than a known way.

The eyes of the Lord thy God are always upon it, from the beginning of the year unto the end of the year.

DEUTERONOMY 11:12

LIST OF JEWISH BOOKS CITED

Bible

Genesis, Exodus, Leviticus, Deuteronomy, Joshua, Isaiah, Jeremiah, Ezekiel, Obadiah, Jonah, Micah, Habakkuk, Zechariah, Malachi, Psalms, Proverbs, Job, Ecclesiastes

Apocrypha and Pseudepigrapha

II Esdras, Ben Sira, Wisdom of Solomon, Testaments of the Twelve Patriarchs (Gad; Joseph), Letter of Aristeas

Mishnah

Avot, Eduyot, Kelim, Sanhedrin, Yoma

Tosefta

Berakhot, Bava Kamma

Minor Tractates

Avot de Rabbi Nathan

Babylonian Talmud

Avodah Zarah, Bava Batra, Bava Kamma, Bava Metzia, Betzah, Berakhot, Kiddushin, Makkot, Megillah, Pesahim, Sanhedrin, Shabbat, Sukkah, Taanit, Yoma

Jerusalem Talmud

Berakhot, Hagigah, Kiddushin, Shabbat, Taanit

Midrash

Genesis Rabbah, Exodus Rabbah, Mekhilta, Midrash Tehilim, Numbers Rabbah, Pesikta Rabbati, Seder Eliyahu Rabbah, Seder Eliyahu Zuta, Song of Songs Rabbah, Tanhuma, Yalkut (Shimoni)

Medieval Legal, Ethical and Mystical Works

Shulkhan Arukh, Me'il Tzedakah, Menorat HaMaor, Sefer Hasidim, Tikkunay Zohar, Zohar